# *The Experts Pick*

## BASKETBALL'S
# BEST
# 50
## PLAYERS
## IN THE LAST
# 50
## YEARS

### Kenneth A. Shouler

ADDAX
PUBLISHING
GROUP

Published by Addax Publishing Group
Copyright © 1998 by Kenneth Shouler
Book Design by Melanie J. Tull
Cover Design by Christine Kossow
Photos Courtesy Basketball Hall of Fame - Springfield, Mass. and Dick Raphael

For information address:
Addax Publishing Group
8643 Hauser Drive, Suite 235, Lenexa, KS 66215

ISBN: 1-886110-45-X

Distributed to the trade by
ANDREWS McMEEL PUBLISHING
4520 Main Street, Kansas City, Missouri 64111-7701

Printed in the United States of America

Library of Congress Cataloging - in - Publication Data

Shouler, Kenneth A.
    The Experts pick basketball's best 50 players in the last 50 years
  / by Ken Shouler
      p. cm.
    Includes bibliographical references (p. )
    ISBN 1-886110-45-X (alk. paper)
    1. Basketball players--Rating of--United States. 2. Basketball
  players--United States--Biography. I. Title.
  GV884.A1S46 1998
  796.323'092'273--dc21                                        97-51882
                                                                   CIP

To My Wife,
Rose Marie

# CONTENTS

Foreword . . . . . . . . . . . . . . . . . . . . . . . . . . . . . . . . . . . . vii

I. THE GUARDS

    1.      Michael Jordan . . . . . . . . . . . . . . . . . . . . . . 2
    2.      Earvin "Magic" Johnson . . . . . . . . . . . . . . . 13
    3.      Oscar Robertson . . . . . . . . . . . . . . . . . . . . . 17
    4.      Jerry West . . . . . . . . . . . . . . . . . . . . . . . . . . 24
    5      George Gervin . . . . . . . . . . . . . . . . . . . . . . . 28
    6.      Walt Frazier . . . . . . . . . . . . . . . . . . . . . . . . 32
    7.      Isiah Thomas . . . . . . . . . . . . . . . . . . . . . . . 40
    8.      Bob Cousy . . . . . . . . . . . . . . . . . . . . . . . . . 44
    9.      John Stockton . . . . . . . . . . . . . . . . . . . . . . . 49
    10.      Clyde Drexler . . . . . . . . . . . . . . . . . . . . . . . 52
    11.      Dave Bing . . . . . . . . . . . . . . . . . . . . . . . . . . 55
    12.      Pete Maravich . . . . . . . . . . . . . . . . . . . . . . . 59
    13.      Nate Archibald . . . . . . . . . . . . . . . . . . . . . . 62

II. THE FORWARDS

    1.      Larry Bird . . . . . . . . . . . . . . . . . . . . . . . . . 67
    2.      Elgin Baylor . . . . . . . . . . . . . . . . . . . . . . . . 80
    3.      Bob Pettit . . . . . . . . . . . . . . . . . . . . . . . . . . 87
    4.      Julius Erving . . . . . . . . . . . . . . . . . . . . . . . . 91
    5.      Rick Barry . . . . . . . . . . . . . . . . . . . . . . . . . 98
    6.      John Havlicek . . . . . . . . . . . . . . . . . . . . . . 103
    7.      Karl Malone . . . . . . . . . . . . . . . . . . . . . . . 107
    8.      Charles Barkley . . . . . . . . . . . . . . . . . . . . 110
    9.      Elvin Hayes . . . . . . . . . . . . . . . . . . . . . . . 113
    10.      Kevin McHale . . . . . . . . . . . . . . . . . . . . . . 116
    11.      Scottie Pippen . . . . . . . . . . . . . . . . . . . . . . 119
    12.      Dolph Schayes . . . . . . . . . . . . . . . . . . . . . 122
    13.      Jerry Lucas . . . . . . . . . . . . . . . . . . . . . . . . 127
    14.      Billy Cunningham . . . . . . . . . . . . . . . . . . . 130
    15.      Paul Arizin . . . . . . . . . . . . . . . . . . . . . . . . 132
    16.      Dave DeBusschere . . . . . . . . . . . . . . . . . . 136
    17.      Dominique Wilkins . . . . . . . . . . . . . . . . . . 138
    18.      Adrian Dantley . . . . . . . . . . . . . . . . . . . . . 141
    19.      Bernard King . . . . . . . . . . . . . . . . . . . . . . 143
    20.      Dan Issel . . . . . . . . . . . . . . . . . . . . . . . . . 146
    21.      Alex English . . . . . . . . . . . . . . . . . . . . . . . 148

## III. THE CENTERS

| | | |
|---|---|---|
| 1. | Bill Russell | 153 |
| 2. | Wilt Chamberlain | 163 |
| 3. | Kareem Abdul-Jabbar | 173 |
| 4. | Hakeem Olajuwon | 180 |
| 5. | Moses Malone | 184 |
| 6. | George Mikan | 190 |
| 7. | Willis Reed | 195 |
| 8. | Dave Cowens | 200 |
| 9. | Wes Unseld | 204 |
| 10. | Patrick Ewing | 208 |
| 11. | David Robinson | 211 |
| 12. | Nate Thurmond | 215 |
| 13. | Walt Bellamy | 219 |
| 14. | Bob McAdoo | 224 |
| 15. | Robert Parish | 227 |
| 16. | Artis Gilmore | 230 |

Ten More . . . . . . . . . . . . . . . . . . . . . . . . . . . . . . . . 233
Up and Coming . . . . . . . . . . . . . . . . . . . . . . . . . . . 238
The Regular Season and Playoff
Statistics of the 50 Greatest Players . . . . . . . . . . . . . . . 239
Bibliography . . . . . . . . . . . . . . . . . . . . . . . . . . . . . 246

# ACKNOWLEDGEMENTS

I have benefited from conversations with many former and current NBA players, coaches and broadcasters. I would like to thank them here.

Special thanks to Hubie Brown, Matt Guokas, Jack Ramsay, Bob Ryan, Phil Chenier, Bill Walton, Mike Gminski, Ernie Grunfeld and Tommy Heinsohn.

Thanks also to Bob Cousy, Isiah Thomas, Chuck Daly, John Havlicek, Red Auerbach, Cal Ramsey, Nate Thurmond, Kareem Abdul-Jabbar, Red Holzman, Moses Malone, Walt Frazier, Larry Bird, Robert Parish, Hakeem Olajuwon, Don Chaney, Kevin McHale, Dick McGwire, Mitch Kupchak, Satch Sanders, Jerry West, Jim Cleamons, Butch Beard, Willis Reed, Gar Heard, Connie Hawkins, Tom Van Arsdale and Paul Westphal.

The photos are courtesy of the Basketball Hall of Fame in Springfield, Massachusetts and Dick Raphael.

White Plains, New York
1998

# FOREWORD

I listened to and learned from the experts whose opinions helped in completing this book. But the book is not a simple recitation of their views. I ended up discarding some of my own inconsistent views, the ones I could no longer defend while researching this book. And I ended up not agreeing with all the experts' views either. For one, I found that their opinions were at odds most of the time. So there is no way to form a single *master list* based on what they said. They did agree *some* of the time.

Among the experts, there was nearly a universal consensus on the greatest nine players of all time. Those nine included four guards, who more often than not were in this order: Michael Jordan, Magic Johnson, Oscar Robertson and Jerry West. The two agreed upon forwards were Larry Bird and Elgin Baylor and the three centers were, in some order, Bill Russell, Wilt Chamberlain and Kareem Abdul-Jabbar.

After those nine, there was no consensus. That's right. Agreement is boring; disagreement, interesting. So this book on the 50 greatest reflects much of the disagreement among the experts on the final 41 players. I found their reasoning to vary as widely as their picks. Some stuck close to the statistics, others valued those players who played a key part on a championship team. Still others chose players for their all-round play. Others seemed to rank their picks on a combination of all these factors.

Perhaps the most refreshingly idiosyncratic opinion was given by Bob Ryan, the long-time columnist for the Boston Globe. Said Ryan: "The simple definition of who your best players are comes down to this. You're playing one game against Mars for the championship of the universe. The loser begins eternal servitude, and I have the first pick of all the earthlings who have ever drawn a breath. Without hesitation I take Bill Walton, Bird, Baylor, Magic and Jordan and I'd take my chances with that team." Not much of a chance for eternal servitude there.

I agree with Ryan's definition of greatness -- who do you want for a single game? -- and with most of those five selections. But not all of them. And you may not either. And you certainly won't agree with all fifty of the selections here. But the book will help you to do your own rankings, since it supplies you with relevant facts and information to help you reach conclusions.

Researching the players, choosing my own list and talking to all these experts afforded me a sense of the history of the game that I didn't have before. I hope the book does the same for you.

# The**Guards**

# Michael**Jordan**

There is not now, never was, and probably will never be another basketball player like Michael Jordan. The statement is true whether he plays five more years or quits tomorrow. Jordan is not only the greatest guard that ever lived but the greatest player that ever lived. To label him a great "shooting guard" or a great slasher or a great defender or a great this or that is to limit his magnificence and detract from it. "Jordan defies categorization and takes care of whatever needs you have," says Bob Ryan, columnist for the *Boston Globe*.

How can we know that he will remain number one? How can that conclusion be stated with such assurance? Sure, other great players have been on more championship teams — Bill Russell, and Kareem Abdul-Jabbar just to name a couple. Scoring titles? Wilt Chamberlain won seven consecutive. But Jordan ran off seven in a row from the Reagan eighties through the Clinton nineties, with the NBA at its apex. And in 1997 he won his ninth. Jordan did it *while* raising a team to championship mettle for five years. As great as he was, Chamberlain was on championship teams only twice in fifteen years

(1967 and 1972). He seemed to have difficulty mastering the balance of individual excellence and team play.

People could say the same of Jordan for his first six years in the league. But then he brought Chicago three consecutive championship seasons from 1991 through 1993. Jordan has achieved things that no one has *ever* done.

Consider: he holds the all-time record for points per game at 31.7, nearly two points ahead of Chamberlain. More impressive — but less known — is his lifetime playoff average of 33.6 points per game, also first all-time, a full 4.5 points per game ahead of runner-up, "Mr. Clutch," Jerry West, who averaged 29.1. And eight of those nine scoring titles were posted while appearing on the NBA All-Defensive First Team.

In the 1996-1997 season he was named to the NBA All-Defensive First Team for the eighth time and named to the NBA All-First Team for the ninth time. Eight times Jordan has earned the two distinctions in the same year. No one else has nearly as many. West earned both awards in four separate seasons (West would probably have won more but the defensive award was not given until 1969). Walt Frazier and John Havlicek also accomplished the feat four times. Kareem Abdul-Jabbar did it three times and so has Pippen. Aside from doing it fewer consecutive years, these Hall of Famers weren't taking home scoring titles while accomplishing the feat.

The following chart shows the players who have won both awards the most in the same season.

**\*ALL-FIRST TEAM AND ALL-DEFENSIVE FIRST TEAMS IN SAME SEASON**

| PLAYER | YEARS RECEIVED BOTH HONORS | NUMBER |
|---|---|---|
| Michael Jordan | 1988, 1989, 1990, 1991, 1992, 1993, 1996, 1997 | 8 |
| Walt Frazier | 1970, 1972, 1974, 1975 | 4 |
| Jerry West | 1970, 1971, 1972, 1973 | 4 |
| Kareem Abdul-Jabbar | 1974, 1980, 1981 | 3 |
| John Havlicek | 1972, 1973, 1974 | 3 |
| Scottie Pippen | 1994, 1995, 1996 | 3 |

*\* First Team All-Defense Award not given before 1969*

The point is that winning both awards eight times in the same year shows just how great an all-around player Jordan is. Jordan has played both ends of the floor more superbly than any other player in history. And the entire Jordan package is more notable than the individual achievements. With Jordan the whole is even greater than the sum of the parts. As much as broadcasters sell his impact on a game, he is still undersold. "Usually a player has a weakness; even the great players," says Cousy. "Jordan, however, has no perceptible weakness. He rebounds well above his size. He's not creative in passing but does what is required."

Over his career he has bettered himself at defense and outside shooting. His career free throw shooting is 84 percent, far above average. It can be argued that this flawlessness cannot be found in any of the other candidates for the all-time greatest player.

"You can make a case for several guys being the greatest ever," says NBA patriarch Red Auerbach, who coached the Boston Celtics to eight consecutive titles from 1959 through 1966, a record that will probably never be broken. "There's Russell, Kareem, Bird, Erving, Magic, Oscar and Jordan," continues Auerbach, whose list makes Wilt Chamberlain conspicuous by his absence. Certainly Chamberlain merits a place on the list. But an analysis of Auerbach's grand list shows that neither of these other seven greats were the equal of Jordan.

Consider them in turn. Bill Russell was a great winner. Russell's Celtics won 11 titles in a 13-year span. He was also one of if not *the* best defender ever to play, a distinction for which there are no adequate statistics. He averaged 22.5 rebounds per game. But Russell wasn't a great scorer, since he averaged just 15.1 points per game on 44 percent shooting.

Kareem Abdul-Jabbar is the greatest scorer in league history, having scored 38,387 points. He won six MVP awards, more than anyone in league history. But in a 20-year career, Abdul-Jabbar captured just one scoring title. While he did play on six championship teams in his career, he played on only one of them in his first ten years, winning five more only after hitching his star to Magic Johnson.

Larry Bird was probably the most complete forward and therefore the greatest ever at the position. He was an astounding passer and deadly perimeter shooter, not to mention being a career 89 percent free throw shooter. But he was neither fleet of foot, nor a great defender. His regular season scoring average (24.3) and playoff average (23.8), while great, were far below Jordan's.

Julius Erving was one of the great players of the 1970s. But his scoring average from 1971 through 1976 in the ABA (28.7) is much better than his 22 points per game from 1976 through 1987 in the NBA. And for all his high-flying, above-the-rim-poetry, Erving was not a lethal perimeter shooter. Nor was he the equal of Jordan on the defensive end — never being named to the NBA All-Defensive First Team. Despite playing in the NBA for 11 years, he took home only one title. That title came in 1983, when Moses Malone, the best center that year and league MVP, joined the Philadelphia 76ers.

Oscar Robertson, like Erving, didn't win until late in his career, in 1971, his 12th year in the league. No doubt, this was largely due to playing with a perennially lackluster team, the Cincinnati Royals. As Hubie Brown put it, "Oscar was once universally regarded as the best in the game." The only person who didn't think so, he adds, was Red Auerbach, who was ever loyal to his perennial meal ticket, Russell. No doubt there were also some votes for Chamberlain. At least outside Boston. But even Robertson was not the defensive equal of Jordan. For all Robertson's numerical magnificence — he averaged a triple double in 1962, his second year in the league, and missed doing it by less than a rebound or assist per game in four other seasons! — Robertson is somewhat reminiscent of Erving and Chamberlain. He won too infrequently. His ability to take his teammates to another level must be questioned. In his defense, of course, it can be said that he didn't play on good enough teams.

Magic Johnson was one of the greatest winners in league history. He was also second lifetime in assists with 10,141. But Jordan scores you about 32 points a game to Johnson's 19. While Johnson was a superior passer to Jordan and the greatest point guard ever to play, in no manner was his package of skills as full as Jordan's. Jordan is superior driving, superior on the perimeter and on the defensive end. Johnson was never a great defender.

But Jordan still has much in common with Johnson and Bird, the other two thirds of the "Holy Trinity." Like them, Jordan has had an enormous impact on games.

And it's been true since his rookie season in 1984. Selected third in the NBA draft behind then "Akeem" Olajuwon and Sam Bowie, Jordan led the Chicago Bulls to the playoffs in their first year. He was the league's third leading scorer with 28.2 points per game and also pulled down 6.5 rebounds and gave out 5.9 assists. He was also fourth in the league in steals with 2.39 per game. He thus became the first player to lead his team in all four categories since Larry Bird did it in the 1982-1983 season. He easily finished first in the Rookie of the Year voting.

In the 1985-1986 campaign, when he missed 64 regular season games with a foot injury, Jordan returned to his team in time to establish his reputation for clutch play in big games. In just his second year in the league, Jordan scorched the Celtics for 63 points in the first round of the playoffs. He knew that Boston Garden on Causeway Street was still the St. Paul's of pro basketball and the place to have such a game. The Celtics won the game and the series due to superior balance on their squad. But even in Jordan's sophomore year, Larry Bird knew he was watching a great one. Sitting in the Celtics' locker room after the 58-minute marathon, Bird said "God played today and it was Michael Jordan." God and the Bulls lost.

The following season Jordan scored 61 points in a victory against

Detroit on March 4th and another 61 in a defeat to Atlanta on April 16th. In the Atlanta game he also set a league record by scoring 23 consecutive points, breaking a mark of 18 he had set earlier in the season against the Knicks. The 24 year-old had now scored 60+ points in three games and his team had lost two of them. That little fact reveals much about Michael Jordan's early years in the NBA.

By his fourth year, the Cleveland Cavaliers' general manager and former NBA center Wayne Embry proclaimed, "he plays higher than anybody's ever played. He plays so high that even the big guys can't challenge him."

Someone asked the Knicks' Hall of Fame guard Walt Frazier how he would have guarded him. "I would start off by giving Michael the outside shot, and hope he didn't hit it," said Walt. And if he did hit it? "I would be in for a tough night," was all he could offer.

Celtics' Hall of Famer Bob Cousy also pondered the question. "I would put two guys on him," said Cousy. "And if that didn't work, then three guys or four guys. I'm not kidding. I'd put as many guys on him as I could, until I stopped him, or until I ran out of guys."

In 1988 Jordan won his first MVP award and in 1991 he took his second. But by 1991, his seventh year, frustration had set in for Jordan. Individual honors by themselves were unsatisfactory. Sweeping the Pistons in the conference finals was a larger prize. And storming past the Lakers four games to one in the Finals was the ultimate. In the Finals Jordan was miraculous, averaging 31 points, 7 rebounds and 11 assists. If you add those three numbers, you get Jordan's Total Offensive Production (T.O.P.) was 49. By comparison, Magic Johnson averaged 19 points, 12 assists and eight rebounds, for an impressive T.O.P. of 39.

Jordan clutched the championship trophy and was on top of the world. As I watched the 1991 finals I knew that the torch had been passed. The Lakers and Celtics of the nineteen-eighties would give way to Jordan's Bulls not just for a year or two. Individual honors passed over to Jordan, too. The debate about whether Johnson or Bird was the game's greatest player was old. Those two had lifted the NBA from its no live TV, tape-delay doldrums in the early eighties and set a standard that will never diminish. But neither was the league's best any longer.

By the end of the 1993 season, Jordan's Bulls had won three titles in a row. Jordan had taken on Johnson, Drexler and Barkley in succession, leading his team to a dominating 12-5 record in the three Finals.

In his individual battles with Johnson, Drexler and Barkley the numbers were also in his favor:

### INDIVIDUAL BATTLES IN THE FINALS, 1991-1993

|      |         | FG% | PPG  | RPG  | APG  | T.O.P. |
|------|---------|-----|------|------|------|--------|
| 1991 | Johnson | 43% | 18.6 | 8.0  | 12.4 | 39.0   |
|      | Jordan  | 56% | 31.2 | 6.6  | 11.4 | 49.2   |
| 1992 | Drexler | 41% | 24.8 | 7.8  | 5.3  | 37.9   |
|      | Jordan  | 53% | 35.8 | 4.8  | 6.5  | 47.1   |
| 1993 | Barkley | 48% | 27.3 | 13.0 | 5.5  | 45.8   |
|      | Jordan  | 51% | 41.0 | 8.5  | 6.3  | 55.8   |

He not only outplayed Johnson, Drexler and Barkley — three future Hall of Famers — but completely dominated each one. Barkley made the best showing, but Jordan's overall game was superior. Michael Jordan sat high atop the basketball world.

Then Michael's father, James Jordan, was found shot to death in North Carolina. Distraught over the murder of his father, and tired of the unceasing media intrusion into his private life, Jordan retired from the game. He said he had "nothing left to prove" in basketball. He would try baseball, the game that was his first love as a boy. His fans, teammates and coach mourned. And NBC mourned just as much, knowing that without Jordan they would never capture the casual fan and see TV ratings like the 17.9 rating they saw in the 1993 Finals between Phoenix and Chicago.

Dave Cowens was prophetic. The Celtics Hall of Fame center wrote an editorial to the *New York Times* on November 5th, 1993. "Not to compare my career to yours, but when I retired unexpectedly in 1980, I did it because I had lost my enthusiasm for the game and for winning," Cowens wrote. "It was like a candle going out inside of me. But after a while, I longed for competition and the fierceness it brought out in me. Two years later, I came back to the game.

"Michael, you were born to fly, and you are going to want to go nose to nose with the next player who threatens to take over the game." Cowens said that Jordan should come back and "extinguish himself" through competition, rather than going "out on top."

Though unaware of Cowen's editorial, many of us thought the same way. Lions will hunt because that is what lions do. And Jordan would play again.

People began to sum up his nine-year career. Hubie Brown noted that in a *USA Today* poll taken during the 1992-1993 season, Jordan was selected by 98 percent of the coaches as the player they'd most like to see take the last shot and defend the last shot in a game.

"With a two or three-on-one against Jordan, you don't have a guaranteed score," Brown marvels. "He can block the shot, steal the pass or force you to take a jump shot. Aside from winning the scoring title seven years in a row,

Jordan shoots around 50%, he shoots the three-pointer, rebounds from the guard position and gets assists. No guy can guard him."

In arguments over the greatest player ever, many will counter-attack and says that the Celtics and Lakers of the eighties would have beaten the Bulls of the Nineties. That may be true. This argument, however, is a double-edged sword. Even if it is true, it hardly detracts from Jordan's preeminence. In fact, it adds to it. Consider: replace Jordan and put Larry Bird or Magic Johnson on Chicago in his place. Could they have carried the other 11 players on Jordan's Chicago squads from 1991-1993 to three consecutive championships? How about the 1996 and 1997 teams? It is doubtful. Neither of the five Chicago championship teams had a dominant center or a consistently dominant second scorer. Bird won three titles in his 13 years with the Celtics, but played with six players who are either in the Hall of Fame or on their way: Nate Archibald, Pete Maravich, Robert Parish, Dennis Johnson, Kevin McHale and Bill Walton. Magic Johnson played with James Worthy, Abdul-Jabbar and Byron Scott — who between them have tallied some 70,000 points in their careers!

How the Bulls would do against those Los Angeles and Boston squads is a matter of conjecture. No doubt the Bulls played far better defense than either the Lakers or the Celtics. This has been abundantly evident in the play-offs against Orlando in 1996 and Miami and Utah in 1997. Perhaps the Bulls would lose to the twin giants of the 1980s. But that is hardly the point. The Bulls, with team defense, number 23 at guard and Pippen at forward, beat everyone around. And Jordan earned his claim to the throne by being an insuperable individual talent at the same time that he was winning.

And then there's the matter of his play in the clutch. Teammate Steve Kerr made that case for Jordan. "Jordan is a luxury we have," Kerr smiles. "No other team has it. When we really need a basket, we can get it."

And in April 1995 at Madison Square Garden — the sidelines swelling from an extra 300 press credentials issued for Jordan's third game back from retirement — His Airness soared over, around and through the Knicks for 55 points. It was the 34th time in his career that he had hit for 50 or more points. And he made it 37 times when he scored 51 against the Knicks in January 1997. As usual, Jordan's sense of the dramatic was incredible. To New York fans it must have felt like they had been here before.

When the press irritated Jordan with allegations of his out-of-control gambling habits after the Bulls went down two games to none against the Knicks in the 1993 playoffs, Jordan retreated and granted no interviews to the press. The Bulls circled the wagons and Jordan smoked the Knicks for 54 in game four. New York didn't win another game.

In the Finals against Phoenix that year Jordan laid 55 on the Suns in game four, eliminating any doubt that Charles Barkley was on his level. A true superstar, Barkley had a phenomenal series, toasting Horace Grant for 27 points per game. But Jordan averaged 41 for the series (see table on page 6). Chicago won in six, winning every game on Phoenix' court.

If you had to guess, you would think that the Bulls have had the best record in the league since 1991. And you're right, as the following table shows.

**NBA TOP 5: TEAM RECORDS IN THE LAST SIX YEARS**

| SEASON | CHI | UTAH | SEA | NY | PHO | HOU |
|---|---|---|---|---|---|---|
| 1990-91 | 61-21 | 54-28 | 41-41 | 39-43 | 55-27 | 52-30 |
| 1991-92 | 67-15 | 55-27 | 47-35 | 51-31 | 53-29 | 42-40 |
| 1992-93 | 57-25 | 47-35 | 55-27 | 60-22 | 62-20 | 55-27 |
| 1993-94 | 55-27 | 53-29 | 63-19 | 57-25 | 56-26 | 58-24 |
| 1994-95 | 47-35 | 60-22 | 57-25 | 55-27 | 59-23 | 47-35 |
| 1995-96 | 72-10 | 55-27 | 64-18 | 47-35 | 41-41 | 48-34 |
| 1996-97 | 69-13 | 64-18 | 57-25 | 57-25 | 41-41 | 57-25 |
| TOTAL | 428-146 | 388-186 | 387-187 | 366-208 | 366-208 | 359-215 |
| | .746 | .676 | .674 | .638 | .638 | .625 |

The table shows that the Bulls have been far and away the top team during the run of Chicago's championship years that began in 1991. It also shows that five other teams have had a fair chance to win. Add San Antonio, playing 347-227 (.604) over the last seven years. Then throw in Orlando, who has posted a 253-157 (.617) record for the last *five* years. All told, the NBA has had eight teams with excellent records, all with a chance to walk off with the NBA title.

But NBA titles are not rationed to the needy. They are there for the taking. Only those teams who have the ability and the desire to sustain in the grueling marathon known as the NBA season can grab them. But no other team has Jordan and no other player in recent years can match Jordan's steady internal fire. As Kevin McHale said after the 1997 playoffs, "the Bulls have five championships because of Michael Jordan. 28 teams haven't won because they don't have him."

By now Jordan has made a career of murdering the hopes of several teams. He slays the Knicks annually, having led the Bulls to five playoff victories and a combined playoff record of 19-8 against them since 1989. He has also haunted the dreams of another Eastern Conference team, the Cleveland Cavaliers. In four different years he ended the Cavaliers' season, leading the Bulls to a combined 14-6 record against them. Now add Utah to the road kill.

Jordan has scored 50 or more points eight times in playoff games. His most prolific game ever: regular season or playoffs? He scored 69 points against the Cavaliers in Richfield, Ohio on March 28th, 1990, the ninth highest total in league history. After being knocked to the floor so hard on a drive that he thought he might have broken his tail bone, he scraped himself up and made 23 of 37 field goal attempts and 21 of 23 foul shots. He also had a career-high 18 rebounds, plus six assists and four steals. Despite Jordan's super human effort, it took Chicago an overtime period to win that night, 117-113. It was the fourth time in his career that he had scored 60-plus in a game. "This would have to be my greatest game," Jordan said in the locker room afterward. "When I scored 63 against Boston (in April, 1986), we lost." Three other players are responsible for the eight highest scoring games. Wilt Chamberlain scored seventy or more six times (100, 78, 73, 73, 72, 70); David Thompson (73) and Elgin Baylor (71).

Following his return to the game in March, 1995, after hitting .202 and failing to hit his weight on the Birmingham Barons, Jordan led the Bulls to a 13-4 record in their last 17 games. Though he averaged 27.5 points per game until season's end, he was not in top shape and hit on just 41 percent of his field goal attempts. And though he improved to 31.5 points per game in the playoffs and shot 48 percent from the field, he made several bad plays down the stretch that caused the Bulls to lose to the Orlando Magic. Mind you, no one was comparing Jordan to anyone else. They were only comparing him to what he was before retiring.

At the close of the playoffs in 1995, Brown denied any notion that Jordan had lost his ability. "If you're naming the All-NBA Team, he still makes the first team. There was hardly a drop-off in his playoff stats and his career stats. He was out for a year and nine months, played a foreign sport and then had to recondition his body and everyone demands that his performance be perfect. Well, the true test will be at the end of the playoffs in 1996."

Right. We had to wait a year to see if he could come back. Mission accomplished. Averaging 30.7 points per game, he lead the Bulls to a 15-3 playoff record. In all, the Bulls won 87 and lost 13 for the entire season, a gaudy .870 percentage over 100 games. And while the team is no longer referred to as "Michael and the Jordanaires," there were still nights when number 23 had to do it by himself. Scottie Pippen is *sometimes* missing in action. Tony Kukoc is *frequently* missing in action. The 1996 second round series against the Knicks furnished a good example. When Jordan hit for 44 points in game one, Pippen, who connected on only 4 of 15 field goal attempts, was second in scoring with just 11. Kukoc was just one-of-eight from the field. It frequently goes this way in Chicago. Though winning 72 regular season games was a great team achievement, the paragraph recaps in the morning papers didn't lie. Jordan frequently had to score 13 or 15 or 17 fourth quarter points for the Bulls to win many of those record 72. So Jordan ended up winning his fourth MVP award.

And as Jordan goes, so goes the league. Hubie Brown noted the seismic waves sent out by Jordan's return to basketball in the spring of 1995 and his continuing effect on TV ratings whenever Chicago is playing.

"Before his return, NBC and TNT were below their predicted TV ratings. Once Jordan returned, the regular season balanced the books and the playoffs far surpassed any anticipated ratings for NBC and TNT. It was staggering, absolutely staggering. What happened was his coming back whetted the appetite of the lackadaisical NBA fan and the disgruntled baseball fans and captured new playoff highs for TNT — doing 45 games in 30 nights. "The two highest rated games ever for TNT were a Chicago-Charlotte game and a Chicago-Orlando game. Everyone piggybacked on that. Everyone rode the wave. The casual fan was brought back in and couldn't leave. At TNT, we immediately added three Chicago games to our coverage when we learned of his return."

In the past, even second round games between the Knicks and the Bulls have drawn ratings as high as 18.5.

Forgetting the TV ratings, what is *Brown's* rating now, on Jordan the player? "He is still far and above everyone else," surmises Brown. "He's taken the test of time. When you step back from it all — the nine scoring titles, the championship rings, the MVPs, the consistency in the scoring, regular season and playoffs, the eight times First Team All-Defense — it's never been done before. When you lay it all out there he has to be the best ever."

His impact on games, his will to win and knowing what to do to win — these things can't be measured. In the 1996 playoffs against Orlando, Jordan provided a paradigm example of what it means to know how to win. Jordan surveyed the scene. He knew what mix of offense and defense would be necessary to take the Bulls over the top. In four games he exacted sweet revenge for what had happened against Orlando in 1995, when Horace Grant was carried off the Bulls' home court, his fist pumping in Jordan's face, after the Magic's six-game triumph.

For the next 12 months Jordan kept his eyes on the prize and then averaged 32.3 points in leading the Bulls past Utah. He won game one at the buzzer and in game five he hit the game winner despite having flu symptoms the entire day. In game six he scored 39 points and grabbed 11 rebounds, leaving no doubt about who the real MVP was.

Jordan defines himself by winning. He turned 35 in February, 1998. He still needs to win, just as his body needs air and water and food. This singular combination of skill and will add up to an insuperable athlete.

11

It was once said of Babe Ruth, "we shall never see his like again." Sixty-three years after the Bambino's retirement, the statement is still true. Behold these coming last three or five years of Jordan's career. Sit back in an easy chair and push a videotape into your VCR. After he's gone, we will never see anything like him again.

# Magic**Johnson**

Magic Johnson is the second greatest guard ever to play. I think that is true and most of the experts I've spoken to think so. Why is Johnson placed in such regard? His lofty place is due to his leadership and his balanced contributions as a scorer, rebounder and legendary assist man. Moreover, it is true because he ran the Los Angeles Lakers and directed them to title after title in the nineteen-eighties. The mental picture of Johnson bent slightly at the waist, surveying the floor, dribbling with one hand and calling a play with the other is an indelible image.

When you think of Magic Johnson you might think of two things. His real name is Earvin but he was called "Magic" because of the pizazz in his play. Blind passes that found their mark, switching the ball from hand to hand on drives to the hoop, even sky hooks — Magic sure earned his nickname.

And then you might think of the championships. Between 1980 and 1988 Magic's squad won five of them. Magic orchestrated the wonderfully choreographed Show Time Lakers, the fast-breaking, high scoring purple and gold.

"Johnson obviously had the court vision and total awareness," said Bob Ryan, columnist for the *Boston Globe* and panelist on ESPN's the *Sports*

*Reporters.* "He was a consummate half-court and full-court guard. He was the greatest end-to-end guard ever, ran classic fast breaks and expanded and adapted his game to become an all-around scorer."

Red Auerbach thought that Magic rivaled his own Bob Cousy when it came to running the fast break.

NBC basketball analyst Matt Guokas also chose Johnson as second best all-time. "Magic came along at the time when he was needed for the league. He and Larry Bird brought TV and the NBA together and made basketball popular. He was one of the most entertaining players and had great flair. Whereas Jordan was 90 / 10 a scorer, looking to get points first, Johnson was 20 / 80. He came out to pass the ball and make good plays for his teammates."

Ryan also adds that Magic played the single greatest game of playoff basketball ever. It was game six of the 1980 Finals between the Lakers and the Philadelphia 76ers. The Lakers led three games to two, but Kareem Abdul-Jabbar, who had dominated the series, was sidelined with a badly sprained ankle. Magic jumped to center for the sixth game.

"We all thought we were going back to Los Angeles," recalls Ryan, covering the game for the Globe. The 76ers were lead by "The Doctor," Julius Erving. "Johnson just took over the game," recalls Ryan. "I wrote in my notes that no one of his first five baskets remotely resembled the other."

With a dazzling array of drives, hooks and jumpers, Magic poured in 42 points, dished out 15 assists and grabbed seven rebounds. "All that at 20 years old," Ryan marvels.

And if one can measure sheer love for the game and an unmatched joy in playing it, then I'd like to find a player who loved basketball more than Johnson. He so loved the game that he came out of retirement, knowing full well that the rigors of games, planes and automobiles would shorten his life, because of his H.I.V. virus.

Speaking of his desire to play, one look at the nineties basketball scene will tell you that Magic's desire is rarely matched by many of the current 348 players in the league. After Cedric Ceballos up and disappeared from the Lakers for a four-day spell to go water skiing in the spring of 1996, the team lost back-to-back games for the first time in months. So Ceballos lost his co-captaincy by a unanimous team vote. Then Van Exel was suspended for seven games for shoving a referee. Los Angeles still managed to win 37 of its last 50 games before losing to Houston in the first round of the playoffs.

Johnson summed up the situation for a reporter. "I've been through more stuff in this one year than I went through in 12 years with my other squad," he said. He talked with his mates, telling them 'I know what you want. You want respect, you want commercials, you want sneaker contracts. You want fame. All those things come with winning." Johnson belonged to the older generation of NBA players, the generation that thought of winning first and money second.

It was on March 23rd, 1994 that Magic Johnson announced that he would return to coach the Lakers. The previous coach Randy Pfund had been fired and Johnson took over the team as a favor to Lakers' owner Jerry Buss. Not a month later, on April 15th after the team had lost five straight games, Johnson called the team "quitters" and announced that he would not return as coach the following season. "I take losses too hard," he said. "I hurt and take it home with me. It's been a tough decision," Johnson said. "I've enjoyed it. This has been great for me, working with 12 guys and trying to get them to understand the Laker tradition." Reading between Johnson's words one could see that he was unsuccessful in getting his players motivated.

He was not used to the attitudes of spoiled players. If players were late and fined $50 it "didn't have meaning to them," he said. During his own playing days, Magic said that "those other 11 guys ragged on you until you couldn't be late anymore. If someone had a baby, everybody had a baby. If someone had a tragedy, everybody had a tragedy. [Now] everything is 'I, I, I. Where's my minutes, where's my shots, what about my game?' I don't like that side of the game." For Magic Johnson, love of the game was never an issue. Neither was winning.

And even when he returned to the Lakers for the stretch run in 1996, he gave the team a shot in the arm. "We went from long shots to contenders that quick," said Cedric Ceballos. By now, however, Johnson's game has come down a notch. He contributed 14.7 points, 7 assists and four rebounds per game off the bench for the Lakers that last season. He retired at season's end. He is 38 years old and he probably won't be coming back.

His bottom line is one that only a 6'9" guard might have. He averaged 19.5 points, 7.2 rebounds and 11.2 assists. At his size he revolutionized guard play. In addition to the five championship squads he played on, Johnson was selected All-NBA nine times.

People talk about Penny Hardaway becoming as great as Magic Johnson. In argumentation there is something called "the burden of proof." And in this argument the burden of proof is on Hardaway. In his first three years Hardaway's charges were swept out of the playoffs three times. They were also unimpressive against Miami in 1997. In his first three years Magic led his mates to two titles. Hardaway seems wise enough to know this and is not given to such comparisons. Too bad that Shaquille O'Neal made statements like "me and Penny are the Kareem and Magic of the nineties." People who have been around long enough to know the game are apt to grow nauseous at such remarks. If people wonder why older players sometimes grow bitter, they need look no further than these kinds of fatuous comparisons. Players like Hardaway and O'Neal should earn their comparisons to Johnson and Jabbar instead of talking about them.

There are few guards in the history of the game who deserve to be mentioned in the same sentence with Magic Johnson. If anyone wants to challenge Magic for the second spot, the burden of proof is on him.

# Oscar**Robertson**

Upon hearing the name Oscar Robertson, the new basketball fan in the nineties will naturally think, 'Oh yeah, Oscar; he's the guy who averaged a triple-double for an entire season.' That's true. But that truth is not the whole truth.

Yes, in the second year of his career, as a 23-year-old, 6-5 guard with the Cincinnati Royals, he averaged a "triple-double" — a phrase coined by the late Lakers PR man Bruce Jolesch. Robertson averaged 30.8 points, 11.4 assists and 12.5 rebounds. But he had a "just-missed-triple-double" for the other first four years of his career.

In fact, Robertson's first five years look like this:

| YEAR | RPG | APG | PPG |
|------|-----|-----|-----|
| 1960-1961 | 10.1 | 9.7 | 30.5 |
| 1961-1962 | 12.5 | 11.4 | 30.8 |
| 1962-1963 | 10.4 | 9.5 | 28.3 |
| 1963-1964 | 9.9 | 11.0 | 31.4 |
| 1964-1965 | 9.0 | 11.5 | 30.4 |

In essence, Robertson missed averaging five triple doubles in a row by a rebound per game here or .3 assists there. Take the average of those five seasons and he *did* average a triple-double.

"When you say to Oscar that Jordan is the best ever, he gets incensed," laughs Jack Ramsay, former coach of the 1977 championship Portland Trailblazers and current basketball analyst for ESPN. "He says 'no, I am.' He's that confident of his ability." While people might smirk at Robertson's opinion, no one laughs for long. "Look at his numbers," Ramsay continues. "Oscar made people around him better also. He was the guy who made it happen in Milwaukee" (in 1971, when the Bucks won their first title). But none of the experts I spoke to — including Jack Ramsey — chose Robertson first. No doubt, his all-around game lacked flaws. He passed, scored, rebounded. But whether he was equal to Jordan as a defender, a scorer or in making his teammates better is debatable.

On defense, it is not easy to tell. We must rely on the testimony of people who saw both him and Jordan play. There are few defensive statistics or awards to appeal to, since steals and blocked shots were not kept until the 1973-1974 season. And NBA All-Defensive First and Second team awards were not given until 1969. But having interviewed about 25 coaches, players and analysts I have found no one who said Robertson was a better defender than Jordan. Said Ramsay, "He's certainly not the defender that West and Jordan were."

Looking at Oscar's career Total Offensive Production (T.O.P.), we see it rates among the best ever at the guard position:

| | PPG | RPG | APG | TOTAL OFFENSIVE PRODUCTION |
|---|---|---|---|---|
| O. Robertson | 25.7 | 7.5 | 9.5 | 42.7 |
| M. Jordan | 31.7 | 6.3 | 5.6 | 43.6 |
| J. West | 27.0 | 5.8 | 6.7 | 39.5 |
| M. Johnson | 19.5 | 7.2 | 11.2 | 37.9 |

Oscar's offensive production rates second, a mere .9 in production behind Jordan. He is 3.2 ahead of Jerry West and 4.8 ahead of Magic Johnson. Further, since T.O.P. is a fluctuating statistic and since Jordan's statistics are beginning to decline, it is conceivable that Jordan's T.O.P. might eventually fall below Robertson's.

"Oscar is without a doubt the greatest basketball player I have ever played against," said Jerry West, after his and Oscar's retirements in the 1970s. "To me he is the closest player I have ever seen to being perfect. I think more significantly, he helped establish the importance of guard play in the NBA."

Still, many people, indeed most experts, rate Robertson third, behind Jordan and Johnson. There is at least one salient reason for that rating.

Both Johnson's and Jordan's teams won and won often. Johnson's Lakers and Jordan's Bulls have won a combined 10 championships — indeed, of the last 18 NBA titles, 10 have gone to Los Angeles and Chicago. Oscar Robertson played 14 NBA seasons with the Cincinnati Royals and the Milwaukee Bucks and won one title. The obvious rejoinder is that Oscar Robertson didn't play on good teams. That is true to a degree.

It is true that he did not play on Philadelphia, Boston or Los Angeles — the three best teams of the 1960s. But he did play with forwards Jack Twyman and Jerry Lucas, both Hall of Famers and Wayne Embry, a center who from Oscar's rookie year through his fifth year averaged double-figures in points and rebounds with Cincinnati. Embry appeared among the league's rebounding leaders and top 20 in scoring for several years. For Oscar's first three years Twyman was also among the top scorers. And rebounding master Jerry Lucas joined the Royals for the 1963-1964 season. Year in and year out Lucas was among the top rebounders in the league, averaging between 17.4 and 21.1 rebounds per game from 1964-1969.

For the 1964-1965 season Adrian Smith joined the Royals. Between 1965 and 1968 Smith averaged between 15.1 and 18.4 points per game. For the 1966 and 1967 seasons Happy Hairston chipped in 14+ points per game. From the 1968-1970 seasons, Robertson's last three years with the Royals, 6'10" Connie Dierking contributed 16+ points each year and between 8 and 9 rebounds per game. And further scoring help came from guard Tom Van Arsdale, who in Oscar's last two years contributed 19.4 and 22.8 points per game.

Thus to claim that Oscar played with no one for his tenure in Cincinnati is nonsense. His was not a solo act. Still, four times during Oscar's stay the Royals were under .500. All told, the Royals in the Oscar years played to a .523 percentage. It is thus not easy to contend that he elevated the play of his teammates. That's his career, B.K. — Before Kareem.

Magic Johnson, by comparison, played his last two seasons, the 1990 and 1991 seasons, *without* Kareem. Without the big guy in the middle, Johnson led the Lakers to a 121-43 won-lost record. That's a .738 winning percentage. Those two seasons were not title seasons for the Lakers. They made it to a Conference final in 1990 and a Championship final in 1991. But, as usual, Magic raised the level of everyone around him.

So winning is the most obvious reason that Johnson — and Jordan, for that matter — get elevated above Robertson.

One rather strong reply can be made in Oscar's defense. In 1959, when Oscar joined the NBA, the league had only eight teams. The NBA was dominated by Boston and Philadelphia in the Eastern Division and by St. Louis and then, with the flourishing of West and Baylor, by Los Angeles in the West. Teams played 79 games in a season, 13 against the other three teams in their own divisions and 10 against each of the four teams in the other division. No expansion teams existed and therefore there was little opportunity to pad your record with easy wins.

The Chicago Packers did join the league in 1961, giving the league nine teams and an eighty-game regular season. In 1963 the Philadelphia Warriors' franchise moved to San Francisco and the Nationals' franchise could no longer make a go of it in Syracuse and moved to Philadelphia to become the 76ers. Baltimore then entered the league. In those years the Knicks and Chicago Packers were as inept as the Vancouver Grizzlies. Still, there were fewer poor teams in the league in those years. In 1997, 11 of the 29 teams won less than 35 games — Boston, Dallas, Milwaukee, New Jersey, Philadelphia, Toronto, Denver, San Antonio, Vancouver, Sacramento and Golden State. Teams that poor provide big opportunities for good teams to rack up easy wins. The opportunities for easy victories were not as frequent in Oscar's early years.

Cincinnati played .600+ ball with Oscar for the first time in the 1963-1964 season, winning 55 and losing 25 during the 1964-1965 season. The following year they played exactly .600, winning 48 and losing 32.

But even in those two years when the team was competitive, they were not formidable in the playoffs. Oscar and the Royals beat Philadelphia three games to two in the first round in 1964, then were drubbed by the Celtics four-to-one in the division finals. Despite the fact that *8 of 12* teams were eligible for the playoffs for the 1968 and 1969 playoffs and 8 of 14 teams for the 1970 season, in Robertson's six years between 1965 and 1970 in Cincinnati the Royals would never win *a single* playoff series, not even making the playoffs for the three years from 1968-1970. In his ten years with the Royals, Oscar-led teams played in eight playoff series and lost six of them. Their record in playoff games was 15-24 for those years, a horrendous .385 percentage. Thus, even though it was harder on Robertson because there were fewer bad teams, he demonstrated little ability to raise the level of other Cincinnati players.

So the most compelling case can be made that Robertson, a player with assembly line efficiency, is the third greatest guard of all-time.

Even without winning, however, "The Big O" could dominate a game. Straight from a gold medal showing in the 1960 Rome Olympics, on a U.S. team that also included Walt Bellamy, Jerry West, Jerry Lucas, Adrian Smith, Terry Dischinger and Bob Boozer, Oscar joined the Royals. He immediately put up huge numbers in the NBA. If a measure of how great a player is can be seen by measuring his dominance right out of college, then Oscar was truly dominant. Only Elgin Baylor, Wilt Chamberlain and Kareem Abdul-Jabbar began their careers with as much thunder as Oscar.

Let's take the three greatest centers, six forwards and six greatest guards that ever lived and measure their first three years in the NBA. Many great players are hyped after their college careers, but few put up great figures right off the bat in the NBA.

### THE FIRST THREE SEASONS OF THE 15 GREATEST PLAYERS IN NBA HISTORY

| NAMES | YEARS | 3 YEAR GAMES | PPG | RPG | APG | TOT. OFF. PROD. |
|---|---|---|---|---|---|---|
| **3 CENTERS** | | | | | | |
| K. Abdul-Jabbar | 20 | 245 | 31.8 | 15.7 | 4.0 | 51.5 |
| W. Chamberlain | 15 | 231 | 42.3 | 26.5 | 2.2 | 71.0 |
| B. Russell | 13 | 187 | 16.1 | 22.0 | 2.7 | 40.8 |
| **6 GUARDS** | | | | | | |
| O. Robertson | 14 | 230 | 29.8 | 11.0 | 10.2 | 51.0 |
| M. Jordan | 11 | 182 | 31.7 | 5.6 | 5.0 | 42.3 |
| J. West | 14 | 209 | 24.8 | 7.6 | 5.0 | 37.4 |
| M. Johnson | 13 | 192 | 18.9 | 8.7 | 8.5 | 36.1 |
| G. Gervin * | 14 | 244 | 26.6 | 5.2 | 3.1 | 34.9 |
| J. Havlicek ** | 16 | 235 | 17.5 | 5.7 | 2.6 | 25.8 |

*\* These are Gervin's first three years in the NBA, not the ABA*

*\*\* John Havlicek was Boston's "Sixth Man" for the first three years of his career*

| NAMES | YEARS | 3 YEAR GAMES | PPG | RPG | APG | TOT. OFF. PROD. |
|---|---|---|---|---|---|---|
| **6 FORWARDS** | | | | | | |
| E. Baylor | 14 | 213 | 29.8 | 17.1 | 4.2 | 51.1 |
| R. Barry | 14 | 240 | 27.8 | 10.0 | 3.6 | 41.4 |
| B. Pettit | 11 | 215 | 23.6 | 14.9 | 2.6 | 41.1 |
| L. Bird | 13 | 241 | 21.8 | 10.7 | 5.3 | 37.8 |
| K. Malone | 11 | 245 | 21.4 | 10.4 | 2.4 | 34.2 |
| J. Erving* | 16 | 234 | 21.8 | 7.4 | 4.0 | 33.2 |

*\* These are Erving's first three years in the NBA*

Benjamin Disraeli once quipped, "there are lies, damned lies and statistics." But the numbers above aren't telling any lies. Oscar Robertson hit the NBA with gale force. None of the other five greatest guards came even close to putting up the three-year numbers that Oscar did. No one else is close to putting up a Total Offensive Production total of 50. The only other players to reach a T.O.P. of 50 in their first three seasons were Elgin Baylor, Kareem Abdul-Jabbar and Wilt Chamberlain.

Robertson explained his early success. The co-captain of the U.S. Olympic squad credited his high school coach, Raye Crowe, with instilling his fundamentals. "Even the so-called 'natural' has to work on things," said Oscar. "I did have the fundamentals down when I entered pro ball. Once you get into pro ball, you don't have time to think, 'If a guy does this, I do that.' You do things instinctively."

And thus the incredible quality of his first five years.

Even while still at the University of Cincinnati — where he averaged a staggering 33.8 points and 15.2 rebounds in four years! — one writer labeled Oscar "basketball's Willie Mays." As a fourth-year pro in 1964 he won the league MVP. It was a time when West, Chamberlain, Baylor and Russell made competition for the award fierce every season.

He was relentless on offense and lead the league in scoring once, with a 29.2 average in 1968. He also led the league in assists *eight* times, including six straight years from 1964 through 1969. The frustration he caused on offense was legendary, "Oscar always made the big play, the right play" said Laker forward Elgin Baylor. "When you played against Oscar you not only faced an opponent with a tremendous amount of talent and physical skills, but you were also up against a finely tuned pro basketball mind. Oscar was smarter than any pro player I have ever faced. It was always a thrill to watch Oscar not only outplay but also outsmart his opponents. The Big O was truly a basketball master, a performer without equal."

By the time he had retired he led the league in lifetime assists (9,887) and free throws (7,694). He played on the All-NBA First Team for a staggering 10 consecutive years, from 1961 thorough 1970. He had also won the NBA Rookie of the Year Award and won the All-Star Game Most Valuable Player three times, having averaged 23 points per game in his first 10 All-Star Games!

Oscar boasted a career line of 26,710 total points, 25.7 points 9.5 assists and 7.5 rebounds per game. Robertson's point total is first all-time among guards, though Jordan is lurking just 2,221 points behind him. No wonder that Chamberlain once said, "If I had my pick of all the players in the league I'd take the Big O first."

And two other Hall of Famers chimed in with similar opinions. Both were guards who played against Oscar. Said the Pistons' Dave Bing, "Oscar is without a doubt the all-time everything basketball player. His tremendous offensive ability has overshadowed his great defensive skills."

Lenny Wilkens had enough trying times trying to guard Oscar, too. When his career was winding down with Cleveland in 1973, he said "If there is one complete player, it's Oscar Robertson. He does everything flawlessly and is a perfectionist."

"He was tough on defense too," recalled Connie Hawkins. "He had great physical strength and was big and strong and would beat guys up." Even one of the great stylists like Connie Hawkins could appreciate Robertson's no-frills approach to the game.

At 6-5 and 210 pounds Oscar was bigger than the other guards of his time. He used that height in backing defenders down, not settling for a 17-footer when he could get a 15-footer or a 15-footer when he could get a 12-footer.

That's the man who was known as the Big O. O as in Oscar. O as in offense. O as in outstanding.

# Jerry**West**

For those of us who remember nineteen-sixties and early-seventies basketball, Jerry West was a steady-going terror. If only a few minutes remained and number 44 was coming downcourt against your team, it was time to check the score. Time in and time out he could back your best defender down and shoot over him. West would wipe out a ten-point lead in a four-minute spurt like no other player.

For these kinds of endgame exploits — and his spectacular playoff performances — he earned the name "Mr. Clutch." He owns a 29.1 points per game average in the playoffs, second only to Michael Jordan in basketball history. He also finished with 25,192 points and a per-game average of 27, 4th highest in basketball history. He was selected to the All-Defensive team four straight times. "He was second only to Jordan as a two-way guard," says Bob Ryan, *Boston Globe* columnist. "He's starting to fall through the cracks of history and we've got to do something to rescue him. There was no tougher competitor."

Those who know best won't let what he accomplished fall through the cracks of history. But West is less given to talk about himself than almost any other great athlete. As an executive with the Lakers he has been so great that some people now think of him only in those terms. "West had grit and fire that Oscar never had," says Ryan, who actually places West third above Oscar Robertson. So does TNT analyst and former Piston's coach Chuck Daly.

"West was all-everything," recalls former Knicks' guard and present director of scouting with New York, Dick McGuire. "You go down three on two on the fast break and he'd steal the ball. He played the passing lanes, knew how to play. He had some great battles in New York with Frazier." And in 1972 the battle was won by West. But the road to that point was too long.

Before his stellar career as an NBA guard, Jerry West was on the 1960 Olympic Team that took home gold from Rome. Right from the start, he and Elgin Baylor teamed up for 30 and 35 or 35 and 40 points per night. They are still the greatest one-two scoring punch in the history of the NBA. Later on, for the 1972 and 1973 seasons, West and Gail Goodrich also gave Los Angeles between 45 and 50 points per night.

But West was not only a point scorer. He was interested in excellence in all aspects of the game. Since he and Robertson came out of college in the same year and both played for the Rome Olympic squad, their careers formed a pair and a thought of one led naturally to a thought of the other.

Jerry West was very gracious for the comparison, picking Oscar to be put on various "best player" lists but never picking himself. Toward the end of his first year in the league, West reflected on his experience in the eight-team league. "Now that I have been around the league a little bit, I have begun to have my own impressions of some of the various players. Naturally the gifted play of such men as Bob Pettit, Wilt Chamberlain and Bob Cousy was no surprise, since they have been highly publicized for several years. But the overall high level of play was more consistent than I had really figured on. There are no weak players in the league."

His first year was the only year in his career that his average was under 20, and one can almost see this young man from Cheylan, West Virginia feeling out the competition and finding his place on the Lakers, a team in a new city after moving West from Minneapolis, where George Mikan helped to bring them five championships in the forties and fifties, at the dawn of the NBA. He was also joining a team with the great Elgin Baylor, one of the first players who performed with hang time. Baylor was in his third year and in West's rookie campaign the 6-5 all-everything averaged 34.8 points and 19.8 rebounds. No "small" forward will ever play that big again. As the playoffs approached, West surmised "the one man in the league who impressed me more than any other had to be Elgin Baylor."

But statistics do tell a story and in West's case the story won't shut up. Though he averaged 17.6 points in his first year the kind of average he could have posted with a sprained ankle for the next 13 years — West was gearing up for the spring tournament. As the Lakers took the Detroit Pistons 3-2 in the Western Division semis, West was finding the range. In a tough series again, St. Louis — with their three 20+ scorers Bob Pettit, Cliff Hagan and Clyde Lovellette — Los Angeles lost a seven-game series in which the widest margin of victory was six points. The Lakers even led three games to two before suffering an overtime loss at home and a two-point loss in St. Louis. West's average climbed to 22.9, five points ahead of his regular season average.

Both the loss and the average began patterns. For nine consecutive years, West's playoff average would exceed his regular season average, even climbing to a staggering 40.6 per game for the 1965 playoffs. Thus the legend of "Mr.Clutch" was born. "He was the captain of the all-clutch team," Jack Ramsay stresses. And it's there in print to see. He was consistent, glorious even in defeat.

But a more disturbing pattern was also begun that year. West's teams would make the playoffs all 14 of his years in the pros, a remarkable record of consistency. But in the sixties his teams never had enough to get them over the top. Six different times in the playoffs — 1962, 1963, 1965, 1966, 1968 and 1969 — the Lakers ran out of gas against Boston. Three of those series went the agonizing seven-game limit. With each year's loss a part of Jerry West died.

But no one blamed the Lakers or any other team of the time. After all, the annual road to the NBA title went through Boston Garden and Boston, with a raging Russell in the middle, won 9 of the 10 NBA championships in the 1960s. The Lakers were the second best team of the nineteen-sixties.

And those seeking ammunition for West in the West-Robertson comparison will find plenty of hardware in the playoff evidence. If one argues that the most important games are those played in the post-season, then one can argue that West is second only to Jordan among guards.

And in 1972 he got the reward he deserved. Not only did the Lakers shatter the Bucks' record of 19 consecutive wins by running off 33 games in a row from November 5, 1971 through January 7, 1972, but they finished that season with a 69-13 record. They averaged 121 points a game, with Goodrich and West averaging a combined 52 points every night. And on defense they were sixth best in the league with 108.7 per game. The differential of 12.3 was best in the league that year.

They stormed through the playoffs. They trounced Chicago four-zip. They exacted revenge for losing to Milwaukee in 1971, besting Abdul-Jabbar and Oscar Robertson four games to two. And in the Finals they paid back the Knicks for the 1970 Finals, this time clobbering them four games to one after the Knicks took the opener. For the season they went 81-16. It was a kind of last hurrah for Chamberlain and West, both of whom enjoyed excellent seasons.

While most people I spoke to chose Robertson over West for the third spot, a case can be made that West was a better player. Here's the case. West averaged 27 points for his career to Robertson's 25.7. He also led Oscar in NBA All-First Team selections, ten to nine. And in NBA All-First Team Defense selections it wasn't even close. West was chosen four times to Oscar's none. West was also superior as a clutch performer and in playoff competition. On Robertson's behalf it could be argued that his all-around play was better. His 42.7 T.O.P. is superior to West's 39.5. This is due to his averaging two rebounds and three assists per game more than West.

But it is splitting hairs to choose one over the other. "West could do it all," says Hall of Fame coach and ESPN commentator Jack Ramsay. "I never saw him make a bad pass. He handled the ball a lot on the break and was very fundamental. He could shoot it from the perimeter, drive to the basket, post you up. He was a great clutch player." I'm sure that Jerry West didn't observe a mantra for the near 1,000 games he played. But if he had followed one I know what it would have been: be consistent, play for every advantage, respect the game with your effort.

Recently the subject of the greatest teams ever was raised. Naturally, the 1972 Lakers found their way onto the list. How nice that the man who shot arena lights out for 14 years finally drew recent praise for something other than being the best executive in basketball.

# George**Gervin**

Gervin won four scoring titles, notes former coach and TNT basketball analyst Hubie Brown. This means that only Jordan with nine titles, and Chamberlain with seven, won more. Hubie Brown is right. "The Ice Man" deserves the fifth spot more than anyone else. He averaged 25 points a game for his career.

I found that Gervin gets little credit from most of the experts, probably because the San Antonio Spurs squads on which he played didn't win much of the time. And Gervin, when he played defense at all, played with disinterest. Some experts left Gervin off their lists completely. "Winning is always a criterion for greatness," said Isiah Thomas. "How many rings you have is important. So in this kind of survey that hurts George." Still, Thomas chose Gervin as fifth best, explaining that George was the "best pure scorer" of the entire group of guards.

The criticism of Gervin for not winning must be considered part of his record. But it should not be made the whole record. Are the players who won titles the only truly great players? Probably not. Players who don't win must be questioned, because they may be purely individual players who couldn't help their teammates. On the other hand, they may be players who just didn't play on teams talented enough to win. Gervin may fit both categories.

A guard on the championship 1978 Washington Bullets, Phil Chenier, remembers playing against Gervin. "I used to have to guard him year in and year out," Chenier complains. "He was phenomenal. He was tall (6-7, 185 pounds), so I thought I could steal the ball on him and pressure him from the outside. But he played so effortlessly. He was smooth and could score in a heartbeat." Gervin shot over guards and was quick enough to go around forwards.

After a 1982 game in which Detroit beat San Antonio, Thomas marvelled at the Ice Man's varied talents. "I wish I was on San Antonio's team just to watch him every night. He's so good. When he gets the ball it's two points. You don't know how he'll get it but he always finds a way."

And few players could score in the variety of ways that Gervin could score. "From the outside he could literally drill the ball in the basket," recalls Gene Shue, who played in the 1960s and coached several teams, including the Baltimore Bullets. "George Gervin was a magnificent offensive player who could score from anywhere. It was uncanny; he had such a soft touch, a beautiful touch. He was an unstoppable offensive player."

Ice was known for his cool from the outside and his "finger roll" on the inside. In a recent TV commercial, Gervin sat in a barber shop, while David Robinson and Tim Hardaway were laughing at Gervin's seventies fashions, including a silver number that looked like a space suit that would fry in the Texas heat. Gervin finally piped up, "One thing I could do is finger roll." Everyone convulsed in laughter.

Finger rolling wasn't all he could do. You don't lead the league in scoring for three straight years — with averages of 27, 30 and 33 — by just finger rolling. The ridiculously thin Gervin had twisting, fall away jumpers and even spinning no-look reverse layups. When the Ice Man got hot, no one could touch him. Only six players in history have won three consecutive scoring titles and Gervin was one of them. The other five are George Mikan, Neil Johnston, Wilt Chamberlain, Bob McAdoo and Michael Jordan. And Gervin separated himself from three members of the club by winning a fourth scoring title in 1982 — his fourth in five years! — when he averaged 32.3 points.

By then Gervin had grown tired of just being a player who was known for filling it up. No better example of his frustration could be found than in a game the Spurs played against the New Orleans Jazz in 1978. Gervin scored 63 points that day, but the Spurs still lost 153-132. The Jazz starting lineup alone scored 121 points. "Four scoring titles got me four watches," he said. "I don't want any more watches. I want that championship ring."

But Gervin could never quite get the ring. He played on two teams that had a chance but both came up short. "The 1979 team was the best I ever played for," Gervin said. "It was great. We developed a run and gun style and we got real good at it." That year Gervin and James Silas teamed at guard, with All-Star Larry Kenon in the front court with Mark Olberding and 6-11 Billy Paultz in the pivot. That team won 48 games but got eliminated by the Washington Bullets in the Conference Finals after jumping out to a 3-1 lead. The 1983 team won 53 games. That year Gervin teamed with Johnny Moore at guard and Mike Mitchell and Gene Banks at forward. Artis Gilmore played the pivot and chipped in 18 points and 12 rebounds a game. But the Spurs lost a tough six-game series to the Lakers on their home court. They trailed by one point when a Mitchell jumper bounced off the rim. The Lakers had Norm Nixon, Magic Johnson and Kareem Abdul-Jabbar that year.

Gervin's lifetime average of 25 points per game is eighth in NBA history, but is fourth among guards, behind only Michael Jordan, Jerry West and Oscar Robertson.

But Gervin's records, including his 26,595 points, do receive short shrift because he scored them in the wide-open west, where defense appeared optional and because Gervin didn't win any championships.

But Gervin's teams did make the playoffs nine different years and Gervin upped his average to 27 points for those games. He also increased his assists and rebounding during the playoffs. But those teams never seemed to have enough. So in 14 seasons in the NBA and ABA Gervin played in only 84 playoff games.

In 1979 Gervin averaged 28.6 points per game in the playoffs. The scoring punch of Gervin and Kenon was not enough to overcome their porous defense. In the following year, the 1979-1980 season, they allowed 119.7 points per game, thus wasting the 119.4 points that they averaged.

Since he exerted three times as much energy on offense as he did on defense — he once explained, "our offense is our defense" — Gervin is taken down a notch or two in the minds of many experts. Still, he was All-NBA first team five times and shot an amazing .511 from the field for his career. Few guards in league history have done as much.

"George was never a defensive player," Shue agrees, and Shue then knocked him down a few notches, down to eighth on his list of the greatest guards.

But the image that Gervin's name evokes for many of us is the image that Chenier and Thomas leave us with. "You thought you had him stopped baseline and he'd squeeze in and dunk on you," Chenier recalls.

"He was so effortless," Thomas says. "He'd have 40 points and not even break a sweat."

Chenier has the last word: "He gave me fits."

In the end, Gervin was traded to Chicago to team in the backcourt with Michael Jordan. Fans in San Antonio protested, saying that they should have traded the team president, not the beloved Ice Man.

After 12 years, the Ice Age had ended in San Antonio. Gervin played 82 games for Chicago in his last year. But Michael Jordan missed 64 of those games because of a foot injury. So Air and Ice never took flight together.

Gervin retired at season's end, leaving behind a shopping bag of goodies. 3 ABA All-Star Games, 9 NBA All-Star Games, 5 All-NBA First Team selections and four scoring titles were just a few of his achievements. Want more? He scored 50 or more 4 times, 40 or more 64 times and once scored 20 or more points in 53 straight games. "I played like I loved the game," he said. "I always loved it."

For people who enjoyed offensive artistry, number 44 gave you something to remember.

# Walt**Frazier**

"Dreadful." The word came quickly to Walt Frazier as he sat in the media production room at Madison Square Garden. Looking resplendent, even thinner than in his playing days, Frazier sports a maroon jacket and black pants and black suede shoes. His voice is quiet, almost reverent, as he drifts back to a time 26 years ago, recalling how the felt the night of Game 7 against the Lakers, May 8, 1970.

"How could we stop Chamberlain without Willis? As always, I sat around the hotel, conserving energy for the game. I went over to the Garden early, trying to find out if anyone knew of Reed's condition. Nobody knew...

"During warmups Reed came onto the court, and we felt we had a chance. Then he hit his first two shots and I believe we all thought we could win." The Knicks jumped in front 9-2 and led 38-24 at the end of the first quarter.

During the second quarter, Jerry West slowed his dribble just before mid-court. In that moment of hesitation the ball was suddenly separated from him, flicked away by a 24-year-old having the night of his life and lunging toward the Hall of Fame. Frazier drove to the basket a step ahead of West and laid — not dunked — the ball over the front rim and got fouled. With his deliberate, over-the-back-of-the-head free throw motion, he completed the three-point play.

The Knicks went into the fourth quarter leading the Lakers by 24 points. "I was thinking, 'Tick clock, tick.' the entire game. Not until the beginning of the fourth quarter did I think we had a chance. I mean, they had Baylor, West and Chamberlain," Frazier recalls, stressing each Hall of Famer's name. "I knew they'd make a run."

Knicks' broadcaster Marv Albert put it into perspective on the radio: If the Knicks score just 16, the Lakers must score 41 to win." On that night, the whole was less than the sum of the parts for the Lakers. The three most pro-lific scorers in Playoff history, to that point — Chamberlain, West and Baylor — could not make up the deficit. The Knicks won 113-99, and though Reed was voted NBA Finals MVP for his heroics, it was Frazier who laid down the line that night: 36 points, 19 assists, 7 rebounds and 5 steals.

The media was certain to want to learn more about the guy trainer Danny Whelan had named "Clyde," due to his yen for wide-brimmed hats.

26 years later, Frazier remains one of the all-time Knicks. He is the greatest guard ever to play in a New York uniform. His number 10 is retired and hangs from the Garden rafters. He was traded to Cleveland for Jim Cleamons in 1976. And in the 20 years since that time the Knicks have looked for a player who could hit an 18-footer consistently.

If Clyde the wordy WFAN color analyst were to sum up his career accomplishment in one of those Frazier Phrases which have become his broadcast trademark, he might decline. But the summation would have to be: Clyde, swishin' and dishin' on offense, reelin' and dealin' on defense.

Anyone who knows those Knicks from 26 years ago knows they won not because of drivin' and jivin' but because they played harder and smarter than everyone in sight.

"No doubt that 69-70 championship team was the highlight of my career; the 1972-1973 season (when Frazier and the Knicks won their second NBA title) is rather vague in my mind. I think of the events of the 69-70 sea-son — the record 18-game winning streak, the 6 points in 16 seconds to beat Cincinnati and keep the streak alive, the playoff with Willis getting hurt and us pulling out the games," Frazier recalls.

And his personal highlight?

"I'd have to say that seventh game against the Lakers. I always tried to hit the open man; that night I was the open man. I'd come off a pick, and the shot would be there. I didn't say to myself 'You have to pick up the slack for Willis.' It just happened."

Could the 69-70 Knicks play the Lakers, Celtics, Pistons or Bulls of the eighties and nineties. The temptation is to say no, that speed and athletic ability have passed that old team by.

"We could play with them," said Frazier, in about the same time it took for him to flick the ball away from an opposing guard. Two reasons: perimeter shooting and defense. Well, they might have problems matching the size of stars like Larry Bird, Magic Johnson, Michael Jordan and Kevin McHale.

Whatever. The Knicks got excellent perimeter shooting from their starting five of Frazier and Barnett at guards, Bradley and DeBusschere at forwards and Reed at center. Then they had Mike Reardon, Dave Stallworth and Cazzie Russell off the bench. And defensively they regularly held teams to less than 100 points and lead the league by allowing only 105.9 points per game.

"Guys today, because they can jump out of the gym, often don't develop the skills they should have," says Frazier. "We boxed out on the rebounds. Many players today don't. And guys who can drive often can't shoot from the perimeter."

And Debusschere, who came to New York in the key trade involving Walt Bellamy and Howard Komives in December, 1968, seconded the motion. "I believe that that team — for a period of four or five years — will be recalled as the most intelligent one ever to play the game." Coach Red Holzman agreed. "We had a philosophy that if you want to win, the selfish thing is to be unselfish. We had some good thinkers out there, and of course Clyde was one of them. He became a great player. He was always a hell of a defensive player, but he also developed into a great shooter."

This notion of the Knicks as a high IQ team of their time doesn't sit well with everyone. In his book *Elevating the Game*, Nelson George looks at the Knicks of that period as an over-hyped, over-endorsed NBA quintet.

> *Boston dominated pro basketball for more than ten years. Yet in the 1969-1970 season alone the Knicks may have generated more national press coverage and endorsements for their players than the Celtics enjoyed in a decade. Books like Pete Axthelm's The City Game celebrated Walt Frazier's flashy wardrobe, Bradley's Rhodes Scholarship, Debusschere's beer drinking, and Reed's leadership, as if one season of outstanding basketball made them all-time greats. Knick team slogans — "find the open*

*man" and "see the ball" were intoned with amazing reverence by fans and sportscasters. The Knicks rise solidified the NBA's national television contract with ABC and led folks to hype basketball as "the game of the seventies."*

*In actuality, this much-heralded championship five won only one NBA title and would last as a unit only another year and a half. This is not to say the Knicks weren't gifted — it's just that in the great flow of basketball history, they never exerted dynastic control of their era, as the Celtics had and the Lakers would.*

True, the Knicks were oversold, the way any team from New York gets oversold. True also, the Knicks from 1969-1974 were not a dynasty. But they won titles in 1970 and 1973 and in 1972 lost in the finals to the Lakers.

In fact their six-year run of excellence beginning in 1969 does rate a second look. Their records were as follows:

| | |
|---|---|
| 1968-1969: | 54-28 |
| 1969-1970: | 60-22 |
| 1970-1971: | 52-30 |
| 1971-1972: | 48-34 |
| 1972-1973: | 57-25 |
| 1973-1974: | 49-33 |

That's 320 wins and 172 losses for .650 percentage. And their playoff record was 51-34, a .593 percentage. They were a team for a time. No they were not the Celtics, but who was? Would George's point be that all non-Celtic teams are worthless? From 1946, when the league began, through 1974, there were just two dynasties. The Minneapolis Lakers had won five titles between 1949 and 1954 and the Boston Celtics had won 12, from 1957-1974. That's two teams sharing 17 of the 29 titles. Besides the Knicks, the only other city with two titles was Philadelphia, with the Warriors (1956) and the Philadelphia 76ers (1967).

And Frazier was the mainstay on those Knicks for six years, playing 472 games out of a possible 492. Willis Reed, the Knicks' give-no-quarter force in the middle, played 335 games, missing 157, most of them due to injuries to his knees. That means Frazier played 79 games on average for the six seasons while Reed played just 56 games per year.

But Frazier didn't get an MVP. Reed deservedly won the league MVP in 1970. Reed also won the Finals MVPs in 1970 and 1973. Reed was the spiritual leader in 1970 and he had the superior numbers in the playoffs, laying down a line of 23.7 points, 13.8 rebounds and 2.8 assists in 18 post-season games. Frazier had a more rounded but less impressive line of 16 points, 7.8 rebounds and 8.2 assists. But in the 1973 post season there should have been no doubt.

Reed was the team's indomitable captain, their bulwark in the middle, and that reputation, perhaps as much as anything, got him the second MVP, even though his pro career had so diminished that he would play just 19 more regular season games and 11 playoff games before he would retire.

It is beyond question that Frazier is the Knicks' greatest guard, if not their greatest player, in the team's 50-year history.

How does he stand against the rest of the all-time guard corps? The question would produce some arguing.

It always occurred to me in recent years that the best four guards were fairly obvious. In some order they had to be Jordan, Johnson, Robertson and West. After that, selecting the remaining greats in order gets very tricky. Gene Shue agreed, saying, "you can join all the rest of the guys; it gets very difficult to choose after the first four."

The first four guards are Michael Jordan, Magic Johnson, Oscar Robertson and Jerry West. Then there is a drop-off in talent. In fifth place is George Gervin. Thereafter, the best candidates are Bob Cousy, Isiah Thomas, John Stockton, Earl Monroe, Clyde Drexler, Nate Archibald and Pete Maravich. And Walt Frazier.

It can be argued that Frazier's all-around game was better than any of these other magnificent seven. He was certainly a better defender than all of them, having been selected seven consecutive times to the NBA All-Defensive first team. None of the others was selected even *once* for the honor. There is some truth to Bob Ryan's point that Frazier was overrated on defense and underrated on offense. But he was still better defensively than the other seven players mentioned here.

Here are the lines on these seven guards:

| NAME | G | FG% | FT% | REBS | ASTS | PTS | RPG | APG | PPG |
|------|------|------|------|------|-------|--------|-----|------|------|
| Drexler | 1016 | .474 | .788 | 6331 | 5743 | 20,908 | 6.2 | 5.7 | 20.6 |
| Thomas | 979 | .452 | .759 | 3478 | 9061 | 18,822 | 3.6 | 9.3 | 19.2 |
| Monroe | 926 | .464 | .807 | 2796 | 3594 | 17,454 | 3.0 | 3.9 | 18.8 |
| Cousy | 924 | .375 | .803 | 4786 | 6955 | 16,960 | 5.2 | 7.5 | 18.4 |
| Maravich | 658 | .441 | .820 | 2747 | 3563 | 15,948 | 4.2 | 5.4 | 24.2 |
| Stockton | 1062 | .520 | .821 | 2233 | 12,170 | 14,468 | 2.1 | 11.5 | 13.6 |
| Archibald | 876 | .467 | .810 | 2046 | 6476 | 16,481 | 2.3 | 7.4 | 18.8 |
| **Frazier** | **825** | **.490** | **.786** | **4830** | **5040** | **15,581** | **5.9** | **6.1** | **18.9** |

Stockton is the best assist man by far. But Frazier and Cousy are the only two that are strong in all three major categories — points, rebounds and assists.

Frazier speeds ahead of Cousy on the strength of field goal percentage and his overall defense. Cousy connected on 38% of his shots, while Frazier hit 49% of his.

NBC studio analyst and *New York Post* columnist Peter Vecsey chose Monroe ahead of Frazier in print, begging the obvious question, 'how long have Vecsey and Monroe been friends?' Pete, get thee to a record book. There is really no contest here. Their scoring averages are virtually identical, but Frazier was clearly the better playmaker, dishing out 6.1 assists to Monroe's 3.9.

From there it gets worse. Frazier essentially doubled Monroe in rebounds — 5.9 to 3.0. He outshot him 49% to 46% and then the playoff performances must be dealt with. Here are the post-season records:

|         | PPG  | APG | RPG | FG. PCT. |
|---------|------|-----|-----|----------|
| Monroe  | 17.9 | 3.2 | 3.2 | 43%      |
| Frazier | 20.7 | 6.4 | 7.2 | 51%      |

Not even close. That is even more embarrassing for Vecsey's selection. More? Frazier was All-NBA First Team 5 times to Monroe's 1 time. The score on NBA All-Defensive selections? Frazier wins in a seven-love whitewashing. A Hall of Famer and one of the most exciting players that every lived, Monroe possessed feints and spin moves that no one could foretell. "Earl didn't know what his next move was going to be, so how could I know?.," said Frazier, explaining his exasperation at guarding Monroe. But despite his arsenal of moves, Monroe was in no shape or form better than Frazier.

Isaiah Thomas versus Frazier makes for an intriguing argument. Both led their teams to two championships. But again Frazier, the better all-around player, must be given the nod. Frazier exceeds him significantly in field goal percentage and just barely in free throw percentage. Thomas, meanwhile, enjoys a substantial edge in assists — 9.3 to 6.1. But Frazier's edge in rebounding, though not as wide, is notable. Both improved their performances during playoff time, with Thomas increasing his points per game to 20.4 and rebounds to 4.7, while his assists, 8.9, remained constant. Thomas and Frazier are two of the greatest clutch players of all-time.

Two distinct advantages fall to Frazier. He had five All-NBA First Team selections to Thomas' three and 7 NBA All-Defense selections to Thomas' none. The verdict: edge to Frazier.

Clyde also rates ahead of one of the flashiest offensive players of all-time, "Pistol" Pete Maravich. Playing for the New Orleans Jazz in the mid-seventies, Maravich put up consecutive seasons of 25.9, 31.1 and 27 points per game. But while a far greater scorer than Frazier, his overall game was never equal. He was selected All-NBA First Team for two of those high-scoring seasons, but that's less than Frazier's five and again it's seven-nothing on defense.

Frazier is one of the greatest and historically undersold athletes ever to play in New York. And his song was certainly more than one note. On the way to their second title in 1973, Frazier had to steer the team past several bumps in the road. Ahead of Boston three games to one in the Eastern Conference Finals, the Knicks lead late but lost game five and then lost game six at home. They had to go to Boston to win a seventh game, where no team had ever won a seventh. But Frazier lead the Knicks past Boston and into the record books, 94-78.

Then the Knicks - now with Lucas and Monroe — spotted Los Angeles the first game in the Finals, before sweeping the next four. Frazier improved on his regular season line, putting up 21.9 points, 6.2 assists and 7.3 rebounds in the playoffs. The Lakers had a starting five of Goodrich, West, McMillan, Bridges and Chamberlain, all of whom scored between 13.2 and 23.9 for the season. Chamberlain averaged 18.6 rebounds and Bridges chipped in another 10.9 boards. West was the assist man, dishing out 8.8 per game.

No matter, Frazier rose to the occasion. Listen to long-time NBA scribe Bob Ryan describe Frazier in the *Boston Globe* when the time came for Frazier to retire.

> *They can talk about Jerry West being Mr. Clutch, but I feared no NBA player down the stretch as much as Frazier. He could shoot from the outside or drive, and he seemingly never, ever took a shot from outside his range, which happened to be 18 feet. He thrived on both hometown crowd noise and enemy arena silence. Apparently nerveless, he seemed to be wired into some mystical message the others could not receive.*

> *He never was much of a runner, but since he never played with runners (until his last year with Cleveland) it hardly mattered. Anyway, Clyde and his vintage mates generally made you play their game.*

> *When NBA future histories are published, they had better include lengthy references to Frazier's contributions. I won't soon forget Walt Frazier, nor will anyone who followed the NBA during the last ten years. He enhanced the league with his on-court performances, and he attracted untold amounts of publicity for the league with his flamboyant life style. In time, Clyde gobbled up Walt Frazier, and it seems to me that when Clyde died, Walt Frazier did, too.*

> *Sure, there was a lot of ragtime attached to Frazier, but it was all harmless. The man was a superb basketball player in his prime. There wasn't a basketball team which ever took the floor that he couldn't have helped. He was a most worthy opponent and he will be missed.*

In a baffling move before the 1977-1978 season, Frazier was traded to Cleveland for Jim Cleamons. His numbers were never the same after that. He did score 28 against New York in his first game back, leading the Cavaliers past his old teammates.

But Frazier and his cool style of play were made for New York. And in the 20 years since he departed, the Knicks haven't come close to finding his equal.

To many New Yorkers who watched during that most special time, it would be alright if they never did.

# 7 <sub>guard</sub>

# Isiah**Thomas**

How many bad things can you say about a guy whose middle name is "Lord?"

Isiah Lord Thomas III is the seventh best guard that ever lived. I should say that most of the experts I interviewed make him the sixth best guard, ahead of Walt Frazier. I would not, for reasons explained in the previous section about Walt Frazier. I would maintain, however, that he is the greatest *small* guard that ever lived, ahead of impressive company like Bob Cousy, Nate Archibald and John Stockton. And I concede that one can make a very strong case that he is as good or better than Frazier. I chose Frazier for his all-around play.

Isiah Thomas, in the words of *Boston Globe* columnist Bob Ryan, "is second all-time to Jordan as having the greatest highlight film material." His first notable highlight reel was his game five effort against the New York Knicks in the first round of the 1984 playoffs. In a 90-second period in the fourth quarter Thomas scored 16 points. He hit threes, jumpers off the dribble, foul shots, everything. It seemed that the Knicks had the game won in regulation time, but Thomas' exploits tied the game before Bernard King, in the midst of an unstoppable five-game run of his own in which he averaged 43 points, lead New York to an overtime victory.

In Game Six of the Finals against the Los Angeles Lakers in 1988 he again went off. As he limped about on one good ankle and one badly sprained one, he poured in jumper after jumper, scoring 43 points. He set a record with 25 points in the third quarter alone. Anyone witnessing the game had to conclude that it was one of the gutsiest, most remarkable efforts they had ever seen. No player ever showed more heart than Thomas did in that game.

Much has been written about athletes' "peak experiences" and "being in a zone" on such occasions. Thomas adds his own feelings on the subject. In both games he recalls feeling something similar. "I just felt that the whole game came together. I remember being so emotional in the Knicks' game that I was crying tears. It's almost like a spiritual thing; I don't know how to describe it. People refer to those games all the time." Unfortunately, the Lakers came from behind to win this game and tie the series at three games a piece.

It is a lead pipe cinch that Thomas, who in 1989 and 1990 won consecutive championship with the Pistons, will enter the Hall of Fame.

Bob Ryan selected Thomas as his fifth greatest guard of all-time. "I thought it took Isiah too long to get to his peak," he said. "Maybe because he was too young and too physically gifted. I've talked to him about this. But he 'got it' in 1987. He was a devastating player, full and half-court."

For the four years from 1984 through 1987 Thomas was indeed a devastating offensive player. He averaged 20-21 points per game and 10 to 13.9 assists per game. But Detroit lost to the Celtics in seven games in 1987, due in large part to Thomas' soft inbound pass in game five. Larry Bird intercepted the pass and fed it to Dennis Johnson for the winning basket. Then in 1988 the Pistons stopped Bird, holding him to 35% shooting for the series, and won four games to two. Though the Pistons lost in seven games to the Lakers in the Finals, the Detroit "Bad Boys" were about to hit their stride.

With Joe Dumars, Dennis Rodman, Bill Laimbeer and Rick Mahorn, the

Pistons employed a stingy, in-your-face defense that was third in the league in points allowed in 1988, second in 1989 and first in 1990. To stop Michael and the Bulls in the 1988, 1989 and 1990 playoffs, coach Chuck Daly employed the "Jordan Rules," a strategy designed to funnel Jordan into traffic on offense, run him off picks on defense and basically bounce him around like an NBA ball as often as possible. As physical defense and Thomas' leadership went, so went the Pistons.

On offense they had Thomas and Dumars, Laimbeer with his tippy-toes three pointers and Mark Aguirre down low. Off the bench they had a man who in stature resembled a human fire hydrant, the "microwave" Vinnie Johnson. They swept Los Angeles in the 1989 Finals and ambushed the Portland Trailblazers four games to one in the 1990 Finals. Not bad. History has not yet given this team — on which the whole was greater than the sum of the parts — its proper due. In 1990 Thomas averaged 20 points, eight assists and five rebounds a game and was awarded the MVP for the Finals. "I felt that we had a lot to prove. The four guys competing at the time were Magic, Bird, Jordan and myself, and Magic was the only one who had won back to back. I wanted to do something the other two hadn't done," Thomas says, explaining his motivation.

Then he sums up the last ten years of NBA basketball. "Everything we became, we became because of the Celtics. Everything that Chicago became, they became because of us. They may not want to admit that, but that's the way it was."

In all of his first 12 years Thomas was selected to the NBA All-Star team. He was awarded the game's MVP in 1984 and 1986. Without a doubt, he was one of the most flamboyant and electrifying players ever. Aside from the legendary highlight film bursts, Thomas also was one of if not the greatest dribblers at the position. He honed this ball handling skill on Chicago playgrounds.

"He was a floor general, could run the floor and one of the best *ever* at getting his own shot," said Matt Guokas. "And he seemed to get that shot all the more in clutch situations. He is one of the great big-game players of all-time."

His two greatest solo efforts, as already noted, were in games the Pistons lost. In Thomas' 25-point third quarter against the Lakers, the Pistons would have won the game if not for a foul called against Bill Laimbeer for bumping Kareem Abdul-Jabbar on a sky hook from the baseline. Abdul-Jabbar calmly sank the free throws and the Lakers had a one-point victory. Had the Pistons won that controversial game, we'd be talking about a Pistons' team that won three consecutive world championships.

Winning was hardly a new experience for Thomas. Playing for Bobby Knight at Indiana, he was chosen Outstanding Player of the 1981 NCAA tournament, leading the Hoosiers to the championship.

Many of us felt that Thomas could have played beyond the age of 33, but he ruptured his ankle in a 1994 game. Some may wish he hadn't quit so suddenly. But then why should a man who had it all hang on? Had he continued playing, maybe that ever-present boyish smile would have turned to a laborious grimace. Perhaps everything would stop being fun. Some things are better left alone.

As someone who watched Isiah Thomas in his rookie year in 1982, I have a lasting impression of his grinning face. As it was for Magic Johnson, the game was usually fun for Isiah Thomas. That smile sometimes changed to a smirk, as if he had just gotten the better of an opponent.

Usually that was the case.

# 8 <sub>guard</sub>

# Bob**Cousy**

It was November, 1980 and the nostalgia in the air at Gallagher's Restaurant in New York was as thick as the red steaks being served. It was a gathering of sportswriters, coaches and players — including Bill Russell, Oscar Robertson, John Havlicek and Red Auerbach — to celebrate the NBA's 35th anniversary. The Basketball Writers of America Association announced their selection of an all-time 11-man squad. The squad included Bob Pettit,

Elgin Baylor, John Havlicek and Julius Erving at the forwards. The centers were George Mikan, Bill Russell, Kareem Abdul-Jabbar and Wilt Chamberlain. Rounding out the team, the guards were Oscar Robertson, Jerry West and one more. Bob Cousy.

If you judge a man by the lofty company he keeps, then Bob Cousy, the 6-1 guard from Holy Cross College, had done alright for himself. But what had he done, exactly, to be rated with these giants of the hardwood?

Consider that in the 1990s the game is as full of flash as ever. Then remember who started all the flash. It was Bob Cousy, a wee lad from Andrew Jackson High in Queens, New York. You have to earn nicknames and Cousy earned his. He entered the pros in 1950 and soon earned the moniker "Houdini of the Hardwood." His stylish game included so many razzle dazzle plays that he was often reprimanded by coach Auerbach. It is one thing for the defense to be fooled by blind passes. It is quite another thing to have those passes fool one's own players. A passing pioneer, Cousy was ahead of his time, and his theatrical deliveries often caught his teammates by surprise and could be seen bouncing off arms, backs, even heads. "I had to curtail him so that he wouldn't throw the ball away," said Red Auerbach. Cousy was also an indefensible dribbler, keeping the ball low to the floor where it couldn't be stolen. In grainy black and white film footage one can still see him dribbling around the Boston parquet floor like an elusive cat ahead of the pursuit of five dogs.

NBC analyst Matt Guokas began his career in 1966, three years after Bob Cousy retired, but he saw enough of the Celtics' playmaker. "I grew up watching Bob play and watching the Celtics. He was more in the mold of John Stockton," Guokas recalls. "He was the floor general and in total control of his team and the game. Cousy was extremely intelligent. He knew how to get people involved and was very much a team player and tough competitor."

For the first six years of Cousy's career the Celtics made the playoffs. In five of those years, 1952 through 1956, Cousy put up playoff scoring averages of 31, 25.5, 21, 21.7 and 26.3. All of those numbers were better than his regular season averages! But the Celtics never made it to the Finals. They were lacking something. In crucial spots the Celtics couldn't get a defensive stop when they needed it most. A fast break is only effective if you can get the ball off the boards. "We couldn't get the ball and lost a lot of close games," coach Red Auerbach recalls.

Then during the 1956-1957 season it all changed for them. "I remember Arnold (Cousy always referred to his coach Arnold "Red" Auerbach as "Arnold") saying to me 'we're getting a player who is going to change things.' " That player was Bill Russell, a spidery 6-10, 210-pound center who had anchored the 1956 United States Olympic squad that won a gold medal in Melbourne, Australia. His University of San Francisco team also won 55 straight games and back-to-back NCAA titles. With his fierce defense, shot blocking and dominance of the backboards, Russell made the Celtics an instant contender.

Cousy was awarded the league MVP in 1957. Now in his seventh season, he got to play on his first championship squad as the Celtics beat the St. Louis Hawks in a grueling seven-game Final. There were two overtime games, including game seven when the Celtics prevailed 125-123.

It was just the beginning. Between 1957 and 1963, when Bob Cousy retired, Boston won six NBA titles, including five in a row from 1959 through 1963. For his part, Cousy kept on taking home the league assist title, winning eight in a row from 1953 through 1960. How well did he rate among his peers at the guard position? Very well. He was selected All-NBA first team 10 years in a row from 1952 through 1961. No one else came close. Cousy was head and shoulders above the others guards of his time. Not until Jerry West and Oscar Robertson entered the league in 1960 did Cousy relinquish his title as the league's best guard.

These days it is common for commentators like *Boston Globe* columnist Bob Ryan and Matt Guokas to try to give people an idea of Cousy's game by comparing him to John Stockton, the Utah Jazz playmaker. But Hall of Fame forward Tommy Heinsohn, a teammate of Cousy's between 1956 and 1963, disagrees. "Cousy's game was five times better than Stockton's," says the man they called "Tommy gun," because he rarely saw a shot he didn't like. "Cousy was the floor general and it was fundamental basketball and he was Mr. Offense on teams that consistently won championships. Cousy *was* the offense. Nobody ran the fast break better. What he did was what every playmaker should do: first use your full compliment of players. And if that can't be done, score yourself."

Red Auerbach maintains that in the history of the game only Magic Johnson is Cousy's equal at running the fast break.

Cousy's playmaking prowess made the other perennial scorers on the Celtics look better. Guys like Bill Sharman, Heinsohn, Jim Loscuttoff, Sam Jones and Frank Ramsey all scored more points due to Cousy's slick passing. "If you had half a step on your man, Cousy got you the ball," Heinsohn recalls. And on defense? "Cousy was not a great defender," Heinsohn says.

Many people who talk about Cousy these days didn't actually see him play. Oh, they may have seen only a minute or two of old film clips. Then they jump to the conclusion that Cousy would not be able to compete in today's fast-paced game. Some also think that he dribbled with just one hand. Actually he didn't. Cousy dribbled the ball with both hands but only did so when he needed to. He only went behind the back with the ball if there was some advantage to doing it. Many players of the fifties and sixties tended to think of putting the ball behind the back and between the legs as "hotdogging," plays where you were trying to show up your opponent.

"Cousy was a great big-game player and instrumental in what popularity the league had in the nineteen-fifties," says NBC broadcaster Marv Albert, who watched as a ball boy on the New York Knicks' bench. "The Cousy flair was not just showing off; he would make the fancy play when necessary."

Could Cousy compete in today's game? Listen to another great small guard, Isiah Thomas. "If Cousy played now he would have elevated his skills to do what these guys do; he would have still had the flair."

Indeed, few people on the Celtics great teams had any more physical stamina that Cousy had. Cousy routinely looked to push the ball up and down the court. When Cousy coached the Cincinnati Royals in the late sixties, Guokas played for him. "Bob would tell me stories about the old days. Boston was one of the greatest running teams of all-time. And they were so good at running because of Bob. He used to tell me that he wanted to get guys like Heinsohn to run more, so he would throw the ball five inches over their head on the fast break so they had to go run and get it."

Many people are skeptical of Cousy's shooting prowess because he shot only 38 percent from the field for his career. "Players from that era didn't shoot for a high percentage," Guokas explains. "They didn't get as many layups then. Bob took a lot of running shots. He would make a running hook and then miss three or four. But he got the team to play better. He would be like Stockton today; the same type of body, the same court awareness."

"Cousy and Magic ran the fast break to the ultimate," said Red Auerbach. "Cousy was good at that break right off the bat. Then he could stop and shoot, penetrate and dish off. He got the ball up court so fast that everybody else would play better. They'd be embarrassed if they didn't hustle and make it to the foul line."

But would Cousy have been as effective in the West-Robertson era or in today's game? "As long as they played on a team that ran," Auerbach explains. "A coach would have to be dumb to coach a man of his ability and not use the fast break."

Cousy's career is not a career defined by numbers but by winning. Along with Bill Russell, he was the most important part of the 1950s and 1960s teams and what is called the "Celtics' Mystique." Actually, the "Celtics' Mystique" was not that mysterious at all. The Celtics played to win and knew how to win. Their players — including their string of "sixth men" — were less interested in leading the league in scoring and rebounding and more interested in winning championships.

In going back through the history of basketball one finds oneself rating the great Celtics differently than other NBA teams. Individual greatness is not the measuring stick to be used on the Celtics. Players like Heinsohn, Russell and Sharman put up great numbers but they thought more about the championships than they did about their personal stat lines. So did Cousy.

This is not to say he didn't have a great individual career. Aside from the assist titles, Cousy had a balanced bottom line. When he retired in 1963 — fittingly a year when Boston won the championship — his average numbers were 18.4 points, 7.5 assists and 5.2 rebounds per game. In the playoffs those assists climbed to 8.6 per game. But the number that Cousy would remember best is six, because that's the number of championship squads he played on.

Because of his contribution to Boston's winning seasons and because of his great stats, Cousy must appear on the top ten list of the great guards. NBC analyst Pete Vecsey rates him lower, placing him 14th among the all-time great guards, behind, among others, John Stockton, Len Wilkens, Earl Monroe, Clyde Drexler, Pete Maravich and Hal Greer. Like Cousy, these six are all great players. But not one of them had the two things that Cousy has: great numbers and championships. That combination gives Cousy the edge.

"I played against him all the time," said Gene Shue, a 5-time all-star whose ten year career began in 1954. "He was a fabulous player, a very exciting open court player, very flashy with the ball. In a day when passing was popular, Bob was wonderful for the game. He created such excitement on the fast break and was very good at scoring on the break."

"Cousy is still the standard by which all point guards have been judged and are being judged," says Bob Ryan. "He wrote the book on point guard play and dominated an era."

# John**Stockton**

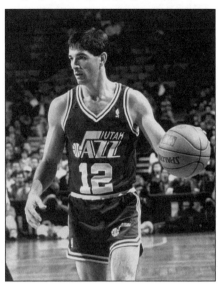

John Stockton belongs in the ninth spot among all the guards that ever played. Once he passed Magic Johnson on the all-time assist list in February of 1995, Stockton was guaranteed a place on the all-time list of guards. He broke the record of 9,921 in just 860 games, taking 14 less games than Johnson took to amass that total. But while Stockton's name is synonymous with "assist," he has also put up surprisingly good scoring numbers.

Consider: in a 13-year career he averages 13.6 points per games, to go with his 11.5 assists per game. But it is the field goal percentage that really jumps out at you. Despite being a guard, and a small guard at that, Stockton's lifetime field goal percentage is .520. There are few guards in the history of the NBA who hit even 50 percent of their shots!

If that isn't impressive enough to get him into the top ten, consider the defense. Four times Stockton has been selected for the NBA All-Defensive First Team. So you have a very rounded player in Stockton, a player who led the league in assists nine consecutive years (Indiana's Mark Jackson finished first in 1997) and led the league in steals three times.

One knock against Stockton is that he hasn't won a title. True enough. His teammate Karl Malone must also deal with that criticism. Stockton's reply is that "we've never been the best team" and "the world would have been shocked if we had won." In the 1997 playoffs he averaged 16 points and ten assists per game and hit 52 percent of his shots. What else is he supposed to do? If you choose an all-time team of the best players who haven't won titles, it might look like this:

| | |
|---|---|
| Guards: | John Stockton |
| | George Gervin |
| Center: | Patrick Ewing |
| Forwards: | Elgin Baylor |
| | Karl Malone |

These players have played a combined 61 years without a title. Yet they are all great players. It may diminish them somewhat that they didn't win, but it would be foolish indeed to overlook their greatness completely on that account. One might as well say that Ty Cobb, Harmon Killebrew, Ernie Banks and Ted Williams weren't great baseball players because their didn't play on any World Series winners. It's absurd to make such a statement. "They just haven't been good enough," says Hall of Fame coach Jack Ramsay, speaking of the Utah Jazz teams that Stockton and Malone have played on.

Stockton's always been an unselfish kind of player, content to pass the ball first in the true point guard fashion. Jim Chones, ten year pro and color analyst with the Cleveland Cavaliers, was quoted in the New York Times as calling John Stockton "the most unselfish player in any major sport." "He's a small Magic Johnson," added K.C. Jones. Well, that is a hyperbole. But we do get Jones' point. Both Johnson and Stockton look to pass first and score second. Both can run the break to perfection and always have had a knack of finding people with their uncanny ability to see the entire floor.

After finishing first in assists last year, Mark Jackson said it was an honor to finish ahead of Stockton, "the second greatest point guard of all-time." Who is Jackson's choice for first? "Well, there was this guy from Lansing," he said, alluding of course to Magic Johnson.

Stockton's former teammate David Benoit said he's seen a lot of guys say 'I can take that little white guy easy.' And the result? "He makes dead meat out of them," says Benoit.

How Stockton was chosen sixteenth in the first round in 1984 is anyone's guess. One can almost hear the buzzing and booing around the auditorium as Utah announced they'd be picking the smallish guard from Gonzaga College.

Houston had already picked Olajuwon, Portland chose Sam Bowie and

Chicago chose that guy Jordan. Dallas got Sam Perkins next, followed by Philly's selection of Barkley. After Melvin Turpin, Alvin Robertson, Lancaster Gordon, Otis Thorpe, Leon Wood, Kevin Willis, Tim McCormick, Jay Humphries, Michael Cage and Terence Stansbury came Stockton. 1984 was the richest draft in basketball history, since it included one of the best centers ever, a great forward and two of the best guards ever. As rich as that draft was, the order of selection suggests that several scouts or GMs may now be out of jobs.

After the draft, the story goes that Stockton took home Utah game films and came to camp knowing where Darryl Griffith and Adrian Dantley liked the ball. At first he was a back-up point guard but then beat out Rickey Green in his third year. He's had the job since.

Stockton's place in basketball history is secure even if he never plays another game. No one will break his assist record for some time to come. No active player is even close to him.

Matt Guokas likes to compare Cousy with Stockton and the comparison is instructive. Cousy was a kind of predecessor to Stockton, even though that claim may aggravate some old Celtics. He had the same kind of game. Stockton was probably not as flashy as Cousy. But he really looks to pass first and run the floor, just as Cousy did. While Cousy may have made more dazzling passes, it could be argued that Stockton saw the whole floor as well as Cousy did. In fact, Jack Ramsay says that Stockton enjoys a "razor's edge" advantage over Magic Johnson as the greatest passer. "Stockton is the Cousy of the eighties and nineties," agrees *Boston Globe* columnist Bob Ryan. "He is the modern point guard reference for point guards." He also shot for a much higher percentage than Cousy. Is he hurt by not winning more? "They've never been favored in the West," Ryan explains. "I'll defend him and Malone against the charge that they haven't won."

Stockton has had Karl Malone and Malone has had Stockton, but Jack Ramsay is right. They haven't always had much else. Jeff Malone and then Jeff Hornacek have provided a third scorer at different times. But they've gotten little help from the small forward spot since Dantley left in 1986. And they've gotten even less from the center position.

Stockton is 35-years-old and he may not see that title that he and Malone hanker for. But if it doesn't happen, it won't be the first time that it happened to a great player.

# 10<sub>guard</sub>

# Clyde**Drexler**

Clyde Drexler versus Nate Archibald makes for yet another very interesting argument. To all those people who collected baseball cards back then and would "battle" Mays against Mantle by comparing the statistics on the back, this battle is one of those good ones. Both Drexler and Archibald have one NBA title. Archibald had three All-NBA selections to Drexler's one. And Drexler never had a peak season quite like Archibald's 1973 season, when he became the only player ever to lead the league in assists and scoring.

So how then can anyone choose Drexler ahead of Archibald? Because his numbers indicate that Clyde's game is more rounded than Tiny's.

Here is Archibald's career line:

| Points | Assists | Rebounds |
|--------|---------|----------|
| 18.8   | 7.4     | 2.3      |

Now here is Drexler's:

| | | |
|--------|---------|----------|
| 20.6   | 6.2     | 5.7      |

Drexler's overall production is slightly higher, even though Archibald, a deserving Hall of Famer, is a better assist man.

Still, "Clyde the Glide" makes the top 50 (and eventually the Hall of Fame) the way that some baseball players make the baseball Hall of Fame. They make it not because they are the best players that ever played or even the best of their era. They make it because they accumulated enough distinctions in their career that they simply cannot be overlooked.

So it is with Drexler. He has scored 20,908 points. Only five guards have ever scored more. And fewer guards have rebounded more than his 6.2 boards per game. Some of the greatest guards ever have less assists than Drexler's 5.7 per game. Want to know a few? George Gervin (what a surprise!), Hal Greer, Walter Davis, Gail Goodrich, Calvin Murphy and Earl Monroe are a few. Want more? How about Pete Maravich, Dennis Johnson, Sam Jones, Jo Jo White, Reggie Miller, Joe Dumars, Mitch Richmond and Bill Sharman?

So what exactly is the problem?

Nothing really. Except that at three notable times during his career, Drexler was the second best guard on the floor. The first time was the 1990 Finals, an instance when Isiah Thomas lead a mentally tough and extremely physical Detroit Pistons team past Portland, four games to one. In 1992 it was Jordan's turn to lead the Bulls past Portland, four games to two. Last year, in the Western Conference finals, Stockton stole the show, leading Houston's Eddie Johnson to rave about how Stockton dissected Houston in the fourth quarter of game six.

1992 was one of Drexler's best years as a pro. He averaged 25 points, 6.6 rebounds and 6.7 assists and was selected, with Jordan, to the All-NBA First Team. He had a good Final series, too. He averaged 25 points, 8 rebounds and 5 assists, though he did shoot only 41 percent from the field. But as fine as he played, his performance didn't measure to what Jordan did. Jordan averaged 36 points, 7 assists and 5 rebounds, on 53 percent shooting. And Jordan's Game One exploits will forever be remembered. In the opener he buried six three-pointers and scored 35 of his 39 points in the first half, as Chicago cruised to a 122-89 win.

And then in game 6 Portland led by 15 points entering the fourth quarter. But they scored only 14 points in the fourth as Chicago won 97-93. It was a devastating loss for the Trail Blazers. They dribbled the ball off their feet, double-dribbled, committed offensive fouls and basically fell apart. Jordan, who had sat out during a Chicago 14-2 spurt for the first part of the fourth quarter, still finished with 33 points. No one was remembering Drexler's performance at series end. It was Chicago and Jordan, Jordan, Jordan. Again Clyde was second best. At Barcelona that summer Jordan and Bird and Johnson were the players of the moment. And why not? Over the previous 13 years, the threesome owned ten of the world championship rings. So Clyde, quiet as is his wont, got little of the press as the United States easily won the gold.

There is a little of Erving in Clyde, though Erving was a far greater player. Clyde Drexler is as good on the drive and at finishing the fast break as most any who ever played. It was said of his and Olajuwon's 1983 University of Houston squad that the team would have won the NCAA Final game had their coach missed the bus. So if coming in second was a Drexler calling card, it started then.

Until recently. Many argue that if the Houston Rockets hadn't made the Otis Thorpe for Drexler deal they would not have won their second consecutive title in 1995. Drexler gave Houston points, assists and rebounds (22, 6 and 5). He also gave them a guard who could fast break and provide some of the rebounding to replace Thorpe. In his 12th season, Drexler won his first world title.

Besides the fact that he reached 20,000 points at the end of 1996, Drexler's never been known as a great shooter. His perimeter shooting waxes and wanes. Despite that, he was only the 27th player in the history of the game to score 20,000 points.

That's pretty impressive for a guy who has usually come in second.

# Dave**Bing**

There's an attitude in basketball that scoring isn't really scoring unless you do it for a winning team in important spots. Alex English, Adrian Dantley and George Gervin are a few players whose reputations have, in varying degrees, suffered from this attitude. So has Hall of Famer Dave Bing.

From his rookie year through his seventh season, Bing averaged between 20 and 27 points per game every season. But his Detroit Pistons were a frequent cellar dweller and only once in those seven years — the 1970-1971 season — did the Pistons rise above .500!

So this Washington, D.C. product was overlooked by those "experts" who put their stamp on the truly great players. A graduate of Spingarn High in D.C., Bing then went on to Syracuse University. The 6-3, 185-pound guard averaged 25 points and 10 rebounds in his four years for the Orangemen. So great was his career at Syracuse that in a letter nominating Bing for the Hall of Fame, Syracuse coach Jim Boeheim gave him his highest praise. The letter, dated August 25th, 1983, said "Dave is certainly the best college basketball player that I've been associated with in my twenty years in the college game."

And as great as he was in college, Bing did not disappoint at the pro level. He was the second pick overall in the first round of the 1966 NBA draft. Only Michigan standout Cazzie Russell was chosen ahead of him. In the pros, Bing got busy right away. He won the NBA Rookie of the Year award for the 1966-1967 season. And he earned it. He averaged 20 points, 4.5 rebounds and 4.1 assists. So on a personal level, the season was satisfying. But the Pistons finished 30-51 that year, ranking dead last in the Western Division. There were just 10 teams in the league and Detroit had a worse record than every one of them except for the Baltimore Bullets. For Bing, it was the start of a trend that would continue throughout his 12-year career. His personal excellence was beyond question most every year he played. But his teams never made it deep into the playoffs.

In just his second season he really made his mark. He led the league in scoring (27.1) and total points (2,142) and was selected All-NBA First Team. Amazingly, he was the first backcourt player in 20 years to lead the league in scoring. The last guard to do it before Bing was Max Zaslofsky, who played for the Chicago Stags and led the circuit with a 21-point average in 1948. If that wasn't impressive enough, consider the competition that Bing was up against. The sixties and seventies were guard rich times in the NBA. Consider: all-time greats Oscar Robertson and Jerry West were in their primes. So were Boston's Sam Jones, Philadelphia's Hal Greer and St. Louis' Len Wilkens. Walt Frazier and Earl Monroe were just reaching their strides. So the competition was stiff. So while other players began to acknowledge Bing's shooting, leaping and grace, it might be said that he was frequently overshadowed by the ink being given to these legends. "Bing had quickness and uncanny leaping ability," recalls Hall of Famer Walt Frazier. "He also had great range on his jumper."

Still, it might be said the graceful guard never really got his due. By 1971 the Pistons were showing signs of improvement. They now had the bulky center with the light touch from St. Bonaventure University, Bob Lanier. They won 45 and lost 37. But the league in the early seventies belonged to other teams.

The Milwaukee Bucks had Kareem Abdul-Jabbar and an aging, hungry Oscar Robertson. The New York Knicks were looking for a second title with their formidable nucleus of Frazier, Willis Reed and Dave DeBusschere. And the following year the Los Angeles Lakers — with Wilt Chamberlain, Jerry West and Gail Goodrich — would win their first title after years of playing second fiddle to the Boston Celtics. In 1971 Bing flourished again, earning his second All-NBA First Team selection. He averaged 27 points, five rebounds and four assists. But only 8 of the league's 17 teams made the post season that year and the Pistons weren't among them. In fact, with Bing suffering from a detached retina the following year, the Pistons slumped miserably, winning only 26 and losing 56 games. Eyesight problems would plague Bing for the duration of his career. Boston forward Satch Sanders said, "there was probably no guard in the league who did not take advantage of the problem. He was constantly being put to the test."

And Bing was up to the test, despite missing 37 games in the 1971-1972 season, it was the sixth of seven straight seasons where Bing averaged 20 plus points per game. The 1973-1974 season saw the Pistons put up their best record in years. For the fifth time Bing made the NBA All-Star team. He was also selected to the All-NBA Second Team. The Pistons won 52 games, but lost a tough seven-game series in the Western Conference semifinals to a scrappy Chicago team. The defensive minded Bulls' squad included Bob Love, Chet Walker, Jerry Sloan and Norm Van Lier.

After one more year with the Pistons, Bing was traded to the Washington Bullets in August of 1975. With Washington he spent his first season as a starter and even won the All-Star game MVP in 1976. He played his second season as a back-up, averaging 10.6 points per game and then was traded to Boston in September of 1977. The trade came a year too soon. Just nine months later the Bullets, with Elvin Hayes and Wes Unseld, won their only NBA championship. Bing was now with a struggling Celtics team. It was the end of the Havlicek era and before the Bird era and no amount of Celtics' mystique could keep them from winning 32 games and losing 50 for the 1977-1978 season.

Now 34 years old, Bing had scored 18,327 points, a career average of 20.3. He also had an impressive 6 assists per game and 3.8 rebounds. If a player's points rebounds and assists total 30 or more, he has had a stellar career. Bing totalled 30.1.

"He was never guilty of an ungraceful move on the court," said Bob Ryan, basketball columnist for the *Boston Globe*. In one column he wrote, "Dave Bing will be remembered simply because he had a style. He never ran, he glided. He didn't jump — and oh, how he could jump as a kid. Rather, he levitated. Year after year, he was captain of the All-Graceful Team. Scorers come and go but few players lend an air of athletic elegance to the game. David Bing did that, and we fans are therefore the poorer for his absence."

"Bing was an outstanding offensive player who could get his shot anytime he wanted," said Matt Guokas, who often found himself trying to guard him. "He was lightning quick. He could shoot the jumper standing still or off the dribble. He was so quick. Often times he had you faked out and he'd be coming back for the next move and you'd still be reacting to the first. He never really played on any outstanding teams."

Eligible for the Hall of Fame in 1983, Bing was finally selected in 1989. On consecutive days in August of 1983, Dave DeBusschere and Red Auerbach wrote letters recommending Bing to the executive director of the Hall of Fame. Then former Knicks' forward, Senator Bill Bradley wrote another the following June. All the letters praised his skills, leadership, effort and personal attributes. And Jim Boeheim's letter even mentioned Bing's success as an entrepreneur, as head of Bing Steel in Detroit. But these letters went unheeded for nearly six years, with Bing finally being enshrined in 1989. No doubt, the hesitation in electing him was due to his being overshadowed by other great guards but also because his ordinary teams did not win.

But other greats like Elgin Baylor and George Gervin never won titles either. And lesser players sometimes get a ring by tagging along, hanging on the coat tails of great teammates. Winning is not always in the hands of the greats.

Dave Bing's career proves it.

Frazier likes to add a final thought. "Like Unseld and Havlicek, Dave was one of the great gentlemen ever to play. He was a person of character."

# Pete**Maravich**

The guy whose nickname was Pistol retired too young and died too young. Since his untimely death on January 5th, 1988 at the age of 41, there has been a fair share of sentimentality about his life and career. That reaction is understandable for an athlete who dies young. But I am not choosing him among the greatest guards for reasons of sentimentality.

Though he played only ten years, Maravich accomplished enough, albeit with bad teams, to merit consideration on the all-time roll call of great guards. Eight of those ten years he averaged more than 20 points per game, five times more than 25 per game and once more than 30 per game. No doubt his best year was the 1976-1977 campaign, when he stayed healthy enough to put together a complete season and averaged 31.1 points per game. In the next three seasons — his last three — he would miss 104 games with assorted leg injuries. So his career was over at the age of 32 and observers were left to wonder "what if?" What if he had played with better teams than the Atlanta Hawks and the New Orleans Jazz? What if he had remained healthy? His last year, 1980, was with the Celtics and that was Larry Bird's first year. But Maravich was cut in training camp in 1980 and he would miss the magnificent Boston teams of the eighties.

Maravich was selected All-NBA First Team twice and picked for five all-star teams. Maravich's style was made for All-star games. When guys like Magic and Isiah sit around they will tell you that Maravich — not themselves or Cousy or Erving or Connie Hawkins — was the game's greatest showman.

Indeed, young Peter Press Maravich did some things on the court that would astound you no matter how many times you saw his act. It was common to see Maravich leap at the free throw line and pass between his legs to a teammate on the wing. Then too, he had several moves that the Harlem Globetrotters would be envious of. In one maneuver, he would break upcourt, purposefully let the dribble get away from him and then fan at it like a handball player whiffing the air with his hand. Then he'd hit the ball with the last wave of the hand, slapping it to a teammate.

A pretty good dribbler in his own right, Isiah Thomas thought that Maravich was without peer as a ball handler. "Nobody did the stuff that Maravich was doing," said Thomas. "If Maravich was playing today he'd be a God. He did things in game situations that you practice on the sand lot. You couldn't pick one move of his as the best because he did twenty different things." "He was the greatest ballhandler I ever saw," said Don Chaney, a defensive specialist who played guard with Boston.

The career of ten-year pro Matt Guokas also intersected Maravich's tenure. "Pete was tremendously gifted. He was way ahead of his time as far as ball handling and showmanship and he could get his shot off any old time he wanted. He was entertaining and an exceptional passer and trying to guard him was a nightmare. He played with reckless abandon. Like Barry he had the license to shoot 30 to 35 times a game. Whereas West and Robertson didn't take bad shots, Maravich did. But he was dazzling. With his head down, he still saw the whole floor and that made him so dangerous."

Bob Ryan also saw enough of Maravich to be impressed. "Maravich was the most underrated great player ever," says Ryan. "Had Bill Fitch stroked him, he would have stayed around a couple of years after 1980. I'm a friend of Fitch but I told him that. Maravich was turned into a freak by his father,

Press Maravich." But while his father could press him, no opposing guard really could.

"His true heart and soul was wrapped up in passing," Ryan continues. "I saw him do things that only Jordan can do. Maravich was tougher than anyone, fearless. He threw his body around with unbelievable disinterest for his own safety. He had a moderate drinking problem in the beginning and had that nice golden sunset moment in one last year in Boston.

"Pete was another guy who was just such an exciting player," said Gene Shue who had a good seat for Maravich's artistry from the bench while coaching Baltimore. "He was a sensational offensive player who you liked to see have the ball. You know he was going to create something that was fun. But again, like Gervin, Pete was a guy who didn't know from defense. He was a colorful and exciting player and I have no fault with that if you can incorporate it into winning. That was the one great thing about Magic; he gave you both entertainment and winning."

"I really came to like Pete so much," Bob Ryan reflects. "He turned into such a good guy, just spectacular. When he died I was crushed."

At the risk of putting a cold spin on this player who generated the heat of lava, I will recite his bottom line. His career averages were: 24.2 points, 5.4 assists and 4.2 rebounds. Those three numbers add up to 33.8, and that's a lot of production. Throw in the entertainment he provided and he was not a two-dollar pistol but a howitzer.

# Nate**Archibald**

Nate Archibald can always say he did something that no one else in the history of the NBA did. In 1973 "Tiny" led the league in points and assists in the same season. In that year, as a member of the now defunct Kansas City Omaha Kings, he tallied 2,719 points, for an average of 34 per game and 910 assists, for an average of 11.4. God if that wasn't enough, he also led the league in minutes, field goals made, free throws made.

As one writer noted, his points and assists essentially gave the team 57 points every night. Only a few players ever did anything like it.

"I was the other guard on that team the year he did that," said Matt

Guokas. "It was my job to stay as far away as I could. He was a tough competitor and he would find you. But that year took a toll on his body. He often initiated the contact on the drive and ended up on the floor a lot."

"He was a great penetrator and took a lot of hits going to the hoop," Auerbach adds. "He had nothing but guts out there. Winning the scoring and assist title in the same year — that's a pretty good accomplishment."

"Guarding him I would call for help all day long," Chenier remembers. "If you played off him he'd shoot it and hurt you."

That season has always been Tiny's calling card, his greatest asset. As it turned out, it was also his greatest liability in terms of what people expected of him. Never again would he put up numbers even remotely resembling those figures. After an injury shortened his 73-74 season to 35 games, he played the full 82 the next year and was for the second time selected All-NBA First Team and then selected again the next year. He also racked up two All-NBA second team selections.

With the Celtics he did some scoring but was primarily a passing guard, racking up high assist totals. Not only that, Bill Fitch had deeper guard rotations and Archibald griped about playing time, despite the best efforts of people like Cornbread Maxwell to cheer him up.

But the experience in Boston included more high points than low ones. In 1980, his first year with the team, he came back to play 69 games for Boston, after sitting the entire season with Buffalo the year before because of a torn achilles tendon. He won "Comeback Player of the Year Award." And, in 1981, he was the All-Star game MVP. He followed that up with a strong playoff run, averaging 15.6 points and 6.3 assists as the Celtics won their 14th World Championship. With the title, the 6-1 Tiny Man now had something that had eluded him for his first ten seasons.

Archibald had taken a route not altogether unlike the one taken by Earl Monroe, who had great scoring games with the Bullets and fit in as one of the team with New York. As a premier gate attraction with the Kings, Archibald had put up big points. But his coach Bob Cousy, who knew a little something about winning, knew that this too would pass.

The day would come, thought Cousy, when Tiny would no longer be a one-man band, playing with Sam Lacey, Tom Van Arsdale and Matt Guokas, who badly needed him to put up points. Archibald related a talk he had with Cousy to Boston sports columnist Joe Fitzgerald. "We talked about what the team needed in order to win, and basically it wasn't a guard who scored a lot of points. It was leadership. He actually predicted the future, because he said the time would come I'd be on a team where there'd be no more scoring 50 points a night and losing."

Eventually Tiny became a big man playing with other big men.With Boston he played with Bird, McHale, Maxwell and Parish. For his drives and acrobatic pump fake drives his teammates called him "scoopola" or scoop.

The Archibald that helped the Celtics win impressed Cousy. "Tiny has it all: instinct, vision, and, most important, attitude — the unselfishness to give up the ball," said Cousy. "And the playmaking and penetrating abilities are ... well, there aren't six kids in the league who can do what he does." Then "Cous" paused.

"Not only would I venture to say that he's the most effective second-round draft choice in NBA history," he added, "but he's gone through a more complete development in terms of personality and playing skills than anyone I've ever seen."

And he also became a legend with kids in the Roxbury section of Boston and the streets of New York City. He visited kids and thousands of them played in Nate Archibald summer leagues. In these neighborhoods he was, as one writer said, "an ever-present touchable deity," known as "skate," because of his slick moves on the floor but also idolized for his participation with children. When the Nate Archibald Youth Development League got started in Roxbury in 1982, Tiny sometimes visited four times a day.

Not only did his game on the court improve, but his universe off the court had expanded.

With a lifetime line of 18.8 points and 7.4 assists per game, he deserves a spot among the 50 greatest players that ever lived.

# The**Forwards**

# Larry**Bird**

Larry Bird was the most complete forward who ever played. His combination of rebounding, passing and perimeter shooting make him the best choice for the greatest forward of all-time. The non-statistical intangibles also favor Bird. Not only was he the obvious leader of the great Celtics teams of the eighties, but he raised the level of those teams from his first year in the league. The year before Larry Bird arrived the Celtics were 29 and 53. In his rookie year they were 61 and 21.

Look at the careers of other great forwards and you will find none as satile as the 6-9, 220-pounder from French Lick, Indiana. Of those experts I spoke to, Bird was the consensus choice as the greatest forward of all-time. He was also selected as the greatest *passing* forward of all-time, though Rick Barry wasn't rated far behind him in this regard. Other than assists, there are no other measures to confirm this. You just had to watch Bird. Bird saw the whole floor and just had a way of finding people. "Bird, like Magic, saw the game as if it was happening in slow motion," said Matt Guokas.

"He was a step or two ahead of anyone else and knew where the play should be, making everyone else better." His assists were an impressive 6.3 per game. No other great forward — not one with 10,000 points or more — averaged that many assists. In fact, Scottie Pippen (at 5.3 assists per game) and John Havlicek (at 4.9) are the only forwards in the top 50 that are even close. That one number will bring to mind another of Bird's greatest attributes: he made players around him better.

Auerbach had drafted Bird on June 9, 1978 in one of his great moves. Auerbach gambled, spending the sixth pick of the first round on the Indiana State Sycamore. The gamble was that this "junior eligible" had the option to sign with the team or finish his senior year and go back into a second draft. "Only Auerbach was bold enough and secure enough to take a chance on Bird," wrote Dan Shaughnessy in *Ever Green*. "You look bad if you've got a top-six draft choice and come away empty-handed." And Auerbach was aware of the risk. "Sure it was a gamble," he said. "But I had to do it. I've always had the philosophy that you pick the best kid that's available in the draft. Worry later." Auerbach would try to sign Bird by selling him on Boston's basketball legacy. "I felt that the reputation of the Celtics was such that every team would want to play here," said Auerbach. After much haggling with Bird's agent Bob Wolff, the Celtics paid $650,000, the most ever for a rookie.

The year before Bird arrived the Celtics had big names aplenty — Dave Cowens, Jo Jo White, Nate Archibald and Cedric Maxwell. But they didn't win.

Bird changed all of that. In camp that first year, forward Cedric Maxwell looked at Bird and made a sarcastic crack to Curtis Rowe, 'hey Curtis, here's our savior.' It wasn't a joke for long. From the outset Bird endured the labels, "too slow, can't run, can't jump." It was such a long running joke that in the 1994 movie *Blue Chips*, Bird, playing himself, repeated the words in a sarcastic tone to actor Nick Nolte.

Slow or not, Bird had already made an impact. Aside from the 61 wins, Bird led the team in scoring and rebounding. His overall numbers were not as impressive as later numbers he would put up. Oh, he scored 21.3, had 10.4

rebounds and 4.5 assists. But the biggest number was 61-21 and like three great Celtics before him — Cousy, Russell and Havlicek — Bird seemed to have accepted the Celtics' organizational philosophy that individuals were subservient to the team. Personal stats were secondary. From then on, Bird's career would be about winning.

But Boston in 1980 was not yet playoff tough. After sweeping Houston, they lost in five games to a seasoned Philadelphia 76ers team with Julius Erving, Doug Collins, Bobby Jones and Moe Cheeks.

But their time was coming. The Celtics before 1980 might be divided into five eras: The Cousy Era, The Russell Dynasty, The Post-Russell Decline, The Havlicek Era and The Second Decline.Now a sixth era was on the horizon: the Bird Era. Aside from the winning that followed him, Bird had a signature-style. He had a deadly perimeter game. He did not think of himself as a scorer first, but as a player looking to do what was required to win games. An assist, a tough rebound in traffic at the end of the game, a perimeter shot — Bird could deliver them all. Had he wanted to score more, it is undoubtedly true that he would have increased his average beyond the 24.3 points per game he finished his career with. On lesser teams his job description may have required him to pour in more points. The history of the league is littered with players that Mike Gminski calls "I.C.B.M.'s" ("intercontinental ballistic missiles"). These guys — like those nuclear warheads — are only offensive in nature. Bird couldn't afford the luxury of being one-dimensional. On the Celtics he had to do a little bit of everything.

What separates Bird from Rick Barry, another high-scoring, slick-passing forward, is the rebounding. While Bird never led the league in rebounds, he was usually among the top ten and even nearer to the top among *forwards*. This has been an under-analyzed part of Bird's career.

The reason it gets short shrift is that Bird's name is associated with winning, first and foremost. People have not always taken the time to break down the various components of his greatness. This is understandable, since his ability cannot be equated with any one skill. With Bird, the whole of his career is greater than the sum of the parts. No simple enumeration of his passing, rebounding and scoring will give you the totality of his achievements.

Still, the rebounding component of his career is worth noting. Here is his ranking among rebounders in the league from 1980 through 1988, the nine seasons prior to 1989, when his back injury limited him to just six games.

| Year | League Rank | Forward Rank |
|------|-------------|--------------|
| 1980 | 10 | 3 |
| 1981 | 4 | 2 |
| 1982 | 7 | 5 |
| 1983 | 9 | 3 |
| 1984 | 9 | 3 |
| 1985 | 8 | 3 |
| 1986 | 7 | 4 |
| 1987 | 18 | 10 |
| 1988 | 12 | 9 |

Not only was Bird's rank among forwards very high, but two further points must be made. One, Bird's rebounding totals were hurt by having to share rebounds with Robert Parish and Kevin McHale.

Two, early in his career he was finishing behind forwards like Kermit Washington, Larry Smith, Buck Williams and others of that ilk, players whose scoring responsibilities were not nearly as great as Bird's. Not playing on the perimeter, they were nearer to the basket than Bird. Bird did not have the luxury to be just a rebounder. In the early eighties he was attempting more shots than Washington and Williams combined. And for a six-year stretch in the early eighties, Larry Smith, the Golden State forward, was only attempting between 5 and 8 shots per game. Responsible for a large part of the Celtics offensive output, Bird was averaging between 17 and 20 shots per game. He handled the ball and passed and shot and so when you look at Boston games in the early eighties, it looked as if Bird had a hand in everything the Celtics did.

The rebounding chart also shows a decline in Bird's rebounding in 1987 and 1988, when he was playing and then visiting an orthopedic therapist after every game. Still, in both of those seasons he outrebounded three prominent centers — Brad Dougherty, Jack Sikma and Patrick Ewing!

In the early eighties the Celtics' chief rival was the Philadelphia 76ers. By the middle-eighties the rival became the Los Angeles Lakers and by the late eighties the Detroit Pistons.

While the Celtics and the Lakers are invariably compared, especially when panelists gather to discuss the all-time greatest teams, the Celtics only met the Lakers in three Finals in the 1980s. The Celtics faced tougher competition in the Eastern Conference playoff rounds than the Lakers did in the Western Conference. In 1980, 1981 and 1982, Bird and the Celtics had to take on the talent-laden Sixers before they could even think about the Finals.

At the outset, the 1981 playoffs looked like a repeat of 1980. The Celtics were down three games to one against the Sixers again. But the 1981 Celtics were not the same team as the year before.

They had acquired Kevin McHale through the draft and Robert Parish in a trade with Golden State. The two added 29 points, 14 rebounds and 4.5 blocks to the Celtics' front line in 1981. An average performer under Al Attles in the Golden State Warriors' lineup, Parish flourished in Boston as a defender, scorer and rebounder. He could throw the outlet pass and get out on the break himself. With a 7-foot Parish and a 6-11 McHale along with Bird, the Celtics had three tall trees. They soon had an invincible front court.

They again fell behind the 76ers three games to one. But they eked out game five in Boston by 2 points, game six in Philly by 2 points and game seven in Boston by a point.

In the Finals they faced the Houston Rockets, who compiled a poor 40-42 record for the season. But the Rockets had come on like gang busters, going through Los Angeles, San Antonio and Kansas City in the Western Conference. Houston coach Del Harris' formula was simple: slow the game down and feed Moses Malone. All shoulders and desire, Malone was over-powering down low and the most dominant center in the early eighties. But Boston held him to 13 points and won game one in Boston, 98-95. Houston rebounded behind Malone's 31 points to take game two, 92-90. Boston won back home court advantage with a 94-71 rout in game three. Behind Mike Dunleavy's 28 points, Houston won 91-86 in game four. For the second straight game Bird had scored just eight points. But he did grab 21 rebounds in each game. The Celtics won game five in a Boston massacre, 109-80. Cedric Maxwell was the hero with 28 points and 15 rebounds. In the clincher in Houston, Boston led by 15 entering the fourth quarter and weren't really challenged after that. Bird scored 27, as did his nemesis on defense, Robert Reid. Maxwell scored 19 more on 7 of 11 shooting, added six assists and was awarded the MVP for the Finals. The Celtics had their 14th world championship.

In 1982, they found themselves against a tough Sixer team and again behind three games to one. Then the Sixers did the unthinkable. After the Celtics got off the mat to bring the series to three games apiece, the Sixers came into the Boston Garden and shot the lights out, winning 120-106. Andrew Toney scored 34 and Julius Erving added 29.

In 1983, Bird's fourth season, the Celtics lost four straight to the Milwaukee Bucks in the conference semis. "Being swept by the Bucks was the worst feeling I've ever had playing basketball," said Bird to Bob Ryan in his bio *Drive*. "At that moment it seemed like the end of the world.

"I sat in that locker room after the fourth Milwaukee game and made a vow. I said that I was taking this loss very personally, that I was going home to work harder than I ever have in my life and I was going to come back and have a great year."

Then Bird talked about his training philosophy. "When I say I'm going home to play ball, that basically means by myself. I never did like to scrimmage against people. Even when I was young I liked to practice by myself or with no more than one other guy. I always felt I could get more work done by myself than with three or four other guys standing around. The way I see it, if I put two hours in by myself, then someone who is working out with somebody else has to put in four hours in order to beat me. That's the way I've always gone about it. That summer I went home and put in more hours and got up more shots that I ever had before. I couldn't get that Milwaukee mess out of my mind."

## 1984-1986

Before the 1983-1984 season, the Celtics had traded Bird's best pal, Rick Robey, for Dennis Johnson. It was thought that Bill Fitch was no longer getting through as coach and was replaced by K.C. Jones. Tiny Archibald was gone, too, picked off the waiver list by the Bucks. The Celtics won 62 games.

Unlike the 1981 Finals, Bird was all everything in the 1984 Finals against the Lakers. It was the first of their historical, eternally interesting series in the eighties. It was a magical time for Boston, the beginning of a peak period during which they would reach four consecutive Finals.

The three years from 1984 through 1986 were the apex of Bird's career, too. In 1984 he won his first MVP award, as he took on an even greater share of Boston's offense, scoring 24.2 points and adding 6.6 assists and 10.1 rebounds. It was a typical bottom line for Bird, balanced and complete.

In the playoffs Bird flew in the stratosphere. In the first series they dispatched Washington and their testy front line players: center, Jeff Ruland and forward Rick Mahorn. Johnny Most, Boston's croaking homer of a broadcaster, labeled the two behemoths "McNasty" and "McFilthy." All the games were close, a credit to a Bullets' team that had won only 35 regular season contests.

Now the Celts had time off before taking on Bernard King and the Knicks. In the New York series the home teams won all the games. At Boston the Celtics triumphed by margins of 18, 14, 22, and 17. Lacking Boston's overall talent, New York eked out three victories at home as Bernard King carried his team.

But Bird had one of the greatest games in his career in Game Seven at the Boston Garden. The Celtics won 121-104, as Bird put up 39 points, 15 rebounds, 10 assists and 3 steals in the finale.

"Bird was the difference," said an exhausted Hubie Brown. "You just saw one of the great performances."

In the conference finals Boston met Milwaukee, their Central Division foe from 1983. Milwaukee had balanced scoring, but for the Celtics it was sweet payback. They won easily in five games.

The 1984 Finals with the Lakers began a classic eighties rivalry, a rivalry that revived the Celtic-Lakers skirmishes of the 1960s. But now, with such heightened media attention on the game's two best young players, Johnson and Bird, the rivalry had all the elements of spectacle. All years considered, Boston-L.A. remains the greatest rivalry in basketball history. It is basketball's answer to the Dodgers versus the Yankees. Ten times they have met in NBA finals, with Boston winning eight of those times.

Los Angeles won game one 115-109, immediately wiping out the home court advantage that Boston had won 62 games to earn. After erasing a 13-point Celtics' lead, the Lakers also led by two points with 20 seconds to go in game two. McHale had two free throws and missed both. The Lakers called time out. Boston pressured in the backcourt and Gerald Henderson stole a cross court pass from James Worthy, drove and scored. Then Magic Johnson inexplicably dribbled out the clock in regulation and the Celtics won in overtime. The Lakers had blown a golden opportunity to go up two games to none.

L.A. won game three easily, 137-104. Bird chastised his mates after the game. "Today, the heart wasn't there, that's for sure," said Bird. "We played like sissies." The words stung his teammates and game four turned the series. When McHale collared Kurt Rambis on a breakaway layup the "sissy play" was over. Benches emptied and several skirmishes followed. The Celtics still trailed by five with less than a minute left but Parish made a three-point play and Bird made two free throws to force an overtime.

There was more controversy in the overtime. With the game tied, Magic missed two free throws, and Bird made a jumper over Magic on the other end. When Worthy missed the first of two free throws, Maxwell flashed him the choke sign. Worthy hit the second. But instead of a tie game, the Celtics were ahead by one and M.L. Carr sealed the game with a steal and a breakaway dunk.

What could have been a four-game Laker sweep was instead a tie series, 2-2. The thoughts of what might have been haunted the Lakers. At tipoff in the Boston Garden in game five, the temperature was 97 degrees. Said Kareem Abdul-Jabbar, "it was like going to a local steam bath with your clothes on, and doing 100 pushups and then running back and forth." The 37-year-old center missed 10 of his first 12 shots and made just 7 of 25 overall for 19 points. Hitting on 15 of 20 field goal attempts, Bird scored 34 and added 17 rebounds. But the Celtics' 121-103 victory was a team effort. Dennis Johnson dropped in 22 points and McHale added 19. The Boston front line accounted for 39 rebounds and the Celtics punished the Lakers off the boards, 51-37. Back in L.A., the Lakers used Abdul-Jabbar's 32 points to win game six, 119-108.

The Celtics took "the red-eye" back to Logan airport and readied themselves for a game seven war. Bird recalls that Maxwell jumped up in the locker room before the game and said, "I am ready. Get on my back tonight, boys. This is my game. Just give me the ball." It wasn't just talk. Maxwell carved up Worthy inside, scoring 24 points, 14 from the foul line. Again the Celtics won with brute strength. Maxwell, Bird and Parish grabbed 36 rebounds, three more than the entire Lakers' team. With 20 points and 12 rebounds, Bird was a unanimous choice for the series MVP. He averaged 27 points, 14 rebounds, 4 assists and two steals for the series.

In 1985, the Celtics rolled up another great record, finishing at 63-19. On March 3rd, McHale had scored 56 points in a victory over Detroit. The total broke Bird's club record of 53 which he registered against Indiana in March 1983. Not to be outdone, Bird broke McHale's record by scoring 60 against Atlanta nine days later. The 60 points equalled Bernard King's total against New Jersey earlier in the year. In the 126-115 victory Bird made 22 of 36 field goal attempts and 15 of 16 free throws. He scored 18 in the fourth quarter, including Boston's final 16 points.

The Celtics beat the Sixers four games to one and met the Lakers in the Finals for the second straight year. In game one at Boston the Celtics shot 61 percent from the field and trounced L.A., 148-114. McHale and Scott Wedman scored 26 each. But L.A. bounced back with a 109-102 victory in game two. Abdul-Jabbar, now 38, had scored only 12 points in game one. But Riley vowed to get him more involved in game two and Kareem scored 34 points, adding 17 rebounds and eight assists.

He again outplayed Parish in game three, as the Lakers won easily on their court, 136-111. The Celtics won game four at the buzzer when Abdul-Jabbar and Johnson double-teamed Bird 17 feet from the basket. Bird passed to Dennis Johnson who nailed a 19-footer. The series was knotted 2-2.

But with a 2-3-2 final, the 5th game was in Inglewood and the Celtics needed another great effort to avoid going down 3-2. The Lakers built a 64-51 half-time lead and were never headed. Abdul-Jabbar scored 36 and the Lakers won 120-111. Back at the Garden in game six the Celtics' front line scored 74 points and grabbed 37 rebounds. But it wasn't enough to overcome Worthy and Abdul-Jabbar, who each scored 29 points in a 111-100 victory. Abdul-Jabbar was unanimous choice as the series MVP. It was the first time the Celtics had lost a championship on their home court and the first time the Lakers had beaten the Celtics after eight consecutive Finals losses against them. "I just think the Lakers played better," Bird said after the game. "They came ready, they wanted to win. The crowd was there but the players weren't."

Bird maintains the difference between the 1984 and '85 teams was Cedric Maxwell. Max had injured his knee and had to have an operation. He missed 25 regular season games and was not a factor in the Finals. After that series, Bird decided to work on his left hand during the off-season.

For the second straight season he was awarded the MVP, making him the only forward ever to win the award back-to-back.

For the 1986 season, the Celtics picked up Bill Walton but lost Maxwell. Still, they were loaded. Walton and Wedman were back-ups, as was shooter Jerry Sichting, and the team really hummed. They finished at 67-15.

In the first round they met up with Chicago. Jordan poured in 49 in game one, 63 in game two and 19 in game three. But his 43.7 average wasn't enough to avoid a Boston sweep. "What was amazing about Jordan's performance (in game two) was that he scored points in the flow of the game," Bird said.

Boston sailed through their next two series and met Houston in the Finals. They won the first two games easily, then lost the third in Houston and took the fourth there. The fifth contest went to Houston but the Celtics returned home for a clinching blowout in game six, 114-97. Bird had a game for the ages, finishing with 29 points, 11 rebounds, 12 assists and three steals. For the series he averaged a triple double — 24 points, 10 rebounds and 10 assists. He took MVP honors for the Finals.

It was June 8th, 1986. The Celtics had won their 16th championship. Now 29, Bird had reached the pinnacle of his career. He had won three consecutive league MVPs, something done only by Bill Russell and Wilt Chamberlain before him and no one since. The future could not possibly look rosier.

The Celtics would return to the finals in 1987, but by then their run of tragedy had already begun. A series of disasters, calamities and near misses that would replace the fabled Celtics' mystique had already been set in motion. Forget the luck of the Irish. The Celtics were about to embark on a path as rueful and more lengthy than the finest Greek tragedies. Those believing in hardwood karma might fold their arms and smirk at a team which had enjoyed more good fortune than any four teams in league history combined but was now about to watch their misery index soar.

Two weeks after they throttled the Rockets and sat atop the world, they would draft Len Bias, a 6-8, 220-pound wunderkind from Maryland. Bias had a 38-inch vertical leap, a powerful inside game and a touch from 18 feet. For the Celtics, he would provide all sorts of answers for the next 10 to 15 years. On June 17th, Bias went to New York to attend the NBA draft.

Cleveland drafted first and chose Brad Dougherty, now retired due to recurrent back problems. Several weeks before the draft, Bias had attended one of the first games of the Boston-Houston series. Before leaving the Garden he shook GM Jan Volk's hand and said "please draft me." Right after Cleveland selected Daugherty, Auerbach announced the Celtics were picking Len Bias. "Praise the Lord," were the first words to leave Bias' mouth.

Two days later Bias was celebrating in Washington Hall on the Maryland campus. As Dan Shaughnessy writes in *Seeing Red*, Bias was pronounced dead on the morning of June 19th at 8:55 a.m. He had ingested enough cocaine to cause cardiac arrest. Auerbach got the shocking call that morning from Maryland coach Lefty Driesell. "It was one of the biggest shocks I'd ever experienced," Auerbach wrote in a release to the press. "It's the cruelest thing ever," said Larry Bird. And that was it.

The autopsy confirmed that Bias had indeed died of cocaine intoxication. Len Cleveland Bias would have been a problem solver in many ways for the Celtics. Like Frank Ramsey and John Havlicek, Bias might have begun as yet another Celtics' "sixth man," a role that Auerbach had perfected. Playing Bias that way would give rest to the Celtics' vaunted front line. Perhaps he would have started 25 minutes a night and worked his way to 40, extending the careers of two future Hall of Famers, Bird and McHale.

Auerbach's brilliant scheming to get Bias should have resulted in at least one more championship banner, perhaps even two or three. He had traded Gerald Henderson to Seattle in 1984 in exchange for Seattle's first-round pick in 1986. He was banking on the idea that Seattle would have a period of decline. He was right. They won 31 and lost 51 in 1985 and did the same in 1986 to set up the Celtics' high pick. And the NBA lottery — instituted in 1985 to keep teams from losing on purpose in order to get a high draft pick — would give Auerbach a chance at the first pick. He drew the second instead. It was Boston's highest pick since Red had traded for the number two pick in 1956, Bill Russell. Len Bias would have been 33 this year. McHale was once quoted as saying that Auerbach's passion for the game was never quite the same afterwards. Seven years later, in the summer of 1993, captain Reggie Lewis died of a heart attack while practicing.

The Celtics came so close without Bias in 1987 that it was easy to imagine how they might have won with him.

In the 1987 Conference Finals, Bird used one of his all-time highlight film plays to win a fifth game against the Pistons. With the Pistons leading by one and five seconds remaining, Isiah Thomas inbounded the ball in the backcourt, hoping to run out the clock. Thomas looped the pass, Bird leapt into the passing lane, snatched the pass and dished to Dennis Johnson for the winning score.

In a grueling seven games, the Celtics won, taking the final game at home, 117-114. For the fourth year in a row they reached the Finals.

Isiah Thomas was starting to form his own opinions on Bird. "Larry Bird is the most competitive person I ever played against," said Thomas recently. "More even than Magic Johnson and Michael Jordan. Johnson was the smartest, Jordan was the best and Bird was the toughest, the type of guy who would meet you in the back alley and beat the shit out of you. He had an undying will and mental toughness. Of those three guys, I feared him the most. He would always find a way."

But the Celtics did not find a way against Los Angeles. Down two games to one they appeared to have game four in hand, leading by 16 in the third period. But L.A. climbed back and McHale lost an Abdul-Jabbar free throw off his hands and out of bounds with seven seconds left. L.A. inbounded and Magic drove across the lane and threw a hook in over the arms of Bird, McHale and Parish. Down three games to one, the Celtics won the fifth game at home but lost the sixth in L.A. Averaging 26 points and 13 assists per game, Magic won the Finals MVP to go with his league MVP. Bird averaged 24 points and 10 rebounds.

We didn't know it at the time, but the best two players of the eighties, Johnson and Bird, would never again meet in the Finals.

Of all the things that Magic said about Bird's playing ability, what he said at the end of Bird's career was most accurate. On the day set aside to celebrate Bird's retirement in February 1993, Magic sat next to Bird at center court and said "you lied about one thing; there will never, ever be another Larry Bird." The crowd roared.

It was therefore absurd, as Les Payne suggested in the pages of *New York Newsday* after Bird's retirement, that Bird was only highly regarded because he was white. Payne pointed out that Bird had never won a scoring title, rebounding title or assist title. True. One can picture Payne, who typically writes political columns, scrambling through a record book for ten minutes before writing a column but knowing little of Bird's career. For Payne to suggest that Bird's accomplishments were only heralded because of his race is pure sophistry. That bit of writing should be commended to the flames.

Bird once told me, "if Red (Auerbach) had a broken arm, he would play. So I felt I had to do the same." He was one of the toughest performers ever.

Even in the late eighties, when the Pistons had gotten the better of the Celtics and Bird's aching back forced him to lay down near the bench instead of sitting on it, he still averaged about 35 minutes a game. In his last five years he missed 148 games due to injuries. He could no longer rebound with the same ferocity. But his averages over those five years were 29.9, 19.3, 24.3, 19.4 and 20.2. And he averaged above ninety percent from the free throw line for the same stretch. He just couldn't play with the pain anymore.

He suffered acute pain, even after undergoing back surgery in the summer of 1991. One day during the Olympics the pain was intense and Bird gazed out the window of his hotel room, realizing the end of his 13-year career was near.

What makes Bird the greatest forward of all-time is his proficiency at most every aspect of the game. Even in the late eighties, when the Pistons got the better of the Celtics, Bird was still an exemplary player. "Toward the end of his career, we learned a lot from playing against him," said Isiah Thomas.

After his stint with the first Dream Team in Barcelona in 1992, Bird announced his retirement on August 18th, 1992 at a hastily called news conference in Boston. "The last couple of years have been very tough on me, on my back and on my body," he said. "It was very hard to deal with, day in and day out. Unfortunately, it all came down to this. I would have liked to have played a little bit longer, maybe a year or two more, but there was no way possible I was going to be able to do that."

After he first signed with the Celtics in June, 1979, Bird addressed the press. "I'm not promising anything except that I will give 100 percent every time I go out on the floor," he said. "And I'll play team ball; I won't sit out with any broken fingernail." Now, 13 years and two months later, he could say he honored the promise. "I gave my body, my heart, my soul to the Celtics," he said.

"I remember when he came here 13 years ago," said Auerbach. "He looked like a country bumpkin. But when you looked into his eyes you knew he was no dummy. He knew what he wanted in life and what he needed to get there."

"Larry was the only player in the league that I feared and he was the smartest player that I ever played against," said Magic Johnson. "I always enjoyed competing against him because he brought out the best in me. Even when we weren't going head-to-head I would follow his game because I always used his play as a measuring stick against mine."

Pat Riley, who coached the Lakers against Bird in their three Finals in the eighties, said, "Pro basketball has just thrown away the mold. He was one of a kind, unique. Not just the best of the best, but the only one who ever did what he did. He was a true warrior. I will never forget the Celtics-Lakers battles."

Bird was also known to talk trash occasionally. On All-Star weekends, during the last of his three consecutive Long Distance Shootout Championships from 1986-1988, he walked into the locker room and said to his rivals, "which of you guys is going to come in second today?"

That was Bird. And he had one more needle for Patrick Ewing. Hearing of Bird's retirement, Ewing said in jest, "It'll be sad that I won't be able to bust his butt on the court anymore, especially after all the junk he was talking during the Olympics."

Bird replied, "as for Patrick, he's had eight years to bust me and he hasn't done it yet. I couldn't stay around a lifetime and wait on him."

Bird's bottom line is 24.3 points, 10 rebounds and 6.3 assists per game. Among forwards, there is no bottom line quite like it.

"He was the consummate offensive package at forward," said Bob Ryan, "and the best passing forward, too."

"He was the consummate *player*, the best in the game today" Julius Erving said at the peak of Bird's career. "He eats, sleeps and drinks basketball."

Said M.L. Carr, Celtics' swingman and unofficial spokesman during the title years, "For any game, Larry shows up to play. For the big games, he shows up to take charge."

These are just a few of the ways he will be remembered.

# Elgin**Baylor**

Elgin Baylor has more unbelievable numbers than you can shake a stick at. If you look at what this forward accomplished at 6-5, 225 pounds, you know well that it will not be accomplished again in your lifetime.

"He was a forerunner of the high-flying acts," said Matt Guokas. "I was in the sixth grade and my coach took us to the old Madison Square Garden to see the Christmas tournament. Baylor was playing for Seattle and had one of those 48-point afternoons. I went home and told my father, 'I just saw the greatest basketball player I've ever seen.'

"He was only 6-5, but incredibly strong," Guokas continues. "He didn't jump particularly high but hung in the air. He was an incredible scorer and rebounder. He had a line-drive jumper from 17 to 18 feet and could put it on the floor."

After setting every record known to man at Seattle University — including points in a game, highest scoring average and a three- year college average of 31.3 points and 19.5 rebounds — Baylor sank his voracious teeth into the NBA. The first draft pick began his rookie year in the 1958-1959 season with the Minneapolis Lakers. His numbers got better each of his first four seasons, until they couldn't get better anymore. While still a junior at West Virginia, Jerry West saw Elgin in his first pro season at the old Madison Square Garden. "Elgin Baylor caught my eye and I watched him most of the evening," West said. "After seeing him, I was skeptical about making it to the pros."

"Baylor invented modern basketball," says Bob Ryan. "He invented the style of play used today. He took a horizontal and vertical game and made it diagonal." Observing the young Elgin Baylor, *New York Post* columnist Leonard Koppett wrote "He is, merely, the best basketball player in the world because he does everything so well."

Don't trust a writer's view of the game? Then try Bob Pettit, Hall of Famer from the St. Louis Hawks. "That guy," said Pettit, "is the greatest player I have ever seen. He makes the most difficult plays look routine." What greats had Pettit already seen? Cousy, Schayes, Russell, to name just a few.

When Baylor began with Minneapolis, not every team had a 6-8 or 6-10 forward. And so Baylor played forward at 6-5. Anyone who marvels at Charles Barkley's tenacity under the boards for his height and insists that Barkley is some historical anomaly, should get to know something about Baylor.

No one his size, no one, ever rebounded like Baylor did. His rookie year saw him average 24.9 points per game, 15 rebounds and 4.1 assists. He also won NBA Rookie of The Year. Minneapolis improved their record over the previous year by 14 games.

The following year, Baylor served notice early on that there would be no sophomore jinx. Scoring 64 points on November 8th against the Celtics, he broke the league record set by "Jumping" Joe Fulks, who had scored 63 points in a 1949 contest. Baylor recalls that Auerbach tried to stop him and preserve Fulks' record. But in their zeal Boston players fouled Baylor before he could shoot and he achieved the record at the free throw line. Baylor upped his points to 29.6 and rebounds to 16.4 that second season.

He then put up 34.8, 19.8 and 5.1 the following year, quite a line. In the process, he scorched New York for 71 points on November 15th, 1960. His teammate Hot Rod Hundley, now a Lakers' broadcaster, recalled the night in Terry Pluto's *Tall Tales*. "He also had 25 rebounds that game. Bob Short gave every member of the team cufflinks with a '71.' We all wore them proudly."

Knicks's guard Richie Guerin saw Wilt Chamberlain's 100-point game and Baylor's 71-pointer. "I was with the Knicks when everyone was setting records against us. Elgin scored his 71, and a few months (actually about 16 months) later Wilt had his 100-point game against us. By far, Elgin's was the better performance, and that 71-point game remains the greatest individual effort I have ever seen. In Wilt's game, they set out to get him the record. There was nothing artificial about Elgin's 71. He got all the points in a natural flow."

His fourth year was the topper, with Elgin outdoing even his own lofty standards. He posted 38.3 points, 18.6 rebounds and 4.6 assists per game. In the fifth game of the Finals he hit for 61 points against the Celtics in Boston. Auerbach desperately tried to stop Baylor, putting Russell on him at one point. But nothing worked. The Lakers won 126-121 to take a 3-2 lead in the series. It may have been Baylor's greatest clutch performance ever. When Jordan scored 63 against the Celtics in April of 1986 to "break Baylor's record," he needed two overtimes to do it. No one has ever broken Baylor's record in regulation time. The Lakers then lost game six at home, and game seven in overtime in Boston, 110-107.

Take a closer look at Baylor's second through fifth seasons. Let's do a "sum analysis" of those years, 1960-1963, simply adding points, assists and rebounds per game to arrive at Baylor's T.O.P (Total Offensive Production). Here are Baylor's best seasons, ranked in T.O.P. order.

## Elgin Baylor

| YEAR | PPG | RPG | APG | TOTAL |
|------|------|------|-----|-------|
| 61-62 | 38.3 | 18.6 | 4.6 | 61.5 |
| 60-61 | 34.8 | 19.8 | 5.1 | 59.7 |
| 62-63 | 34.0 | 14.3 | 4.8 | 53.1 |
| 59-60 | 29.6 | 16.4 | 3.5 | 49.5 |

Now look at the seasons of some other great players, again ranked in T.O.P. order.

## Wilt Chamberlain

| YEAR | PPG | RPG | APG | TOTAL |
|------|------|------|-----|-------|
| 61-62 | 50.4 | 25.7 | 2.4 | 78.5 |
| 62-63 | 44.8 | 24.3 | 3.4 | 72.5 |
| 60-61 | 38.4 | 27.2 | 1.9 | 67.5 |
| *59-60 | 37.6 | 27.0 | 2.3 | 66.9 |
| 63-64 | 36.9 | 22.3 | 5.0 | 64.2 |
| 65-66 | 33.5 | 24.6 | 5.2 | 63.3 |
| 64-65 | 34.7 | 22.9 | 3.4 | 61.0 |

These were Chamberlain's first seven years in the pros. He won the scoring title each of these years. Even in 1973, his 14th and last year, he was getting "double-doubles" in points and rebounds. I have put these seven here because they were the only seasons where Chamberlain's T.O.P. was 60 or above. Baylor had just one such year, with another at 59.7. But we will see how few players in 50 years of basketball history totalled 60.

Before doing that, let's look at the meaning of this total.

While basketball boasts no statistic quite like the "Total Average" that Tom Boswell writes about annually for *Inside Sports*, adding points, assists and rebounds might be looked at as a "Total Offensive Production" average for playing offense. It in no way reflects upon a player's man-to-man defense, steals, blocked shots, tipped balls, or any of the other effort plays on the defensive end of the floor. Defense has never been properly measured with statistics and probably never will be.

But it does provide us with an index for measuring offensive talent. Of course, the statistic can always be refined. One might, for example, *weigh* rebounds, assists and points differently. Fine. I am not opposed to such fine tuning. But fine tuning is only fine tuning. It does not obscure the importance of this number for measuring a player's total offensive contribution. Using this analysis it is easy to see that few people in the history of the game accomplished what Baylor did.

A player comparable to Baylor today, at least in physical stature, is Charles Barkley. Barkley has had several years where his totals were in the forties, but never in the high forties.

Here are Barkley's best three T.O.P. years:

## Charles Barkley

| YEAR | PPG | RPG | APG | TOTAL |
|------|-----|-----|-----|-------|
| 87-88 | 28.3 | 11.9 | 3.2 | 43.4 |
| 92-93 | 25.6 | 12.2 | 5.1 | 42.9 |
| 86-87 | 23.0 | 14.6 | 4.9 | 42.5 |

Comparing Baylor to Barkley is not done to humiliate Barkley. His were three fine seasons. Rather, Barkley's seasons are here to show what an utterly dominant player Baylor was, even at 6-5. Baylor's four best years beat *any* of Barkley's 13 seasons by far. Even a difference in the greater number of available rebounds in the fifties and sixties (due to lower field goal percentages at that time) does not account for the gap between the two players.

In fact, here is the ranking of some of the best career active players by total offensive average, taking their best three years.

## Karl Malone

| Year | PPG | RPG | APG | TOTAL |
|------|-----|-----|-----|-------|
| 89-90 | 31.0 | 11.1 | 2.8 | 44.9 |
| 90-91 | 29.0 | 11.8 | 3.3 | 44.1 |
| 88-89 | 29.1 | 10.7 | 2.7 | 42.5 |

Malone's averages are slightly better than Barkley's, but are not even close to Baylor's. And it doesn't get much closer if you compare Baylor to the greatest forwards in history. Except for one. Here are the T.O.P. numbers for Bob Pettit, the St. Louis Hawks' forward and a contemporary of Baylor's.

## Bob Pettit

| YEAR | PPG | RPG | APG | TOTAL |
|------|-----|-----|-----|-------|
| 61-62 | 31.1 | 18.7 | 3.7 | 53.5 |
| 60-61 | 27.9 | 20.3 | 3.4 | 51.6 |
| 58-59 | 29.2 | 16.4 | 3.1 | 48.7 |

Of all forwards who ever played the game, Pettit comes closest to Baylor in Total Offensive Production. Pettit's career T.O.P. is 45.6, compared to Baylor's 45.2. This .4 difference is insignificant, however, considering that Baylor's T.O.P. was hurt by playing 14 seasons and Pettit's was helped by playing just 11 years. Like a batting average or slugging average in baseball,

T.O.P. tends to decline, even for the great players. And Baylor's peak seasons — 1960-1962 — were far better than any of Pettit's seasons.

Here are Bird's best years on offense:

## Larry Bird

| YEAR | PPG | RPG | APG | TOTAL |
|------|-----|-----|-----|-------|
| 84-85 | 28.7 | 10.5 | 6.6 | 45.8 |
| 87-88 | 29.9 | 9.3 | 6.1 | 45.3 |
| 86-87 | 27.0 | 10.0 | 7.2 | 44.2 |

In the midst of nine consecutive All-NBA first team selections, Bird reeled off these seasons. As Total Averages, they did not even rival Baylor's best. And Bird's career Total Offensive Production — 40.6 — did not rival Baylor's either. Two things might be pointed out here.

One, Total Average does not address intangibles such as team leadership and elevating the performance of your teammates. A consideration of all these factors make Bird superior to Baylor.

On the other hand, it does show the greatness of Baylor. Even for those of us who never saw Baylor play — I did not start watching him until 1969 — we *did* see Bird play and knew how productive he was as a rebounder, scorer and passer. If Baylor not only tops Bird's averages of 24.3 points, 10 rebounds and 6.3 assists but tops them *significantly*, then even those who did not see Baylor at his best can still infer that he was truly great.

The Total Offensive Production numbers of another great forward tell a tale of two leagues. Julius Erving's most productive 3 years as a pro all occurred during his years in the ABA (1971-1976) with the Virginia Squires and the New York Nets. In the NBA, he never reached a T.O.P. of 40.

## Julius Erving

| YEAR | PPG | RPG | APG | TOTAL |
|------|-----|-----|-----|-------|
| 72-73 | 31.9 | 12.2 | 4.2 | 48.3 |
| 71-72 | 27.3 | 15.7 | 4.0 | 47.0 |
| 75-76 | 29.3 | 11.0 | 5.0 | 45.3 |

Even the acrobatic Erving's ABA numbers don't approach Baylor's figures.

The achievements of Rick Barry, another two-league forward, are also notable. One obvious difference between Erving and Rick Barry is that Barry put up stellar numbers in both leagues. Four times he averaged 25+ points in the NBA, and he twice broke 30 points per game. The first of the following three seasons was with the San Francisco Warriors. His second and third best were with the Oakland Oaks and the New York Nets.

## Rick Barry

| YEAR | PPG | RPG | APG | TOTAL |
|------|-----|-----|-----|-------|
| 66-67 | 35.6 | 9.2 | 3.6 | 48.4 |
| 68-69 | 34.0 | 9.4 | 3.9 | 47.3 |
| 71-72 | 31.5 | 7.5 | 4.1 | 43.1 |

While Barry's numbers put him in Erving territory — and if for just one year, Bird territory in the NBA — he too is far behind Baylor.

Baylor carved out a place in NBA history. Too bad that so few people recall his terrific career. And some who have heard of him still know little about the magnitude of his achievements. He is the very model of the modern forward.

All Baylor did in his career — which spanned 1959 through 1972 — was average 27.4 points per game, third best in the history of the NBA. And his bottom line also included an uncanny 13.5 rebounds per game. Try finding one other person at that height to average that many rebounds. Words like "spectacular" and "versatile" arise whenever people weigh in with opinions on Baylor.

Some will point out that Baylor never won a championship. It is commonplace to hear sports radio hosts to talk about "how many rings" a guy has, as if a player could marshall a team to do his bidding single-handedly. John Havlicek doesn't agree. "In my mind that doesn't diminish a player," Hondo says. That being said, it hardly seems persuasive that the difference between a Baylor not winning and a Bird winning three times or a Johnson winning five times can be written off as just luck. It is indisputable that players like Bird and Johnson made those around them better.

Baylor's career was sandwiched between the championship Mikan-Lakers and the West-Chamberlain-Goodrich squad of 1972 which won it all. Baylor retired nine games into the 1971-1972 season, before the championship celebration. Baylor retired on the day that Los Angeles began their 33-game winning streak. The day of his retirement "He was an exceptionally talented guy," says Jack Ramsay. "It was Baylor and West against the world. They were always good enough to win the Western Conference but didn't have enough to win it all." "They just never had a center to play against Russell," adds Tommy Heinsohn, who played with Boston from 1956 through 1965.

While Baylor's teams never won, Baylor was certainly a clutch performer. His 27 points per game playoff average tell us something about the kind of clutch performer he was.

John Havlicek recalls playing against him. "Elgin Baylor was the first guy to have a game similar to a lot of guys today. He could hang in the air, double-pump. He was a terrific scorer, huge rebounder and could shoot inside and outside and lead the fast break."

He was Rookie of the Year, an 11-time All-Star and was selected All-NBA 10 times.

No one who knows the game could ever forget him. He ranks second all-time because his incredible achievements and well-rounded game.

# Bob**Pettit**

If you put together an all-forgotten team in NBA history, Bob Pettit would star on it. Many fans in the nineteen-nineties know little of how Pettit's scoring and rebounding kept the St. Louis Hawks (who moved to Atlanta for the 1968-69 season) right on the tail of the Boston Celtics in the late fifties and early sixties. Pettit was a two-time MVP and was selected to the All-NBA First Team ten different times and the second team once. When he retired after the 1965 season, Bob Pettit was the leading scorer in NBA history with 20,880 points. Twice he lead the league in scoring and even led the Hawks to their only World Championship in 1958.

"Bob Pettit was usually in the top two or three in rebounds," said Tommy Heinsohn, Hall of Fame forward with the Boston Celtics. "He could hit the 18-footer, play in the low-box. He wasn't super quick but he would shoot coming off a pick. He was the master of the half-inch."

Born and raised in Baton Rouge, Louisiana, Pettit was cut from his high school baseball, basketball and football teams. Then his father nailed up a basket in the back yard. Pettit shot for hours on end, sometimes until nine at night. For lighting he put two lamps in the window.

He improved enough to enjoy a stellar college career at Louisiana State and was the Milwaukee Hawks' first pick in the 1954 NBA Draft. But the 6-9 forward had no intention of turning pro and was thinking of playing for two teams sponsored by industrial companies. Good money could be made that way, and Pettit had interviews with the Peoria Caterpillars and Phillips 66 teams. Phillips 66 was offering $425 a month, less than half of what the Milwaukee Hawks were offering. But Phillips 66 offered an opportunity for executive training in the company after he was finished as a player.

Still, Pettit decided to go with the NBA. If he avoided the NBA, Pettit thought, it would gnaw at him never to know how he would have done against the best players.

He and Hawks owner Ben Kerner discussed a salary and Pettit, after rejecting Kerner's offer of $9,000, signed with the Hawks for $11,000. His coach Red Holzman then made the move that was instrumental to his greatness, switching him from center to forward. Pettit said he was "eternally grateful," thinking that "he wasn't strong enough" to play center in the NBA.

As a forward Pettit shone immediately. "He had the most reliable turnaround jumper, a relentless, monotonous turn-around jumper," recalls *Boston Globe* columnist Bob Ryan. "He was also a great rebounder, a banger, a warrior."

To show how different 1950s basketball was, in a 1957 article in the *Saturday Evening Post*, Pettit spent much the article defending tall people and pleading with the public "not to call us freaks."

What Pettit got, he got with determination and guile. Heinsohn, who was 6-7, recalled that it was nearly impossible to block Pettit out. "You could block him out perfectly and then he'd go over your back," Heinsohn said. "He had a cute trick of getting his elbows over your shoulders and knocking you into him. Then he'd shoot the ball and get a three-pointer."

"I had the opportunity to see Bob play about 50 times in my life," recalls NBC TV analyst Matt Guokas. "He always played with the same intensity. He was a hard-nosed player and had more of a post game, a turn-around jumper from about 16 to 17 feet. He was a great scorer and great rebounder."

In his fourth year Pettit led the St. Louis Hawks (the franchise had moved to St. Louis for the 1955-1956 season) to the Finals for the second consecutive season. The 1956-1957 season the year before, the Celtics and

Hawks fought up a seven-game Final. The seventh game was decided in two overtimes, with the Celtics winning 125-123. Heinsohn had 37 points and 23 rebounds. Pettit played 56 of a possible 58 minutes and scored 39 points with 19 rebounds in the game, but he shot just 14 of 34 from the field.

It was Boston's first title, the dawn of the Russell-era in which they would win 11 titles in 13 years. But Pettit had another chance in the 1958 Finals. Boston and St. Louis split the first four games. St. Louis took the fifth and now had a chance to take the series at home. In game six, the Hawks led 83-77 entering the fourth quarter. But even without Russell, who played only 20 minutes because of a badly sprained ankle, the Celtics rallied and went ahead in the last quarter. Bill Sharman scored 26 and Heinsohn added 23. But Pettit scored 19 points in the quarter and iced the game with a 15-footer to put the Hawks up 110-107 with just 15 seconds remaining. Pettit had scored 50 points, breaking George Mikan's 47-point record for a regulation-length playoff game. Bob Cousy had scored 50 in a 1953 playoff contest against the Syracuse Nationals, but it took him four overtimes to do it.

Pettit's 50-point total gave him a 29.3 average for the six-game series. It was a "once-in-a-lifetime thing," he said. "I wasn't sure what was happening. I was getting the ball, shooting it and it was going in. The whole thing happened in a blur and I don't remember any of the individual shots or plays. I just knew I wanted the ball because I didn't think they could do anything to stop me."

The Hawks would meet the Celtics twice more in the Finals, in 1960 and '61, making it four times in five years that the teams met. In 1960 the Hawks lost in seven games as Pettit averaged 26 points. The following year they lost in five as Pettit averaged 28.6 The Celtics had too much fire power for anyone else and went on to win every title through 1966.

By 1965, Pettit was 32 and was plagued by a succession of ailments, including a back injury that had placed him on the disabled list earlier in the season. After recovering, he went back on the shelf with a leg injury.

When he announced his retirement in St. Louis on March 1st, his owner Ben Kerner broke into tears. The fortunes of the Hawks were sagging, mirroring their brightest star. A younger Baltimore team eliminated them in the first round of the playoffs later in March, with Pettit averaging only 11 points per game in the series.

In his 11th year in pro ball, Pettit had scored 20,880 points and recorded 12,849 rebounds. No other player had passed the 20,000 mark. Pettit was also the first player to record 20,000 points and 10,000 rebounds.

His career averages were 26.4 points, 16.2 rebounds and 3.0 assists. The sum of those three numbers, 45.6, is his Total Offensive Production. That is the highest T.O.P. for any forward in NBA history.

The greatest All-Star performer ever, Pettit averaged 20 points in 11 All-Star games and was awarded the game's MVP three times.

It is the sum of these distinctions that earns Pettit third place on the all-time list, behind only Larry Bird and Baylor. His 26.4 points per game is second all-time among forwards, behind only Elgin Baylor (27.4).

"I played against him for three years," said Hall of Fame forward, Boston's John Havlicek. "He was a relentless player. Through smarts and ability to shoot, he was the primary weapon in their offense. It was not uncommon for him to get 20-25 rebounds per game. I never matched up with Pettit that much. When I did, I tried to keep him off the boards."

"He was one of the most respected players ever," says Bob Ryan.

"Pettit was and probably is what the power forward should be," says 14-year forward and Charlotte broadcaster Mike Gminski. "He defined that position in those years when forwards didn't have that size and strength."

"To me, he was second at the big forward spot to Larry Bird," said TNT TV analyst and former coach Hubie Brown.

"He is still the best forward I ever saw play the game," said Heinsohn.

# Julius**Erving**
## (tied with Rick Barry)

If you do the only sensible thing and combine his ABA plus NBA points, then Julius Erving is the third leading scorer in NBA history. In his 16-year career that began with the Virginia Squires in 1971, Julius Erving scored 30,026 points.

Picking his own forward list, John Havlicek said "Julius Erving is the Picasso of the group; his game was more or less an art form." Beyond his statistical markers, it is his style of play that most people bring before their mind's eye when they hear the name Julius Erving. "Erving was doing Jordan-like things before Jordan," says Mike Gminski, who began his career in 1980. "Erving went into a higher orbit than Baylor did. Had there been cable when he was in his prime, we would have witnessed him more often. When he was in his prime he looked like a soaring apparition with a big afro."

After playing the first two years of his career with Virginia, Erving was traded to the New York Nets, along with center Willie Sojourner, for forward George Carter and the draft rights to forward Kermit Washington. The trade paid immediate dividends. Playing on Long Island where he grew up, the good "Doctor" won the MVP and brought the Nassau Coliseum hopeful a championship in 1974. He was co-MVP with George McGinnis in 1975 when the Kentucky Colonels won the ABA title. In 1976 he again won the league MVP and the Nets won the title for the second time. He led the ABA in scoring twice.

When the ABA merged with the NBA for the 1976-1977 season, the Nets sold Erving's contract to the Philadelphia 76ers. While it would appear to be one of the bone-head moves of all-time, Nets owner Roy Boe had no choice. The merger settlement with the new league, which Terry Pluto describes verbatim in *Loose Balls,* required that each ABA team had to pay each NBA team $3.2 million by September 15, 1976. Boe also owned the New York Islanders hockey team. "I had a lot of financial responsibilities," Boe recalls. "But to be hit with $3.2 million to get into the NBA — actually it was over $4 million because there were some extra charges. I owed the Knicks $480,000 a year for ten years in indemnity charges (this charge was because the Nets would be playing in "the Knicks territory"). I needed to get some cash, about $5 million, by September 15. And Julius Erving said he wanted a new contract. He was making $350,000 with several years to run (on his contract). Julius said that we made him a promise that we'd renegotiate his contract if we got into the NBA. Well, we had a 60-some-page contract and there wasn't a word in there about that.

"I offered Julius Erving to the Knicks for a cash settlement and in exchange for dropping that $480,000-a-year indemnity charge.They turned it down. I didn't have the $3.3 million in liquid cash to get into the NBA and it was due by September 15. I was offered $3 million for Julius Erving from Philadelphia and I took it, because I had no choice. The merger agreement got us into the NBA, but it forced me to destroy the team by selling Erving to pay the bill."

Said Erving: "Ask yourself this: who made out? The NBA owners got a great deal. They got all the money from the ABA teams, who wanted to get into the NBA. But they also got all the best ABA players, which made the

NBA a more exciting and popular league. But what happened to the average ABA players? Most didn't get jobs or played maybe a year or two in the NBA. They basically were left out in the cold."

The Nets were certainly left out in the cold. Since the Red Sox' trade of Ruth has been referred to as "The Curse of Babe Ruth," so too can the Nets' sale of Erving be referred to as "The Curse of Julius Erving." Just as Ruth's departure left the Red Sox a sub-.500 team for the next *fourteen years,* in the 20 years since the Erving trade the Nets' franchise has known little joy and mostly despair.

With Philadelphia Julius Erving played on some very, very good teams and one great one in 1983. For the 1976-1977 season he teamed with an athletic bunch that went to the Finals. Julius' skywalker routines came earthbound a bit, going from 29.3 points per game in his last year in the ABA to 21.6 with Philly. That fact might fuel a skeptics' opinion on the differences in talent between the leagues. But the disparity could also be expected. He was now sharing shots with high scoring George McGinnis and two other big scorers in Doug Collins and World (as in "don't call me all-NBA, I'm All-world") B. Free. "Nobody denied Erving the ball more," NBC's Pete Vecsey once said about Free.

Philadelphia emerged from a tough six game series with Boston, the previous year's champion, and a seven-game battle with Houston, to make the Finals. Philly had the most talent and won the first two games at home. Portland then began to play their game, chipping the rust away after laying off nine days, waiting for the Philly-Houston series to end.

Now at home, they trounced Philly by margins of 22 and 32 points. Bill Walton badly outplayed the center combo of Caldwell Jones and Darryl Dawkins and Maurice Lucas was outplaying George McGinnis to an even greater degree. Bill Walton went to far as to say that Bobby Gross outplayed Julius Erving in game six, when Portland closed out the series with its fourth straight victory. Said Walton while narrating an ESPN replay of the game, "they always dribbled before passing. You can't play basketball that way."

Bobby Gross did play well and scored 24 points in the sixth game. But Erving played well, too, scoring 40 points, hitting 17 of 29 shots. But the game was won on the boards. Walton had 20 points and 23 rebounds, three less than Philly's starting front line combined. Said Jack Ramsay, "we wanted to work Julius at the defensive end and give help when he was on offense. We had a good defender in Bobby Gross and good defenders off the bench. We ran a lot of things for Gross and made Julius work."

The year had set one pattern in motion. Julius Erving's teams won a lot of games and made it deep into the playoffs. Beginning with the Virginia

Squires in 1972, here are the records of Erving's teams for the 16 years he played.

| Team | Year | Regular Season | Playoffs |
|------|------|----------------|----------|
| Virginia | 1971-72 | 45-39 | 7-4 |
| Virginia | 1972-73 | 42-42 | 1-4 |
| New York | 1973-74 | 55-29 | 12-2* |
| New York | 1974-75 | 58-26 | 1-4 |
| New York | 1975-76 | 55-29 | 8-5* |
| Philadelphia | 1976-77 | 50-32 | 10-9 |
| Philadelphia | 1977-78 | 55-27 | 6-4 |
| Philadelphia | 1978-79 | 47-35 | 5-4 |
| Philadelphia | 1979-80 | 59-23 | 12-6 |
| Philadelphia | 1980-81 | 62-20 | 9-7 |
| Philadelphia | 1981-82 | 58-24 | 12-9 |
| Philadelphia | 1982-83 | 65-17 | 12-1* |
| Philadelphia | 1983-84 | 58-24 | 2-3 |
| Philadelphia | 1984-85 | 58-24 | 8-5 |
| Philadelphia | 1985-86 | 54-28 | 6-6 |
| Philadelphia | 1986-87 | 45-37 | 2-3 |
| | Averages: | 54-28 | 7-5 |

*Denotes World Championship seasons*

The regular season average record is 54-28 (.659) while the playoff record is .583. But a decline is expected there, since poor teams are not in the playoffs to help pad a team's record. The records also show that Erving's teams did indeed win. In no year did his teams miss the playoffs and in 12 of 16 years they got past the first round.

In those years that the 76ers made the Finals but did not win — 1977, 1980 and 1982 — they didn't have a center to compare with the rival's center. In 1977 it was Bill Walton against Caldwell Jones and back-up, ever erratic Darryl Dawkins. In 1980 and 1982 it was reversed, with Dawkins starting and Jones off the bench, against Kareem Abdul-Jabbar. Again, no contest. Philadelphia finally solved this problem in September 1982 by getting Moses Malone from Houston for Caldwell Jones and a 1983 first-round draft pick. In 1983 they sailed through the playoffs with a 12-1 record, "riding Moses' coattails," as then assistant coach Matt Guokas puts it.

The statistical difference between his ABA and NBA numbers is also curious with Julius Erving. As noted, his first year in the NBA was a decline from his ABA years. But it is also notable that he never really approached the 28.7 average he had amassed over the first five years of his career in the ABA. One reason is the one that Hubie Brown cites, that Erving's knees would not allow him to reach the heights, literally and figuratively, that he attained in the ABA.

A second explanation says that the ABA was tailored to suit Erving's high-flying ways. "I was in Connecticut when they carried Nets' games," says Mike Gminski. "The ABA game was wide open and catered to him purposefully." No doubt, there is some truth to both of Gminski's ideas. The ABA was "wide open," which meant far more flying on offense but also less defense. And Erving was the league's biggest star. With Erving, the ABA could say to the NBA 'see, we have a guy who's as good as any one of yours.'

A third explanation for the decline in Erving's scoring is that many players see their scoring decline after their first five years. Including Robertson, Baylor, Chamberlain and Abdul-Jabbar, many of the greatest offensive players tend to score more in their first five years of their careers than thereafter. Michael Jordan's highest scoring year was his third season.

There are exceptions. Gervin had his highest scoring years in the NBA, in the sixth, seventh, eighth and tenth years of his career. And Jerry West enjoyed his two highest scoring years in his sixth and tenth years. But Erving is one of those who fits the first category, the "young" scorers.

A fourth explanation is that Erving in Philadelphia teamed with players who, to put it kindly, liked putting the ball up. In Erving's first year in Philadelphia, McGinnis took 66 more shots than Erving in three less games! World B. Free also hoisted away, putting up 1,022 shots. Never mind that Erving shot 50 percent and they shot 46 percent each. A habit is a habit and these guys were going to shoot. So Erving, who had attempted between 1,719 and 1,810 shots a year when the offense ran through him with the Squires and the Nets, now was taking just 1,373 shots, about 5 less per game. In fact, Erving was a .509 shooter with Virginia and New York and shot about the same — .507 — in eleven years with the Sixers.

All four explanations show contributing causes to the decline in Erving's numbers. The 76ers had more individual talent. But they didn't always play as a team. In 1980, three years after the loss to Portland, they sailed through the Eastern Conference with a 10-2 playoff record. But then they found themselves against Abdul-Jabbar and a sensational rookie, Magic Johnson. Abdul-Jabbar averaged 33 points for the series, before he hurt his ankle and missed game six. That's when Johnson took over with his 42 points, 15 rebounds and seven assists. Erving averaged 26 for the series, but it wasn't enough to offset the Lakers' advantage at point guard and center.

The 1982 Finals brought the same result. Johnson was again the MVP as Los Angeles won in six games. It was the third Finals' loss for Erving, now in his sixth NBA season. "We are more disappointed this year than any other year," Erving said afterward. "It hurts more than any other year." Then an assistant coach with Philadelphia, Matt Guokas recalls what helped the

Lakers. "We had to double-team Kareem and that hurt us defensively. On defense they came at us with a 1-3-1 trap to slow the tempo. We got wide open shots in the corner for Julius and Andrew (Toney) and Bobby (Jones) and couldn't hit them. It wasn't a case of a team breakdown. They were a better team."

In 1983 Erving did get his first championship. The Moses Malone trade brought the 76ers a center who could outplay the opposing center for the first time in four Finals. Philadelphia swept Los Angeles. Erving averaged 19 points and 8.5 rebounds, but the series belonged to Moses Malone who put up 26 points and 18 rebounds per game, outplaying the 36-year-old Abdul-Jabbar (23.5 points and 7.5 rebounds). When all-time great teams are discussed, the 76ers' team must be included. For the regular season they went 65-17 and then 12-1 in the playoffs for a 77-18 record (.810) In Malone, Erving and Toney Philadelphia had potent scoring at the center, forward and guard positions. Malone's 15 rebounds per game also led the league by a country mile and he was selected All-NBA First Team on defense.

After that championship season, Philly went rather gently into that good night. Inexplicably, they lost in he first round to the New Jersey Nets in 1984.

Boston, Los Angeles or both would appear in every Finals series from 1984 through 1989. The eighties belonged to college and pro rivals Larry Bird and Magic Johnson and their rivalry tended to eclipse every other, until Isiah Thomas and the Pistons won consecutive titles in 1989 and 1990. For his part, Erving appeared in the playoffs four more times, but averaged 20 points in none of them. Perhaps age was taking its toll on Erving's totals but it is also true that the Bird-Johnson era was in full swing beginning in 1984.

The team that the Nets had eliminated in Philadelphia had three twenty-point scorers in Toney, Malone and Erving. And in 1985 and 1986 they had at least two twenty-point scorers in either Malone, Erving or Barkley. But dynastic talent doesn't always produce dynastic results. Boston beat them in five in the 1985 conference finals and Milwaukee beat them in the conference semis in 1986. Philadelphia had fought their way to four of eight Finals from 1977 through 1983. But by the mid-eighties they were an afterthought.

Erving got his 30,000 point in 1987, just the third player to attain that feat.

Who better to rate the Doctor than Matt Guokas, who saw much of Erving's career as an assistant and then as a head coach from the Philadelphia bench. "Doc was such an incredible player and competitor. He brought dignity to the game and played with flair. He was like Michael Jordan in that you would come to a game and see his best effort and two or three spectacular plays."

A highlight film of such plays can be called to mind by calling up our mental files. "He was the supreme aerial artist who did what a great player should do and include and expand his game dramatically," says Bob Ryan, an observer of much of the Celtics-76ers combat. "He became a dangerous outside shooter as he went on. When the knees started to go out, his aerial game was not the focal point. His hit his physical peak in the ABA but had the shot and was better and smarter in the NBA."

Julius Erving's 30,026 points are the most ever by a forward. He also had impressive career averages of 24.2 points, 8.5 rebounds and 4.2 assists. Throw in his 3 ABA and NBA titles and five All-NBA First Team selections and it is apparent that the Doctor operated like few others.

# Rick**Barry**

## (tied with Julius Erving)

Superlatives never cease when the subject of conversation is Rick Barry. Richard Francis Dennis Barry III is a long name for a large talent. He was one of the most gifted men ever to play basketball. Like Erving, Barry switched from the ABA to the NBA. Unlike Erving, Barry started in the NBA, left for the ABA and came back to the NBA in 1973. Because of his switching, a look at Barry's all-time stats in the *NBA Official Register* is like a trip through the virtual reality ride at Busch Gardens. Your mind sizes up columns of data and gaps in columns. There are heads and subheads and more columns.

But Barry did some things in the NBA that Erving did not, like leading the league in scoring (35.6 points in 1967). Rick Barry, as Hubie Brown puts it, "was the full package."

"Next to Bird, Barry is the greatest passing forward ever to play the game," says Mike Gminski. "His assist numbers are the same as John Havlicek's (4.9 per game). And he lifted that 1975 [championship] Golden State team *on his back.*"

In passing, it should be said that only Scottie Pippen (5.3) and Larry Bird (6.3) had more assists at the forward position than Barry. Whereas, Barry's passing came off the drive, "Bird did more of his passing from the perimeter," Guokas says. "He was a great passer off the dribble," Ryan agrees.

And we haven't even talked scoring yet. Four times Barry averaged 30+ points per game, even more times than Elgin Baylor. "Barry is a forgotten man," says coach Jack Ramsay. "But he could shoot it from *anywhere.* He could put it on the floor and was a great passer. And he moved well without the ball."

"Rick gets a lot of credit for being a shooter and once he got going he was, but was more a scorer than a shooter," says Matt Guokas. "He could score 40 or 50. If he realized the jump shot was not going, he would drive to the basket. Like Bird he was a great passer but was not as good a ball handler as Bird. But he was more explosive going to the basket than Bird."

Barry had unlimited range and if he played now could certainly set up shop and bomb away from the three-point line. One recollection I have of Barry was his coming to New York to play against Dave DeBusschere. On defense DeBusschere routinely drew the other team's best forward. His six NBA All-Defensive First Team awards — tie with Pippen among all forwards who ever played — attests that he was pretty good at handling those assignments. But against Barry he was ineffective. Barry would launch from 20 to 25 feet and score forties time and again. New York's team defense seemed clueless against Barry.

And at the free throw line he is second lifetime with a .900 percentage. That underhanded technique of his gave a soft loft to his shot and if the ball did hit the rim, it hit softly, not like a brick. He attempted 4,243 free throws and made all but 425 of them. The only man ahead of him is Mark Price but Price has taken only half as many tosses as Barry.

If you want a primer on Barry the scorer, glance at his first nine years in the pros. And marvel: 25.7 points in 1966; 35.6 in 1967; he sat out his option year in 1968 due to a court order; 34.0 in 1969; 27.7 in 1970; 29.4 in 1971; 31.5 in 1972; 22.3 in 1973; 25.1 in 1974; 30.6 in 1976. Besides the 30+ points in four different seasons, he had between 25 and 30 four other times. He led the NBA in scoring once, and led the ABA once. Six times he led the NBA in free throw percentage and three more times led the ABA.

Barry's irrepressible offense also included some of the greatest outbursts in NBA history. On March 26th, 1974, Barry scored 64 points against Portland, making 30 field goals. Besides Barry, only Wilt Chamberlain ever made 30 field goals in a game. Barry also had a pair of 57-point games, one at New York in 1965 and another in 1966.

What else do you need to know about Barry? How about his playoff performance. Four facts will do.

One, his life-time NBA average is 23.2 and his playoff average went up to 24.8.

Two, his lifetime ABA average was 30.5 and his playoff average jumped to 33.5. In a five-game playoff series in 1970, he averaged 40.1 points for the Washington Capitols.

Then there's the matter of the 1967 NBA finals. The Philadelphia 76ers were legendary for their 68-13 record that season. It was the season that Wilt Chamberlain *didn't* lead the league in scoring, but averaged 24.1 rebounds per game to lead the league, to go with 24 points and eight assists per game. For the first time since 1959 someone other than Chamberlain led the league in scoring. Who was it? It makes a good trivia question. It was Rick Barry, who scored 35.6 points per game and led the league in five offensive categories.

It was Philadelphia's year, but the San Francisco Warriors gave them trouble in the Finals. Barry scored 44 in the final game at the Cow Palace and averaged 41 points for the series, stealing the show. In game three he hit for 55 points, the third highest total in playoff history to that point. Guokas, who played for the winning Philadelphia team, recalls the 23-year-old Barry's performance. "I recall he hit for 55 points in one game," says Guokas. "In that series he was Jordanesque, if you will. He was unstoppable. He had the green light. You've got to remember it was more of an up-tempo game then and more shots were taken in any given game. And you didn't prepare defensively as you would today. Today you would double-team in that situation. A small forward would start on Rick — though they didn't call them small forwards then — and for us that was Chet Walker. Bill Cunningham came off the bench and individual defense was not Billy's forte. I guarded him and shut him down," Guokas laughs. "Actually, I got lucky. For about a 6 to 7 minute span of the game he didn't see the ball. "What made him so hard to guard is that he took all kinds of shots. He had a tremendous ability to put it on the floor and drive to the basket. You would see him hit three-point shots now. Up to about 22 feet he could make them in streaks." Could anyone stop him? "That's why I say he was like Jordan," Guokas continues," if he didn't score it's because he didn't make shots, not because anyone shut him down."

Despite Barry's heroics, there were three keys to the Sixers' victory.

Their starting five badly outplayed the Warriors' five. Philly had the best quintet in the league that year with Chet Walker, Luke Jackson, Chamberlain, Hal Greer and Wali Jones. Between them they *averaged* 97 points a game. In that final game they totaled 99 to give Philly a tough, come-from-behind 125-122 victory. And Billy Cunningham's 13 off-the-bench points in the last quarter helped the Sixers to overcome a five-point fourth quarter deficit. The 76ers also wore the Warriors out at the free throw line, attempting 64 free throws to the Warriors' 29! Barry and the Warriors split their playoff share of $72,500 twelve ways, about $6,042 a piece. The winners earned about $7,300 each.

In 1975 Barry finally got his title. Playing the Washington Bullets, the Warriors were down by 16 in game one, but outscored the Bullets 61-41 in the second half to win, 101-95. With 38 second left, Barry hit a big jumper as the 24-second clock ran down. In game two Phil Chenier gave the Bullets 30 points. But it wasn't enough to offset Barry's 36 as the Warriors eked out a 92-91 victory. With 23 second left the Bullets led 91-90 but Barry was fouled by Mike Riordan and hit both. The Warriors then kept the ball away from Chenier and Hayes and forced Riordan to take a difficult shot that missed as the buzzer sounded.

In game three Barry was at it again, pouring in 38, leading the Warriors to a 109-101 victory in San Francisco. In this unusual 1-2-1 series the fourth game was played in Landover, Maryland and the Warriors had their second one-point victory, 96-95. It was only the third Finals' sweep in NBA history, the first two belonging to the 1959 Celtics and the 1971 Bucks. The Bullets had now been swept in two Finals. The Warriors had just one superstar player, Barry, and won the series because they played better in the pressure situations.

Chenier, who averaged 23 points in the series, recalls Barry's effort. "He was awesome in that 1975 series," says Chenier. "They had some players; Phil Smith, and Cliff Ray did a good job. But Rick set the tone in that series. If they needed a shot, he took it. He had the range. Just imagine how many points he'd have now with the three-point line moved in. His desire to win was at such an incredibly high level."

Barry was the unanimous choice as the Finals' MVP, averaging 29.5 for the series. In his two NBA finals, 1967 and 1975, Barry averaged an incredible 36 points per game, giving him the highest Finals average in NBA history.

Simply put, if you select a team composed of the all-time best playoff performers, Barry would be on it.

Barry's 25,279 points are the seventh highest among forwards in NBA history. Toss in — underhanded, of course — 12 All-Star appearances and 5 All-NBA First Team selections. Barry's bottom line of 24.8 points, 6.7 rebounds and 4.9 assists, though hurt by his final two lackluster seasons in Houston, is still one of the most impressive among forwards in NBA history.

Barry versus Erving makes for an interesting argument. Barry was a better perimeter player and Erving was stronger on the drive. Barry was a better passer and Erving has the better rebounding numbers. Erving had three titles (two in the ABA), while Barry had just one. But Barry's NBA numbers were better than Erving's and he was certainly a superior Finals' performer. Their personal styles were very different but they were about equal in overall effectiveness.

Few players in the future will ever even approach Rick Barry's achievements.

# John**Havlicek**

John Havlicek will be remembered for many things. Many people remember him in the manner that Matt Guokas does. "He had a motor on his back" said Guokas, who played against "Hondo" for ten years. "He may be the best conditioned athlete ever to play," says Mike Gminski. "He was in constant motion," Grunfeld agrees. "He never got tired."

And there are so many other ways to recall this Ohio native's wonderfully rich career.

Celtics' Sixth Man, player on eight Celtics' championship teams, equally adept at guard and forward, great offensive player and great defender — these

103

are some of the epithets that are synonymous with the John Havlicek.

Built as slightly as a matador but as durable as a marathon runner, Havlicek was one of the most important Celtics ever in their run of championships. I would argue that Bill Russell was the most important player to the Celtics' storied success; Bird, second; Havlicek and Bob Cousy tied for third. Havlicek's importance was never more obvious than in the seventies, when he was Boston's best player and invaluable to their 1974 and 1976 titles.

Havlicek also provided a big assist in the 1960s. His marathon career ran — and "ran" is the apropos word to describe Havlicek's activity — from 1963 through 1978. Sure, he will always be remembered for the above-mentioned perpetual motion; that tireless practice of running oval patterns and circles in the front court, never stopping until he had left one defender in the dust or ran another into a pick or two.

Havlicek was also a "swing man," a 6-5 talent capable of playing guard or forward. So great was Havlicek at both positions that Bob Ryan thinks that he should be rated not only among the top ten forwards but among the top ten guards also. "He still remains the most versatile player ever," Ryan marvels. "He played guard, was an All-Star forward, and the definitive small forward."

Then too, "Hondo" Havlicek was a sixth man, a position innovated by Red Auerbach and played to perfection by Frank Ramsey, Sam Jones and Havlicek. "He didn't become a starter until his seventh year in the league," says Ryan. "He had more value to the team that way. But whenever they were in a pinch in those days they started him."

Because of the Celtics' perennial one-for-all, team philosophy, Havlicek did not put up big minutes early in his career. With the Celtics of the 1960s, it was considered selfish, even gauche, to worry about personal achievements. While Havlicek averaged 30+ minutes only once in his first five years, he played when it counted, at crunch time.

Havlicek shuns praise for his sixth man selflessness. "In 1962 I came to a team that had won four straight championships," he recalls. "So I didn't think that I should bust in and expect to start. I wanted to work myself in and become a contributor.

"Red Auerbach had instituted the role of sixth man, having started it with Frank Ramsey. 'It's not who starts but who finishes,' Red would say, and I found myself finishing."

The drafting of Havlicek was another bit of Celtics wisdom. In 1962 most every team in the league was drafting for big men and players like Bill McGill, Paul Hogue, Zelmo Beatty, Len Chappell, Wayne Hightower, Leroy Ellis were all drafted ahead of Havlicek, who was picked 7th in the first round. Havlicek ended up in the Hall of Fame; none of the others did.

A rookie out of Ohio State, Havlicek recalls having an optimistic view on the bench. "When you're young you don't need that warm-up to play," he said. "I looked at it the other way.

The opponents would be tired and I could get a few cheap baskets. And from another aspect I could see how the game was developing and whether we needed offense or defense at that moment."

By the late 1960s, with Bob Cousy and Bill Sharman gone and Bill Russell and Sam Jones on the way out, Havlicek had to play a bigger role. All those people around the league who had suffered through Auerbach's victory cigars thought that now, without his meal ticket Russell, Red would get his comeuppance. "There was a lot of enmity toward Red," says Tom Heinsohn, the Celtics' Hall of Fame forward. With Russell gone, anti-Boston and anti-Auerbach rooters said that the Celts would no longer win. Havlicek recalls coming of age when Russell left the team. In fact, Russell passed the mantle to him. He saw Russell the day after his retirement and Russell said "it's your team now; you're the leader."

Havlicek's minutes had already increased during the 1967-1968 season. Now, with Russell and Jones gone after 1969, his scoring, rebounds and assists jumped too. And what happened as a result?

Havlicek became multi-dimensional. "He was the ultimate team player," says TNT analyst Hubie Brown. "He sacrificed stats to become a team man." Thus Havlicek was chosen All-NBA First Team four times and second team seven more times. "He also played in 13 all-star games," Brown points out. "And he was selected five times All-Defensive First Team and three times second team." And that award wasn't even given until 1969, Hondo's seventh year in the league.

In the 1970s, only two teams enjoyed the distinction of winning two NBA championships. The first to do it were the New York Knicks. The second was Boston.

In 1974 the Celtics beat the Bucks and Abdul-Jabbar in the NBA Finals in a terrific seven-game series. Hondo averaged 27.1 points, 6.4 rebounds and 6 assists in the series, to top all three of his season averages. He was the obvious choice for the playoff MVP. Then an assistant to coach Larry Costello for the Milwaukee Bucks, Hubie Brown recalls the series well. "We had beat them in Boston twice. The difference was we never had a point guard in the series, because Lucius Allen was injured against Detroit when Dave Bing fell across his knee. Fritz Williams and John McGlocklin could not get the job done against White and Chaney.

"At 38 years of age Oscar (Robertson) had to bring it up court. Unfortunately, they wore Oscar down. We shot poorly in game seven and the full court pressure from Chaney got to Oscar and his production. Havlicek was outstanding."

And it was not even Havlicek's best playoff year. All of Havlicek's career averages in the playoffs were equal to or superior to his regular season averages. Two of his best post-season efforts followed Philadelphia's championship in 1967. "In the fifth and last game of the Eastern Division Finals, Philly buried the Celtics, 140-116. Havlicek recalls that day. "The Philadelphia fans were shouting 'The Celtics are dead, Boston's Dead.'" Havlicek showed everyone that they weren't dead.

In the 1968 and 1969 playoffs he posted averages of 25.9, 9 rebounds and 8 assists and then 25.4 points, 10 rebounds and 6 assists. Boston won the title both years, with Havlicek leading in scoring and assists. Russell lead in rebounds.

And of course there was the legendary cry from the ultimate homer, Boston broadcaster Johnny Most in the 1965 playoffs. The Celtics were playing the Sixers in a cliffhanger. It was game seven of the Eastern Conference Finals. With five seconds left, the Celtics lead the Sixers by one point but Boston had the ball on an inbounds play. Mindful that if the play was set for Chamberlain, the Celtics would foul to put him on the line, coach Dolph Schayes called Chet Walker's number in the huddle. With the five-second clock running down, Hal Greer sent a looping pass toward Chet Walker but Havlicek anticipated and jumped between Greer and Walker to tip the pas away to Sam Jones as the clock ran out. Johnny Most's gravelly voice screamed "Havlicek stole the ball, he stole the ball." And that was it. Havlicek had delivered the knock out blow and the Celtics were on their way to their seventh consecutive title.

Fans in the eighties will remember Bird's steal of an Isiah Thomas pass with a few seconds left in the 1987 Conference finals. Bird's play also included a quick dish to Johnson for the winning basket. But Havlicek's steal is every bit as legendary and important as Bird's.

Though his scoring fell off to 13.2 points in the 1976 playoffs, he was the leader of that squad too. They beat the Phoenix Suns in six games.

If Bob Cousy was the "Houdini of the Hardwood," Bill Russell the "Eagle with a Beard," and Larry Bird "Larry Legend" then the name Hondo is just not enough for the 6-5 swingman from Ohio State. He earned a more descriptive, flattering moniker. John Havlicek was the Jack Armstrong of basketball. He was a great player, one of the best Celtics ever. As there are four great guards separate from the rest, so there are six great forwards in an orbit of their own. Without hesitation I would give Havlicek the sixth spot, in the first echelon of all the forwards who ever played the game.

# Karl**Malone**

If NBA careers could be likened to a school achievement, then Karl Malone has earned A's for individual achievement for a long time now. "Malone is the prototype power forward," says Mike Gminski. "The durability is exceptional; he has missed only four games in his entire career." All this for a guy who was drafted 13th in the first round in 1985.

So not only does he get straight A's but the attendance is exemplary. Malone has missed only four games in 12 years, dating back to 1985, the middle of the Reagan administration. He is the Cal Ripken of basketball. He even works and plays well with others, especially one John Stockton. No doubt the twosome are one of the top five one-two punches in the game's history. Karl Malone keeps getting down and dirty, playing with force in the paint, putting up numbers, rolling along like old man river. Though he plays with the Utah

Jazz, there is little jazz or pizazz in his game. His game is like a roundhouse right, swift and lethal.

"He can run the floor and catch and finish," says Jack Ramsay. "It has also helped him to no end that he plays with Stockton." Indeed, at this point it seems that Stockton-Malone are as inseparable as Abbott and Costello. Each would surely not be as good without the other.

The downside of this duo is that they have not won — and may not win in the future — an NBA Final. This is partially due to the Jazz never having a dominant presence in the middle and often not having a third scorer at the two-guard or small forward. That much has been documented, that much is true.

Two other points are less documented. One, the Jazz with Malone (since 1986) have won 627 and lost 357, a .637 record during the regular season and won 59 and lost 58 — a mere .504 percentage — in the playoffs. While it is expected that a team's won and loss percentage will be worse during the play-offs than it is during the regular season, this is an *enormous* discrepancy. Red lights should start blinking and lights should go off with this statistic.

Second, Malone has often faded in big spots. Here are three exhibits for your inspection.

In the fifth and deciding game of the '95 playoffs against Houston, Utah had a 7-point lead at home with four minutes to play. Instead of Malone demanding the ball inside and getting to the basket with a field goal or draw-ing a foul, Utah's offense went into disarray with David Benoit clanging 20-footers off the rim. There was so much bricklaying I felt as if I was attending a mason's convention. Utah lost 95-91, losing its second home game of the series. Can you imagine Jordan, Johnson or Bird allowing the third or fourth best offensive player on their teams to determine the game's outcome?

Exhibit two is the 1996 Western Conference Finals. Malone missed free throw after free throw against Seattle throughout the series, especially in the seventh game, which Utah lost.

Then there was the 1997 Final series versus Chicago. Malone connected on 55 percent of his field goals during the regular season, averaging 27.4 points per game. Against the Bulls he hit only 44 percent of his shots from the field and averaged 23.8. He also connected on an abysmal 60 percent from the free throw line. The MVP award that he'd received in a close vote weeks ear-lier seemed to weigh him down. After he missed two free throws with seconds left in game one, Jordan hit a 20-footer to win the game. Malone took 18-foot fadeaways in big spots instead of going to the basket. In the sixth game he delivered a luke warm 21 points and seven rebounds. Ho hum. For four rounds of the playoffs he averaged 26 points but shot only .435 from the field.

"I can't ignore the achievement, I can't ignore the numbers," says Bob Ryan. "But I find him to be a boring player. And he's not great in crunch time. In both Olympics (1992 and 1996) he's been so tepid."

Matt Guokas defends Malone against the not-winning charge. "Malone is not hurt by not winning. He's had the longevity. He has the strong inside game but is now stepping outside and hitting the jumper. He still goes to the foul line, is a good rebounder and his teams win."

Up to a point they win. But Malone may never deliver them to a title. In fact, when a Utah columnist wrote a piece essentially asking "where is Malone?" during the Houston series, Malone went ballistic. But the columnist's point was well taken: the Mailman had not dominated in several big spots and only Stockton's game six heroics carried Utah past Houston.

If this ranking was based on numbers alone, Malone would land higher than seventh. He became only the 14th player in basketball history to make the 20,000-10,000 club (20,000 points and 10,000 rebounds) when he reached 10,000 early in the 1996-97 season. But there are other distinctions not yet attained.

The first six forwards on this list did more than score points and put up big numbers. His 27.1 points per game in the playoffs is the fifth highest in basketball history, behind only Jordan, West, Olajuwon and Barry. Still, he cannot get the same consideration given to players like Havlicek and Barry whose games were more complete and who could carry teams to victory. Barry carried the 1975 Golden State Warriors to a title without a stellar cast around him. Barry had no teammate as good as John Stockton and was certainly the only great player on that team.

But Malone remains as high as seventh because his numbers are overwhelming. After 12 years his averages — 26.1 points and 10.8 rebounds per game — are very high. His 25,592 points put him in 13th place on the all-time scoring list. His points per game put him 6th all-time. Nine times he has been chosen All-NBA First Team. His field goal percentage is 53 percent.

That is a long list of distinctions.

# Charles**Barkley**

A hefty man like Karl Malone, Charles Barkley has been busy putting up some pretty hefty numbers. Those numbers are now as weighty as Malone's:

| | PPG | RPG | APG | ALL-NBA FIRST TEAM |
|---|---|---|---|---|
| Malone | 26.1 | 10.8 | 3.2 | 9 |
| Barkley | 23.1 | 11.7 | 4.0 | 5 |

Neither player is a great defender, neither owns a championship ring. So they are equal to that point. Malone is a better scorer, is more durable an has been selected nine times to the All-NBA First Team. Barkley is the better rebounder, better passer, better ball handler and perimeter shooter. But since neither of the two players enjoys a significant post-season distinction, you must give the nod to the player with the better numbers. That player is Malone.

I can just hear Sir Charles grousing about that selection and hurtling a scorer's table to chase after me. Mike Gminski played with Barkley in Philadelphia. "I have a bias for Charles because I played with him for years. But at 6-4, he lead the league in rebounding (in 1987 with 14.6 per game). By the time I got there, he had established himself as a perennial All-Star. You don't think of him as a defender but he can play defense, can shoot the ball and can handle it. He may have the best hands in the game, whenever there is a loose ball he comes up with it. If you throw him a pass he snatches it. His hands are not overly large, since most of his dunks are two-handed.

"What he does for his size is unbelievable," says Jack Ramsay. "I was there (as an assistant) when he started in Philadelphia," says Matt Guokas. "Looking at his size, people thought he was too small to play forward and didn't shoot well enough to play guard. There was no way for him to hold up." All those sentiments have proved wrong. Now, 20,000 points and 10,000 rebounds later, a lot of people are eating crow. "He has said that he is most proud of rebounding," Guokas continues. "I get a kick out of it when they call someone the greatest rebounder ever. If Charles wasn't as good a scorer as he is and just a rebounder, he would get 17, 18 or 19 a game. If he just wanted to pass the ball, he would get 7, 8 or 9 assists. He's an all-around player. He gets knocked for his lack of intensity, but when the game is on the line, Barkley turns it up defensively.

"The one time that Barkley came close to an NBA title was the 1993 finals. Against Chicago he averaged 27.3 points per game, to go with 13 rebounds and 5.5 assists. He routinely toasted Horace Grant, turning him into an end-of-the-series basket case. Grant was so distraught that he scored just 1 point (on 0-4 shooting from the floor in game 5 and 1 point (on 0-5 shooting) in game six. Barkley was clearly the second best player on the floor for that series, which garnered the highest TV ratings of all Finals, averaging a 17.9 for the series. But Jordan averaged 41 points. Was it a crime to be second best to Jordan? If so, then Barkley is guilty. Barkley was a far greater force in that Final series than Karl Malone ever was in the 1997 Finals.

Until the 1996-1997 season, Barkley was a 20-10 man for 11 consecutive seasons, more than *any* active player. 20 points and 10 rebounds per game is a major contribution to make for that stretch of time. And his points have been as high as 27.6 and his rebounds as high as 14.6. In the playoffs, his averages stay the same or go up. His points per game jump from 23.1 to 23.5. His assists remain at 4 per game from 11.7 to 13.1. But in the 1997 conference finals Barkley had an uneven, uninspired series. He shot only 43 percent from the field and averaged 17.9 points. To many, Utah seemed vulnerable after Houston tied the series at two games apiece. But Barkley had one of his poorer playoff series.

For what it's worth, he's been the best player on the two Dream Teams, too. He loves to bang bodies and no foreign team has a match for him. In these situations he has gotten ink for his irrepressible personality. Asked what he knew about Angola, a United States opponent in 1992, Barkley said "I don't know much about Angola but I know they're in trouble." In Atlanta, before they played Brazil, someone asked Barkley how they would deal with Oscar Schmidt, the Brazilian legend. "Tonight Oscar will be the 13th best player on the floor," Charles pointed out.

He has become a spokesman for the league now. Like Magic, Bird, Thomas, Stockton, Malone and Jordan of recent times, Barkley represents one of the old-guard of NBA players, players who cared about performing and victory first, and jumping teams for bigger and better contracts later. "I blame my mother," Barkley said in an NBC interview when he was asked about the huge contracts that Juwan Howard and Shaquille O'Neal were getting in 1996. "I was born too early." He is a veritable quote machine for reporters looking to spice up their broadcasts or columns. Basketball for Charles is a fun pastime.

Now that he plays with Houston, it would be fitting if Houston won a title. Charles Barkley has done everything else in his career.

"Charles Barkley is the smallest of this group of forwards but he has played as big as anyone of them," says John Havlicek. "Whatever it takes, he would put forth that effort to succeed. Rebounding, intimidation, defense, shooting — whatever it takes, he'll do."

Some observers think there is something amiss with Barkley's career. Think again. Desire achievements, numbers, rising to the occasion when the games count — all this is there for Sir Charles. In 1993, Barkley's MVP season, the Suns gave the Bulls a run for their money. People forget that in game six the Suns led 98-94 with 49 ticks left and had the ball! Then Frank Johnson missed a jumper and Jordan went coast to coast, making it 98-96, with 38 seconds left. Incredibly, Dan Majerle then shot an airball from 12 feet away on the baseline. Then came Paxson's three to win it.

Barkley moped at his locker after the game. He had finished with 21 points and 17 rebounds. "At a time like this, it's really bad to be an athlete," he said.

A small margin has stood between Charles Barkley and an NBA title. That margin doesn't tarnish a great career.

# Elvin**Hayes**

Across the back of Elvin Hayes' San Diego Rockets shirt was a number 11 and an "E." After all, he was the "Big E." Selected first overall in the 1968 draft, Hayes came into the league like a house on fire. He lead the league in five categories as a rookie. Two of those categories were points (2,327) and points per game 28.4. The next year he led the league in rebounds with 16.9. Hayes gave a lesson on how to enter a league.

In fact, Hayes finished fifth lifetime in rebounds, with 16,279, behind only Chamberlain, Russell, Abdul-Jabbar and Moses Malone. He shows up pretty well in points, too, piling up 27,713.

Hayes averaged 20+ points and 10+ rebounds for a staggering 12 consecutive years. Despite these mammoth achievements, Hayes seems an overlooked man. The experts tend to snub him. Some who mention him say that when the ball went in to Elvin, it wasn't coming back out. Because of his no-pass tendencies, they think he should have been named "The Black Hole" instead of "The Big E." It is often suggested he was selfish and hard to coach. Truth is the San Diego and Houston teams he played on the first four years of his career lost more than they won. But that didn't stop Hayes from burying that turn-around from the baseline, from the left of the lane and from the right.

When he started playing for the Baltimore Bullets in 1973 (who became the Capital Bullets in 1974 and the Washington Bullets in 1975), those teams started putting up better records. In his years with the Bullets he teamed with Wes Unseld, Phil Chenier, Archie Clark, Mike Riordan, Kevin Porter, Bob Dandridge, Kevin Grevey and Mitch Kupchak.

In 1978 the Bullets rebounded from a 3 games to 2 deficit in the Finals to overtake Seattle. Hayes was the team's leading scorer and rebounder that year. But until the playoffs, very little was exceptional about that 44-38 team. In fact, their regular season record was better in each of the five previous seasons.

But in the post-season they rallied for a 14-7 run and capped it with a 105-99 win at Seattle. Hayes fouled out with 8 minutes left in game seven. Unseld was rewarded with the Finals MVP.

Still, not everyone has fond memories of Hayes' career. Ramsay, Heinsohn, Guokas, Ryan and Grunfeld left him out of their top ten picks. Bob Ryan said "the numbers are dramatic, but he is one of the most boring players and worst human beings that ever lived. I'm pleased to know that in 1978 Washington won that game with him on the bench. He fouled out and they put Kupchak in." Others mumbled things about how difficult Hayes could be.

But five observers — Hubie Brown, Mike Gminski, Phil Chenier John Havlicek and Butch Beard — did pick him for their lists. Brown remembers him as a "real power player who could post up and hit the jumper." And then there were the distinctions. "He was All-NBA First Team 3 times and second team 3 times. And he was a 12-time all-star," Brown continues.

"He was just a phenomenal athlete, faster than people realize," said Beard. "He was a greyhound running the court and could score inside and out. I still remember one of his great feats, getting 35 rebounds against the Knicks at Madison Square Garden, an awesome display of toughness. He had one of the quickest jumpers."

"I played against him in the twilight of his career," said Mike Gminski. "He was a big-game player and didn't impress me as a guy who played above the rim. He had a quick turn-around jumper, mid-post, a turn-around bank shot. A good position rebounder, he played center and forward, and probably played a little more defensively at forward and offensively in the middle."

In his first year of eligibility he was elected to the Hall of Fame. Not bad for a player who arouses such mixed emotions.

# Kevin**Mchale**

Not every expert picked McHale for their top ten, but most did. Jack Ramsay maintains that McHale and Karl Malone are tie. Here is one of his reasons. "McHale was the best back to the basket post man ever," said Ramsay. "Among all players, not just forwards. He had such a variety of fakes and pumps and yet was always on balance. He was a great defender as well."

Matt Guokas seconds that notion. "He is probably the best low-post man of anyone that size in the history of the NBA," says Guokas. "His footwork was so good that he got away with extra steps." Guokas laughs. "He claims he had only two moves; if you reacted to one, he did the other. He was so creative and his long arms made him so difficult to guard."

Those long arms also helped to place the 6'10", 225-pounder high among forwards in blocked shots. In five seasons he averaged two or more blocks per game.

Bob Ryan rates McHale fifth all-time and makes a strong case for his selection. "Kevin McHale was the surest two points in the history of basketball," Ryan says. "Throwing him the ball was the surest thing." Ryan loves stats, and came up with a unique one for McHale. "He is the only 60-80 man in the history of basketball." A 60-80 player is one shoots 60 percent of his shots from the field and 80 percent from the free throw line. Sure enough, McHale shot .604 from the field and .836 from the free throw line in 1987. As Ryan says, he was a sure two for his career, hitting 55 percent from the field and .798 from the charity stripe. "He scored 60 against us," says Detroit coach Chuck Daly. "We didn't double-team anyone and he wouldn't miss." Actually he scored 56 against Detroit in that game on March 3rd, 1985.

"He had a lot of moves," says Ryan. "There was no one spot he shot from. He was adept from the right or the left, either side. He didn't have a left hand though, unlike many other great players, like Bird, who was a member of the all ambidextrous team."

Except for Bird, McHale was as instrumental to the Celtics' run of titles in the eighties as any player. This was especially true in 1986, when the Hibbing, Minnesota native posted 24.9 points and 8.6 rebounds in the playoffs to help the Celtics to their last title.

The story of how the Celtics got McHale is another strand in the tapestry of the Celtic legend. The 1979-1980 Pistons finished 16-66, entitling them to the number one pick in the 1980 NBA Draft. But Boston owned this pick and dealt the number one and the number 13 picks to Golden State for center Robert Parish and Golden's State's first-round pick, which was the third pick overall. While Auerbach and others in the organization wanted Joe Barry Carroll, Golden State chose him first. Utah chose second and grabbed Darryl Griffith. Then the Celtics scooped up McHale. In essence, the Celtics got Parish and McHale for the number one and number 13 picks in the land, Joe Barry Carroll and Ricky Brown. In his book *Ever Green*, Dan Shaughnessy explains that coach Bill Fitch should have gotten credit for the deal but never did. Regardless, the Celtics got bigger and better on the front line. The rest is history.

At the outset, McHale played the role of "sixth man." As usual, this Boston sixth man was getting minutes comparable to any starter. McHale won the Sixth Man Award in 1984 and 1985, averaging 31 and 34 minutes a game in those seasons. In 1985 the sixth man began a run of six seasons in which he averaged 20 or more points per game. As the team played its best, McHale played his best. From 1986 through 1988 McHale was elected NBA First Team All Defense. Three other times he was selected to the second team on defense.

And on offense, his repertoire expanded near the end of his career. "As he got older, he stepped away and faced up," recalls Guokas. "His volume of rebounds were never high because of the combination of Bird and Parish." He still finished with 17.9 points, 7.3 rebounds and 1.6 assists. His .554 field goal percentage is tenth best in NBA history.

The seven-time all-star is a cinch Hall of Famer. And getting in won't require any fancy footwork.

# Scottie**Pippen**

Central Arkansas is not a college on the tip of everyone's tongue. But that is where Pippen began and then steadily improved, until he graduated in 1987, with his points and rebounds and assists rising. The Seattle Supersonics had the smarts to draft Pippen fifth in the first round. Give Seattle credit. San Antonio chose first and got David Robinson. Phoenix then chose Armon Gilliam, New Jersey picked Dennis Hopson and the L.A. Clippers chose Reggie Williams. Oh well, some of the worst deals are the ones you don't make.

Or do make. Seattle followed their prudent selection of Pippen with a supreme act of imprudence, trading him for Chicago's 8th pick, Olden

Polynice. Pippen had a better rookie year than Polynice and — in case you hadn't noticed — has had countless better years since.

By now Pippen may have turned into the most singular combination of skills of any forward who ever played. He can soar like Jordan and finish drives. He can get assists at an un-forward like clip. And he dogs people on defense with the best of them, a skill that resulted in six consecutive All-Defensive First Team selections. He led the league in steals in 1995.

His identity to some may always be that of an accessory to Jordan. Clearly, Jordan flies the plane in Chicago. But two things can be said about that. The plane only flew at a championship altitude since Pippen arrived. And when Jordan was away flailing at curve balls, Pippen came within a hair's breadth of taking the Bulls to the NBA Eastern Conference finals.

In game five of the conference semis at Madison Square Garden, the Knicks were down one when Hubert Davis missed a jumper with just seconds left. But outside official Hue Hollins blew the whistle on Pippen. Replays and a photo in The New York Times showed that the ball was off before Pippen hit him on the shooting hand. A pair of free throws by Davis gave the Knicks the victory.

Chicago rolled over the Knicks at home but lost game seven. But the point had been made. Even without Jordan, Pippen had carried the Bulls near to the top.

Next to Jordan, it could be argued that Pippen is the most complete player in the league. This is not to say that he is close to Jordan or even the league's second best player. He isn't. But he does most everything well and is therefore closest to Jordan in having full-blown talent. If I was going to improve one thing, it would be the consistency of his perimeter shooting. At times his outside game looks like long-distance brick heaving. But even without the jumper, versatility is still his calling card.

Most people left Pippen out of their top ten. I have picked him eleventh. Ernie Grunfeld did not leave him off. "Pippen is probably the most athletic forward ever to play the point-forward." Indeed, the combination of ball-handling, speed, man to man defense and playing the passing lanes has made Pippen a terrific all purpose player.

1994 remains the best season for The 6'7" forward. He won the all-star game MVP that year, leading the East to victory with 29 points and 11 rebounds. That was the season he emerged from Jordan's sizable shadow. But the Hue Hollins whistle kept Pippen's season from being complete. "I've seen a lot of things in the NBA, but I've never seen what happened at the end of that game," moaned coach Phil Jackson.

Game three of that series included another unsightly incident. In that game, Pippen would not reenter the game with 1.8 seconds left, after Phil Jackson called a play for Toni Kukoc to take the last shot. Kukoc nailed the winning jumper but the bush action of Pippen had not been obscured. I cannot recall a team's leader sitting in such a big spot. Ever.

But that was a moment. It seems the Bulls have been good for a lifetime. Pippen has been the second most important part on five championship teams.

Still there is a feeling that Jordan must still go it alone much of the time in Chicago. Even when the Bulls posted their 72-10 season in 1996, the morning wire service reports didn't lie. Jordan often needed to score double digits in the fourth quarter for the team to win.

In the playoffs the same pattern was repeated, especially against the Knicks, whose defense always gives the Bulls fits. Jordan's ability to get his own shot often seems the only element keeping the Bulls' offense from complete stagnation. Even in the 1994 playoffs, Pippen shot just .434 from the field. In 1995 he shot .443. Hardly better, Kukoc shot .448 in 1994, .477 in 1995 and an abysmal .391 in 1996. So when defense gets chest to chest, as it always does in playoff contests, Jordan emerges as the only option.

In 1996 Pippen's playoff shooting plummeted to ridiculous levels. He connected on just 112 of 287 shots for a .390 percentage. If that's the supporting cast, one begins to wonder how indispensable they are. Pippen did grab 8.5 rebounds and easily led the team in assists, dishing off for 6 per game in the 1996 post-season. He added 2.6 steals per game. But the shooting was routinely horrendous.

In the 1997 playoffs Pippen averaged 19.2 points, on 42 percent shooting, and 6.8 rebounds. Jordan not only led the team in playoff scoring with 31.1 points per game, but he averaged 7.9 rebounds per game, finishing second on the team and grabbing only 10 less total rebounds than Rodman.

Before a 1997 game at the Garden, Knicks forward Larry Johnson called Pippen "a bum...who just passes the ball to Jordan." Pippen fired back that Johnson has "done nothing but take money since he entered the league." That was one volley too many for grand-mama. Pippen then toasted Johnson with 34 points. Next.

Despite Pippen's offense which ebbs and flows, Jordan has always insisted that Pippen-Jackson-Jordan remain a threesome, saying that he won't sign a contract unless management signs the other two. If Superman knows how valuable Pippen is to the Bulls' dynasty, then who are we to argue?

# 12 forward

# Dolph**Schayes**

In 1958 New York native Dolph Schayes surpassed George Mikan's 11,764 points, then the record for most all-time points. Mikan, who lead the Minneapolis Lakers to five world titles between 1947 and 1954, had been referred to as the "Babe Ruth of Basketball" by some writers.

The 6-8 Schayes was one of the last of the old fashioned set-shot artists — not "the one-handed jump toss," as one writer then described it — featured by other stars of his day like Paul Arizin and Bob Pettit. If Schayes was wide open he would really take the time to load up that shot, getting his feet set just right before releasing a rainbow from up to 30 feet. This outdated technique was enough to net him 18.2 points and 12.1 rebounds per game for his 16-year career with the Syracuse Nationals and Philadelphia 76ers.

Schayes also set a mark for durability. In a nine-year span from February 17, 1952 through December 27, 1961 he played in 764 consecutive games, every Syracuse game played. The Iron Man Schayes finally missed a game after shattering his right cheek bone in a collision with the Philadelphia Warriors' Al Attles.

He provided the "Nats" with scoring and rebounding. Just look at his averages in rebounds, assists and points from 1956-1961.

| YEAR | RPG | APG | PPG |
|------|-----|-----|-----|
| 1956 | 12.4 | 2.8 | 20.4 |
| 1957 | 14.0 | 3.2 | 22.5 |
| 1958 | 14.2 | 3.1 | 24.9 |
| 1959 | 13.4 | 2.5 | 21.3 |
| 1960 | 12.8 | 3.4 | 22.5 |
| 1961 | 12.2 | 3.7 | 23.6 |

If we just looked at the numbers without knowing the player, we might think those numbers belonged to Elgin Baylor or Larry Bird in mid-career.

When he graduated New York University in 1948 there were two pro leagues competing for players. Schayes received bids from each. He wanted to go with the New York Knicks, who then belonged to the Basketball Association of America (BAA), but a league rule prevented them from paying a rookie more than $5,000. Syracuse, at that time in the older National Basketball League (NBL), offered $7,500.

He waited two months before accepting. The league merger the following year brought Syracuse and Schayes into competition with the Knicks in the new NBA. The Knicks reached the finals in 1951, 1952 and 1953, coming close but not winning. "Our failure to win a championship can be traced to our not getting Schayes," moaned Ned Irish, then owner of the Knicks. "We've always missed because we never had a man who could average about 20 points over a season."

Schayes became an ambidextrous shooter when his right wrist was broken in 1952. "Losing the use of my right hand was the best break I ever got," he later said. "I developed a left-handed shot that made me twice as effective."

Though he broke his arm again, Schayes played with the arm in a cast against Minneapolis in the 1954 Finals, inspiring his team by his presence. But George Mikan's team won the see-saw series in seven games.

The following season Schayes paced the Nats to their only title. The 12-time All-Star led the Syracuse Nats to a seven-game victory over the Fort Wayne Pistons, averaging 19 points and 12.8 rebounds.

New York's missed opportunity in not getting Schayes continued to haunt Ned Irish. Several years later he offered Syracuse three "first stringers," Dick McGuire, Harry Galatin and Sweetwater Clifton, in exchange for Schayes. "I don't blame Syracuse for turning down the trade," Irish said. "Schayes has been holding the team together for years. He's the only player close to Bob Pettit as a one-man powerhouse."

And teams wanted a powerhouse not only to win but for box office appeal. In the mid-fifties Syracuse was in the middle of the pack in league attendance, averaging about 4,200 customers a game. This was about 800 less than they needed to break even. But they hung on in Syracuse.

By 1957 Schayes got $14,000 a year in salary, an "upper bracket" salary in the league, he recalls. He deserved it. Double-double is a frequent term employed by sportscasters today. Dolph Schayes averaged a double-double (double digits in points and rebounds) 11 years in a row, from 1951 through 1961, including being a "20 and 10" man for six consecutive years.

When Schayes was about to pass Mikan in scoring, a player who had been selected in the 1950 Associated Press poll as the greatest player of the half century, he seemed hardly affected and made some bold statements. "I'd get a bigger boot out of the record if Mikan didn't hold it," he said in a *Saturday Evening Post* article in 1957. "He epitomized the type of player who I never admired. I've always resented strong-arm guys who are effective just because of their size."

At least he said he was effective. Mikan got his 11,764 points in 520 games. That's an average of 22.6 It took Schayes 615 games to pass Mikan. Schayes didn't appreciate that Mikan scored the majority of his points on low-post, power moves. Said Schayes, "even when I was a half-foot taller than the other players I refused to play the pivot. To me basketball is a game of movement and finesse. The emphasis should be on teamwork and skill, not on size, as it is today. Maybe I'm an ingrate for criticizing Mikan. He helped to turn my height into an asset by proving that all big men weren't goons. He was a tremendous competitor who took as much as he dished out. I wonder, though, how much good he would have been if he was only six feet tall and had to depend on cleverness to get by. That's the test of a real player." Maybe so. But we'll never know if Schayes would have passed that test either, since he was 6-8.

Schayes spent much of his time charging to the basket, and it wasn't unusual to see 30 points on five field goals and 20 foul shots next to his name. "I want somebody to smack me so I can get a three-point play," he once explained. He hoisted them from the perimeter, too. Said Syracuse coach Alex Hannum, "the guy had legitimate 25-30 foot range. You could add five points to his career if they had the three-point shot back then. Because he never hesitated to take a 25 or even a 30-footer." This was referred to as his "sputnik," a fitting name for a shot that came to earth when the Cold War between the United States and Russia was at its peak.

Schayes adopted a strange attitude about the distance shots, however. "I feel I'm cheating when I score from the outside," he explained. "Distance shooting is just a trick, like fancy diving or figure skating. Anyone can perfect it with practice. I prefer to earn points on drives set up by passes and blocking. You're not a basketball player if you can't drive. Sometimes when I miss a couple of long shots I ask myself, 'what the hell am I doing out there? I should be under the backboards, fighting for rebounds.'

"Syracuse hasn't got a lot of height and my job is to get the ball. That's the payoff. A team that throws from the outside will win only by mistake, because they won't get many rebounds on the shots that don't go in. The shot is valuable chiefly for keeping the defense honest by forcing it to send out a man to cover me. That opens up the zone around the basket for my drives."

To sum up this exasperating set of attitudes, Schayes didn't like the power game of the Mikan variety for he saw it as taking advantage of one's size. Nor did he feel right bombing from the perimeter. Despite these contradictory views about the proper way to score, Schayes was regarded by then Knicks coach Joe Lapchick as "something of a revolutionary, because he was the first big man to develop a great outside shot (and the first not to like himself for developing it, Lapchick might have added). Few people — and I wasn't one of them — believed that anyone taller than six-six had the coordination and the fine touch to hit consistently beyond twenty feet. Until Schayes came along, all the good long shooters were little weasels who couldn't get close to the basket often enough to score in any other way." We may be getting close to the reason for Schayes' self-loathing on the perimeter: he was a "weasel" if he succeeded out there.

Kidding aside, in Terry Pluto's *Tall Tales* Carl Braun wrote: "the only big man who had the shooting range of Dolph Schayes was Larry Bird. Dolph's shot was higher, softer. But if you see Larry, then you get an idea of how Dolph was."

Said Tom Gola: "the Bird comparison is perfect. Both guys were self-made players. Both were rebounders who couldn't jump. Both had tremendous range on their shots, yet also could shoot off the run with either hand. Dolph wasn't the passer like Larry. It's just a shame because everyone will always remember Larry Bird and more people should appreciate Dolph Schayes."

The time he played in was light years apart from today's game. "Players are much quicker now," Schayes explained in a recent television interview. "All these teams have tremendous quickness. They don't pass the ball as much or use the high post as much or keep the floor as spread as we did." Schayes was not known as a great defender and often drew the other team's "defensive forward" for his assignment.

When Schayes retired in 1964, the Syracuse franchise had folded and moved on to Philadelphia. His point total was 19,247. Only Bob Pettit had more. Schayes then won Coach of the Year honors for the 1965-1966 season, leading the Philadelphia 76ers to a 55-25 record.

An opposing player once cracked that Schayes was 6-8 and couldn't dunk if he was standing under the basket. And maybe some observers, needing a point of comparison, will label him a 'poor man's Larry Bird.' But Schayes was an All-NBA First Team player for six years. From the mid-1950s to early 1960s he was one of the greatest forwards.

# Jerry**Lucas**

Jerry Lucas was born a 10-pounder in Middletown, Ohio in 1940. Born big, he would later play big. A 6'9" forward, Lucas was outstanding at every level: Middletown High, Ohio State University, the 1960 Rome Olympics and the Cincinnati Royals.

After he had led his Middletown High team to 76 straight victories and two state titles, he was recruited by 150 colleges before picking Ohio State. He could have attended any school from Florida to Hawaii. He turned down offers too extravagant for words, including one which included a new job for his father which would have doubled his salary as a press man. But Ohio State was his choice and he paid his own expenses to travel there and look over the campus. "If Jerry went to all the campuses where he's been invited, he'd be travelling for the next two years," his father said. He led the Buckeyes to a 78-6 record over three years. O.S.U. won a NCAA title and was runnerup

127

during the Lucas era.

After his sophomore season at Ohio State he left for the Rome Olympics, where the United States won five straight contests. Olympic coach Pete Newell usually liked to play ball control basketball. But he had too little time to prepare his team of all-stars for the games and changed his style.

The Americans played fast break ball throughout and scored more than 100 points in three of the five games. In one game they were pressed by the Soviet Union, but ended up winning easily 81-57. And in the final game they crushed Brazil, 90-63. Lucas led the way, scoring 25 points in only 20 minutes. Coach Newell called him "the greatest player I ever coached."

Individual greatness was also his legacy at OSU. He won an unprecedented three straight field goal titles, finishing by connecting on a record 62.4 percent of his shots. Lew Alcindor later broke his record at U.C.L.A.

Following college he signed with the Cleveland Pipers of the ABL but he never played a game there since the league folded. He subsequently agreed to terms with Cincinnati and won the Rookie of the Year Award in 1964. He shot .527 to lead the league and averaged 17 points and 17 rebounds a game.

As time went on, the Lucas name reminded people of rebounds. In two seasons, 1965 and 1966, he averaged 20 points per game and 20 rebounds per game. The only other players to accomplish this feat were Bob Pettit, Wilt Chamberlain and Nate Thurmond.

As Terry Pluto points out in *Tall Tales*, Lucas averaged 19.8 in the four years from 1965 through 1968.

While some people want to write off the greater rebound totals of the day to the 15-20 more missed shots per game during the late fifties and early sixties, Lucas disagrees.

"You can talk all you want about eras and all you want about how guys shot for a higher percentage today and how there are fewer missed shots. But the players of my time simply wanted to rebound more and we rebounded better," said Lucas. "I went into games expecting to get 20 rebounds. So did Wilt, Russell and Nate Thurmond. Now when a guy gets 20 rebounds, it's an event. Back then, it was just doing your job. There were many games where I got 35-40 rebounds, and that felt normal. Only four men ever got 40 rebounds in an NBA game: Wilt (14 times), Russell (8 times) Nate Thurmond (once) and myself (once, on February 29th, 1964 at Philadelphia). In my opinion, those are the four greatest rebounders ever to play the game. We grunted, sweated all over the arena. We would rather get a rebound than eat."

Needless to say, these were not times when broadcasters got slap happy talking about the home team guy who pulled down 12 boards.

In his 1992 book *A View From Above*, Chamberlain agrees with Lucas' high assessment of sixties basketball. He makes two points about the era, both connected with Lucas.

Chamberlain talked about the "big, strong outside shooters" who played forward and "could pound the shit out of you under the boards." Chamberlain blames the loss of the Americans to Yugoslavia in the 1990 Goodwill Games on the loss of that kind of forward. "We've lost Bob Pettit, Dolph Schayes, Jerry Lucas, Dave DeBusschere, Chet Walker and Luke Jackson. Now the guards have taken over the game and the forwards try to play like Julius Erving, swooping to the basket and dunking balls."

He also commented on "how amazed" announcers seem these days when a big man can shoot from 20 feet, as if that were something new. Wilt mentions several fifties and sixties players who could hit from the outside, including Hall of Famers Clyde Lovellette and Dolph Schayes. And he included Lucas, "one of the best shooters in the history of basketball."

Chamberlain has a clear recollection of the kind of player Lucas was. Without laboring the points about Lucas the rebounder much further, Lucas was one of the greatest rebounding forwards in NBA history. He grabbed 1,000 or more rebounds in 8 of the 11 years he played and ended up with an average of 15.6 per game. Among all forwards, only Pettit's 16.2 average was greater!

When Lucas was traded to the New York Knicks in May of 1971, it was to help them rebound and provide a little scoring too. It didn't work in the first year. The Lakers had the horses in the 1971-1972 season and won 69 games, including 33 in a row. Chamberlain led the league in rebounding and shot a remarkable .649 from the field. The Lakers buried the Knicks in the Finals.

The next year Lucas gave the Knicks less minutes, about 28 per game, but developed a folksy reputation for shooting what broadcaster Marv Albert referred to as "the bomb." This was a high-arching shot that Lucas hoisted from his left hip. Lucas reasoned that a shot with a high arc had a greater chance of going in, since shots usually fell short and that a hole, like the opening in a garbage can, is wider from right above and easier to hit than it is from the side.

In the 1972-1973 season Lucas' bomb found its target a great deal, 51 percent of the time. Not that such shooting was new to Lucas. Six times in his career he shot above 50 percent. But 1973 was the 33 year-old's first championship. Now the Knicks turned the favor, burying the Lakers in five games.

The seven-time all-star retired the next season after eleven years in the league. His lifetime line was impressive indeed. 17 points, 15.6 rebounds and 3.3 assists per game. That's good for any position.

And it's great for a 6'8" forward.

# Billy**Cunningham**

People who have been watching basketball for less than 20 years will naturally think of a guy known as "Billy C." in coat and tie, directing traffic from the sidelines with the Philadelphia 76ers. That's not a bad association to make. Cunningham the coach did post an amazing 454-196 record from 1977 through 1985, for a .698 percentage. No slouch in the playoffs either, his teams won 66 and lost 39 (.629).

But that was only the more recent vocation for Billy Cunningham. He started his career as a Philadelphia forward and in his second season, 1967, came off the bench to help the Sixers win the world championship. A 1965 first-round pick by way of Erasmus High in Brooklyn and University of North Carolina, Cunningham could go home after each season knowing that his numbers got better in each of his first five years.

Bob Ryan's voice gets enthusiastic recalling Cunningham. "He was a phenomenal driver and slasher; a quintessential Brooklyn player who you picture playing on a court with the rim bent, net missing and wind blowing and so it made no sense shooting from the outside anyway. So you take it to the hoop!"

That was just the start for the left-hander known as "The Kangaroo Kid." "One of the great white leapers," Bob Ryan remembers. "Billy was a guy who could play in the air with the black guys."

He played eleven years in the pros, 9 in the NBA and two in the ABA. Three times he was chosen All-NBA First Team and was signed by the Carolina Cougars in 1972. In his first ABA season he averaged 24.1 points and won the league MVP. Then he returned to the Sixers in 1974 and played two more seasons, before being forced to retire 20 games into the 1975-1976 season due to a severe knee injury.

Not only did he play on that legendary Sixers' 1967 team, but his hot hand off the bench produced 13 fourth-quarter points in the sixth-game victory over Rick Barry and San Francisco in the Finals.

"By the end of his career he was much a better shooter, and near the end one of the great collaborations in basketball was Billy Cunningham, bouncing that long, beautiful backdoor pass to a young Doug Collins on the baseline." And off the boards? "He played much bigger than his size," Ryan remembers.

In an article he wrote for the *New York Times* in 1983, Cunningham noticed great similarities in the 1967 76ers and the 1983 edition that he coached to a title. "We didn't know if Moses would be able to adjust to our team because he came from Houston, a team that did not run... We also had some apprehension about whether Doc and Moses could play together.

"After two days in training camp we had our answer. Moses would make the adjustments. He did everything we asked of him. Each player changed his game. Doc concentrated more on defense and passing rather than scoring. Moses concentrated more on defensive rebounding and making the outlet pass rather than carrying the load with his offensive rebounding.

"This had happened with Wilt Chamberlain as well. Wilt had averaged 50 points a game one season and he had achieved all the individual goals. But he showed he was a complete basketball player, making passes, blocking shots and rebounding."

By the time of that awful knee injury, the "Kangaroo Kid" had already logged an impressive 21.2 points and 10.4 rebounds per game, to go with 4.3 assists. That's not a bad 11-year line. And that's no left-handed compliment. The Sixers retired his number 32.

# 15 forward

## Paul**Arizin**

I surveyed many experts to pick the great forwards. No one chose Paul Arizin among their top ten of all-time. But Paul Arizin, who starred with the Philadelphia Warriors from 1950 through 1962, was actually the second great NBA scorer ever to come along. The first was George Mikan.

Though he missed two of his peak years to military service during the 1952-1953 and 1953-1954 seasons, Arizin averaged 20+ points for nine consecutive years and finished his career with an outstanding 22.8 points per game. "He is remembered for being one of the early, true practitioners of the jump shot," says Bob Ryan. "That was the focal point of his repertoire in the early days of the NBA. Other guys had jump shots but it still wasn't the number one weapon. The game was still two-hand sets and drives."

Look at a list of the best players who began their careers between 1945 and 1959:

| | |
|---|---|
| Dolph Schayes | Bob Cousy |
| Larry Foust | Richie Guerin |
| Bailey Howell | Red Kerr |
| Ed McCauley | Dick McGuire |
| Vern Mikkelsen | Guy Rodgers |
| Bill Russell | Jack Twyman |
| Max Zaslofsky | Bob Pettit |
| Bob Davies | Harry Gallatin |
| Cliff Hagan | Neil Johnston |
| Sam Jones | Slater Martin |
| George Mikan | Jim Pollard |
| Bill Sharman | Wilt Chamberlain |
| George Yardley | Elgin Baylor |

Where do you think Arizin ranks among these 26? Among them, how many do you think averaged more points than Paul Arizin? Take a guess. Ready? Three. Only Wilt Chamberlain, Elgin Baylor and Bob Pettit averaged more points per game over their careers. If a measure of a great athlete is how he stacks up to his contemporaries, then Arizin was truly great because of his standing. So make room on the all-underrated team; Arizin earns his place.

One writer given to hyperbole said that Arizin's jump shot was "like a Renoir or a Rembrandt — perfection."

Arizin was not nearly so impressed with his own style of shooting. "The truth is," Arizin said, "that it (the shot) came by accident. I was playing in the Catholic Club League in Philadelphia and our games were on a slick dance floor. When I tried to hook, my feet would go out from under me. So I jumped; the ceiling was low and I had to throw line drives. I just never changed."

During his ten productive years he won scoring championships in the 1951-1952 season with 25.4 points and in the 1956-1957 season with 25.6. His two-year hitch with the Marines almost certainly cost him 20,000 lifetime points.

A 6'4", 210 pounder and swingman for the Warriors, Arizin was hampered by what appeared to be asthma. People who watched him wheeze often wondered how he got up and down the court while being forever short of breath. "He wheezed all over the place," says Ryan. Some hastily concluded he was not in shape. Arizin laughed. "That panting and coughing is a sinus condition I've always had. It doesn't hurt my endurance," he said.

When the Warriors played Syracuse, Dolph Schayes remembers the pregame conversations used to try and stop "Pitchin' Paul." "Someone would bring up Arizin's jump shot and we'd try to figure out how to stop him." 'What makes him click?' someone would ask. 'A jump shot,' would be the answer. 'Let's stop it,' we'd say, but we knew we couldn't. His jump shot was perfect. There was no stopping it."

And then Arizin would go out, gulping for air up and down the court. He'd head for the corner, take a pass, then fake and jump, hanging in the air for a split second before firing his line-drive jumper. "He was just 6'4" but had good elevation," Ryan recalls.

Another player attempting to guard Arizin was Paul Rocha of the Fort Wayne Pistons, whose words were recorded in Phil Pepe's book *The Greatest Stars of the NBA*. "I had a five-inch advantage over Paul," Rocha says, "but it was never enough when he leaped for that jump shot."

In the 1950-1951 season, Arizin's first, he finished sixth in the league in scoring, averaging 17.2 points per game. And his 41 percent field goal percentage was good enough for 7th in the league. The following year he outscored Mikan 25.4 to 23.8, breaking Big George's three-year run of scoring titles. Back from military duty for the 1954-1955 season, Arizin finished second to Neil Johnston in scoring. It was the first of three successive seasons in which he finished first or second in scoring.

Still the wheezing seemed to follow him wherever he went and rumors circulated that he had asthma. "I never had asthma," he made clear. "It never really affected my play."

On December 1, 1961 he scored 33 against the Los Angeles Lakers to become only the third player in NBA history to surpass 15,000 points.

When the 1961-1962 season ended he called it quits, but still averaged 21.9 points, good enough for only 12th place in the league. The NBA had entered a new era, an era dominated by guys like Baylor, Chamberlain, West and Robertson.

The Warriors, for whom he had played his entire life, were moving on to San Francisco and this Southern Philly boy, now 34, did not want to accompany them. "To show how times have changed," Bob Ryan recalls, "Eddie Gottlieb sold the team and the Warriors were moved to San Francisco. Arizin did not go, because he thought he could not afford to go and leave his job at I.B.M. in New Jersey. Instead he joined the Eastern League and played for the Camden Bullets from 1962 through 1965. He won the MVP there. Today, that would be like the Knicks packing up and moving to Oklahoma City and Charles Oakley says, 'I'm not going.' Arizin was far from done at the time." Indeed, in his last NBA season the 34 year-old Arizin averaged 21.9 points and 8.6 rebounds.

He had already enjoyed a stellar career. Three times he had been selected All-NBA First Team and in 1952 he won the MVP of the All-Star Game.

In the playoffs Arizin was even better. In 1956, when the Warriors beat Fort Wayne in five games to win the title, Arizin had a 28.9 playoff average. For his career he averaged 24.2 in playoff competition.

In 1977 he was elected to the Basketball Hall of Fame.

# Dave**DeBusschere**

The sound came rolling down from the $5 seats at Madison Square Garden. "Defense, defense." It was the rallying cry of the New York Knicks from 1969 through 1974. Moreover, it was their identity. And Dave DeBusschere was the cornerstone of that identity.

Several years after DeBusschere came to the Knicks from Detroit for guard Howard Komives and center Walt Bellamy, it was known as "the trade." Perhaps the moves that Knicks' president Ernie Grunfeld engineered in the summer of 1996 to get Allan Houston, Larry Johnson and Chris Childs will one day rival the Debusschere trade in importance. But it won't be easy.

From the get go, the DeBusschere move made so many things fall into place. With DeBusschere anchoring the power forward spot, before forwards were called "power forwards," Bill Bradley could move from guard, where he was too slow, to small forward. With Bellamy gone, Reed didn't have to split minutes in the pivot with anyone. And Walt Frazier took charge in the backcourt. To New York, the solar system was realigned with one stroke.

"People should not forget DeBusschere," says Ryan. "Today he would be a monster because he had three-point range. Each of the Knicks forwards had more range than their guards, Frazier, Barnett and Monroe. He was a rugged rebounder and personified the power forward at that time."

At 6'6", DeBusschere would be giving away inches to many of today's forwards. Could he adapt? "I think he would have adapted," says Ryan. "He would be a monster three-point threat."

"He got better every year," recalls Phil Chenier, who played for the Bullets during some of the great Bullets-Knicks' rivalries of the 1970s. "He was a very dominant force; rebounding, blocking shots, scoring."

DeBusschere finished up just shy of 10,000 rebounds (9,618) and logged 14,053 points. The numbers he wants to appear on his bottom line are two world championships, 16 points per game, 11 rebounds, 8 all-star appearances and six consecutive appearances on the NBA All-Defensive Team, a tie with Pippen among all the top 50 forwards. John Havlicek won five awards.

But talk about DeBusschere's assorted virtues leads inevitably to talk about the Knicks' teams between 1969 and 1974. "He had a total, team-oriented game," says Hall of Fame coach Chuck Daly. "He really blended in nicely with all the great skills that that team had."

"They had an awesome team; all five players," says Chenier. "Gene [Shue, Baltimore coach) was very thorough. We would take away their third and fourth options and they would burn us with a fifth. DeBusschere and Gus [Johnson] had tremendous battles; you had to be there to really see it. They were warriors; they didn't look to the referees for calls, never got mad at each other. They were so fierce but they were the epitome of professionalism. I read that after Gus passed (in 1987, at the age of 51), Dave gave Gus a lot of praise. I thought that was very nice."

It was a different time; DeBusschere didn't bark in Johnson's face and Gus didn't stare Dave down after one of his graceful, carpet rides to the hoop. As rivalries went, that rivalry was as good as it gets.

And the other rivalries weren't half bad either. When Baltimore played New York, fans could feast on Johnson vs. DeBusschere, Monroe vs. Frazier, Unseld vs. Reed and Marin vs. Bradley. Matchups for eternity.

Wake me when it gets better than that.

# Dominique**Wilkins**

For the longest time, Dominique has had a rendezvous with numbers. His career is nothing if not a orgy of ink: ink in a record book that shows 13 years in the NBA before he packed up, left Boston and brought his aging offensive package to the cradle of Western civilization in Greece. Then he returned for his 14th NBA campaign and, at age 37, lead the San Antonio Spurs in scoring.

He has already done some major damage. Some wags say that of his 26,534 points, about 25,000 are forgettable. After all, if you play word association with Wilkin's Atlanta Hawks, Boston Celtics, L.A. Clippers and San Antonio Spurs the term that first comes to mind isn't exactly "post-season." These weren't teams worth summoning the spirit of Dr. James Naismith for. "Wilkins appeals more to the uneducated rather than the educated basketball fan," Ryan sums up.

In that light, "Nique's" statement when he was signed by the Celtics in July, 1994 — "I'm a Celtic, a perfect fit for me" — is a bit odd, since his solo act would have upset the balance of great Boston teams. He might have been thinking that the 1994 Celtics, poor as they were, would put up with some one-on-one displays.

In 14 years, Wilkins has still given us a great fourth quarter shootout with Larry Bird in the seventh game of the 1988 Eastern semis. That mano-a-mano duel was one for the ages. And those 26,534 points in 14 seasons, essentially 2,000 per year, must be reckoned with.

So let's start reckoning. The record shows that Wilkin's game peaked just as Jordan's was getting underway in 1986. Wilkins won the scoring title that year, with a 30.3 average. Jordan's foot injury kept him from even qualifying. The year before Wilkins had averaged 27.4. That makes two in a row over 25. Now while Jordan reeled off seven titles in a row, Wilkins was finishing very close to the top. How close? Here are the scoring title leaders and Wilkins' place, for the ten-year period from 1985-1994:

| YEAR | WINNER | WILKINS' PLACE |
|------|--------|----------------|
| 1985 | Bernard King | 6th |
| 1986 | Dominique Wilkins | – |
| 1987 | Michael Jordan | 2nd |
| 1988 | Michael Jordan | 2nd |
| 1989 | Michael Jordan | 7th |
| 1990 | Michael Jordan | 5th |
| 1991 | Michael Jordan | 7th |
| 1992 | Michael Jordan | (injured:did not qualify) |
| 1993 | Michael Jordan | 2nd |
| 1994 | David Robinson | 4th |

So Wilkins was either first or second four times. On average, over this ten-year period he finished fourth in the league. Not once did he fall below 25 points per game. Eight of those years he had 2,000 points, which is a benchmark for a great scoring season.

The Utah Jazz could have had all those points. In September 1982 they traded the draft rights to Wilkins to Atlanta for forward John Drew and guard Freeman Williams. With Utah's perennial problem of getting points out of the small forward spot, Wilkins might have helped.

No one picked Wilkins in the top ten, mostly because they believe that being one of the "best" players means more than just scoring points. Those points had better make people around you better or in some way contribute to important victories, i.e., post-season wins. The point is well-taken. But if you say that about Wilkins, be consistent and make sure you say it about your others who didn't win titles. There are a long line of people who played with teams more talented than Wilkins' Atlanta squads and yet won only once or not at all.

Wilkins doesn't deserve a spot among the top ten players. But if a player scores 26,534 points, fourth place among all the forwards that ever played, that must count for something.

For the NBA to not include Wilkins on their list of the top 50 is unconscionable. Forwards who didn't achieve nearly as much — like James Worthy — were included on the NBA's list. And the NBA included George Gervin, a Wilkins-like scorer who never played on a title team. Quick: who are the three 25,000-point scorers that the NBA left off their list of the top 50? Dominique Wilkins, Dan Issel and Alex English. Should we demand another vote?

In his 14 NBA seasons he has averaged 25.3 points, 6.8 rebounds and 2.5 assists. Those lifetime averages also indicate that he contributed to the teams he played on. If he took all those shots in that great fourth quarter shootout with Bird, doesn't that mean that he was the only one the team wanted to take those important shots?

# Adrian**Dantley**

Adrian Dantley was a great scorer in the 1980s, the same decade in which Michael Douglas unabashedly declared "greed is good" in the film *Wall Street*. Looking at Adrian Dantley's totals, one must decide if he scored out of greed or because his teams desperately needed his contributions on offense.

Inclined toward a principle of charity, I tend to think that his teams needed points and so he delivered. His initials are A.D. but in Utah he did most of his scoring B.M. — before Malone. And many will be surprised to learn that in a seven-year run from 1980 through 1986, he scored at a higher points-per-game rate and had a higher field goal percentage than Karl Malone did in the ten years since then!

From 1981 through 1984 Dantley led the league in scoring twice and scored more than 30 points per game all four years! His field goal percentages in those years were .559, .570, .580 and .558. Talk about two sure points!

And he was dishing off for a respectable four assists per game, too.

What follows is a chart of all those players who averaged 30+ points per game two or more *consecutive* years:

**PLAYERS IN HISTORY WITH 30 POINTS**
**FOR AT LEAST TWO STRAIGHT YEARS**

| Player | Number of Yrs. | Year | Points | Avg. For Period |
|---|---|---|---|---|
| Chamberlain | 7 | 1960-66 | 21,486 | 39.6 |
| Jordan | 7 | 1987-93 | 18,820 | 34.2 |
| Robertson | 4 | 1964-67 | 9,549 | 30.9 |
| Dantley | 4 | 1981-84 | 8,003 | 30.5 |
| Abdul-Jabbar | 3 | 1971-73 | 7,710 | 32.3 |
| McAdoo | 3 | 1974-76 | 7,519 | 32.1 |
| Baylor | 3 | 1961-63 | 7,093 | 35.3 |
| West | 2 | 1965-66 | 4,768 | 30.6 |

The chart shows that Dantley's scoring puts him in a pretty select circle of company, at least on offense.

In 1987, in a hard fought seven-game series against Boston in the Conference Finals, Dantley hit his head on the parquet floor during a fight for a loose ball in the fourth quarter. He had to leave the game and Boston won, 117-114. The next year Detroit went to the Finals and Dantley contributed 19.4 points a game in the post season. But the Lakers won in seven games after Detroit had led 3 games to 2.

The following year the Pistons would go on to win one of two consecutive world championships. But Dantley, in the midst of a 19 points per game season, was traded with a first round pick for Mark Aguirre in February of 1989. He missed the Piston party by four months. Had he won one or two world championships those years, how differently might people look at his career?

With 23,177 points under his belt, a lifetime average of 24.3 points and a field goal percentage of .540, Dantley retired from the NBA after being signed by the Milwaukee Bucks in April of 1991. He then played a year in Italy.

Dantley's omission from the NBA list of the 50 greatest makes two great forwards they overlooked. No, those 23,177 points weren't forgotten. They represent the ninth highest total among forwards in NBA history. If he is ninth highest ever, how many people do you think are behind him?

# Bernard**King**

Bernard King was one of the most exciting offensive players of all-time. Period. "There was a time when the surest way to get two points was to throw the ball to Bernard King," says Bob Ryan. "There was a stretch when Bernard King was a devastating offensive force. First of all, he had an astonishingly quick release. He caught the ball and shot. It was like (Pittsburgh second-baseman) Bill Mazeroski getting rid of the ball to complete the double-play. I don't know how he did it. He had explosive quickness off the blocks and was a great fast-break finisher. He had that relentless, phenomenal, truly high-level desire to score two points. Issel had it, Barry had it. It was an obsession in life at that moment to get the ball in the basket."

One of the more dramatic playoff series ever was played between the Knicks and the Pistons in 1984. King played with two dislocated fingers. "He had the ring finger of each hand taped to the middle finger," Ryan remembers. Still, King put on that game-face scowl and posted 213 points — a playoff record until Jordan wiped it out with 226 in a five-game series against Cleveland in 1988 — in a fabulous five-game series, which even reached an overtime period in game five. It was the same game in which Isiah Thomas brought the Pistons back from the dead, scoring 16 fourth-quarter points in 90 seconds. King led the Knicks to victory with a 42.6 average for the series.

Ryan recalls the entire series with amazement, as if it happened yesterday. "In the first game of the 1984 series against Detroit, in the first period, (New York coach) Hubie Brown, who called every play, called Bernard's number 13 consecutive trips (the call was "power right"). On those 13 trips they got 22 points out of a possible 26! That's what we're talking about."

Before the next series, several Celtics vowed, "he won't get 40 against us." But King scored 46 in one game and averaged 29.1 for the series. The Knicks succumbed to a superior Celtics team in 7 games. Larry Bird was happy to see King out of the way. *In Drive* he recalls:

> *The best thing about that series was saying good-bye to Bernard King for the rest of the playoffs. During those playoffs, Bernard was automatic — the best scoring machine I have ever seen.*

> *His release was amazing. You'd always seem to come within a fraction of getting a piece of his shot, but he wouldn't allow it. He always had you off-balance. And the Knicks seemed to go to him every time. We tried to get the ball out of his hands, but we always seemed to be late.*

> *What's really incredible about what Bernard did in those playoffs was that he was doing it with dislocated fingers on both hands! He seemed to be steering the ball up, shooting it off the bottom of his hands and he'd still get forty.*

If the Knicks had gotten by us, they would have had a good shot at the championship.

"In the beginning of the career he had the drug and alcohol problems," Ryan recalls. Signed as a veteran free agent in September 1982, he played terrific ball with New York for two-and-a half years before obliterating his knee in March, 1985. But he returned to the Knicks for six games in 1987. New York then renounced the rights to him, and foolishly let Washington sign him as a free agent. In his fourth season with Washington, King, now 34, made the all-star team and averaged 28.4 for the season. Ryan recalls King announcing, "I'm the first person to make an all-star game without an a.c.l." (anterior cruciate ligament injury).

What we're talking about is a scoring machine, a player who scored 50 points on consecutive nights against San Antonio and Dallas in 1984. In broadcaster Marv Albert's assessment, "he is the greatest offensive player in the history of the New York Knicks." Watching King in New York between 1982 and 1985 was a dizzying experience. He scored 50 points or more five times and went off against New Jersey on Christmas Day, 1984, when he racked up 60. In three years he scored forty or more 23 times. He would set Madison Square Garden records for points in a game and then break and re-break his own records.

He had scored big points out West, too, as a member of the Golden State Warriors. But this Brooklyn boy saved his best for New York.

"His pinnacle was with New York," says Ryan. "If he could have had an unimpeded career... By 1985 Kareem's hook was on the downside. Until then, the surest way to score two points was on Kareem's hook. But in 1984 and 1985 you'd have to say the surest way to score two was to throw the ball to Bernard King."

Those of us who care about the long-term numbers would liked to have seen King stay around to improve his total of 19,655 points to 20,000. But he had played for 16 seasons — two of which he sat out due to injuries — and went as far as his 36-year old body would take him.

King makes it three forwards in a row that the NBA top-50 voters missed the boat on. "St. Bernard" ended his career with a 22.5 scoring average. Add two more points for the playoffs. That should remind you of some of the frustrations of guys that had to guard him on his deadly turnaround.

# Dan**Issel**

Like Gervin, Barry and Erving, Dan Issel starred in both leagues. While he scored points at a greater pace in the ABA than in the NBA, his total of 27,482 points is almost evenly divided between the two leagues. He scored 12,823 points in the ABA and then 14,659 in the NBA. In addition, he recorded 11,133 rebounds, making him one of just 14 players to record 20,000 points and 10,000 rebounds (Barring injury, Patrick Ewing will likely be the

15th when he grabs his 10,000th rebound)."

"Issel scored his 25,000th point in New Jersey," Mike Gminski remembers. "I was there for that milestone and I remembered it because he scored it off of me! I don't recall the shot, but he abused me somehow. For a guy his size he had incredible mobility. He could shoot the jumper facing up or off the drive." The offensive record is really beyond dispute.

"He was a forward with Kentucky and then a center with Denver," Bob Ryan recalls. "He was a sieve on defense, though, and not much of a passer."

Issel made the all-star team all six of his years with the Colonels in the ABA. In nine NBA seasons he made the all-star game once. But he averaged 20.4 points in the NBA, a respectable figure, though not as great as his 25.6 in the ABA. He was a member of the 1975 ABA champion Kentucky Colonels, coached by Hubie Brown.

Dan Issel, averaging 22.6 points for his career, ended up with 27,482 points, the second highest among forwards in basketball *history*. That many points will compensate a lot of flaws on defense.

Aside from being a member of the exclusive 25,000-point club, a club with only 15 members, Issel appears on the 20,000-point 10,000-rebound list as well. Evidently that wasn't good enough for the NBA top-50 voters. In baffling fashion, they omitted him from their list of the best 50 players.

# Alex**English**

There are far more subtleties in the English language than there were in Alex English's game. That being said, we should still learn our English.

Alex's language was pretty much limited to scoring, but in that language he was awfully fluent.

After playing his first three and a half seasons with Milwaukee and Indiana, Alex found a permanent home in the wide open West, playing for the Denver Nuggets. In Denver playing defense seemed optional. English must have felt wanted there, for he thanked his team with points, points and more points.

Readers of this book who find me frustrating for going on about how many points a player scored will find my analysis of Alex English's game similarly frustrating. That's alright. I can take it. But readers will learn something in the process.

There are few players in the 50-year history of the league to do what English did. What did he do? Perk up your ears, here it comes. Beyond anything he displayed what great athletes are supposed to display: consistency.

Between 1981 and 1989, the lithe 6-7 forward scored and scored and scored. Mind you, he didn't do this by missing more than half of his shots.

He was an All-Star eight consecutive years — from 1982 through 1989 — and the scoreboard lights didn't get much rest during those years. It would be nicer if it was an even ten, but his scoring run lasted nine years. Here are the essence of those years:

| YEAR | POINTS | PPG | RPG | APG | TOTAL OFFENSIVE PRODUCTION |
|------|--------|------|------|------|------|
| 1980-81 | 1,929 | 23.8 | 8.0 | 3.6 | 35.4 |
| 1981-82 | 2,082 | 25.4 | 6.8 | 5.3 | 37.5 |
| 1982-83 | 2,326* | 28.4* | 7.3 | 4.8 | 40.5 |
| 1983-84 | 2,167 | 26.4 | 5.7 | 5.0 | 37.1 |
| 1984-85 | 2,262 | 27.9 | 5.7 | 4.2 | 37.8 |
| 1985-86 | 2,414* | 29.8 | 5.0 | 4.0 | 38.8 |
| 1986-87 | 2,345 | 28.6 | 4.2 | 5.1 | 37.9 |
| 1987-88 | 2,000 | 25.0 | 4.7 | 4.7 | 34.4 |
| 1988-89 | 2,175 | 26.5 | 4.0 | 4.7 | 35.2 |

*Denotes a league leading total*

Before analyzing this amazing — and unappreciated — run of numbers, notice one other thing. In these nine years English missed only seven games. That's right. He played 731 of a possible 738 games. No sore toes or fingers were keeping him out of games.

Now to the numbers. A Total Offensive Production (T.O.P.) of 30 is an outstanding total. In all nine of the seasons above he was well-above 30, and most of the time between 35 and 40. He scored 19,700 points in the 731 games for an average of 26.9. That's a serious average. And in six of the nine years his field goal percentage was above .500. The three times he went below .500 he shot .494, .495 and .491. His lifetime field goal percentage is .507.

His 25,613 lifetime points places him sixth among forwards.

Without many horses, Denver played above .500 for this run of nine years. Twice they won more than 50 games. When English started to decline in the 1990-1991 season, so too did the team's record decline to 20 and 62.

So in this instance I don't care that the experts did not mention him. Alex English had a fabulous NBA career and was rewarded for it with his election into the Naismith Hall of Fame in 1997. When he was elected he complained about being left off the NBA's top 50 list. I don't blame him; 25,000 points should make his selection automatic.

English spoke the vernacular, the most important basketball dialect there is: two points, two points, two points.

# The**Centers**

# The**Big**Three

Among all the great centers, there are three who rise above the rest. They are Bill Russell, Wilt Chamberlain and Kareem Abdul-Jabbar. Though I argue in this chapter that Russell is the first choice, a strong case can be made for either of these three as the best ever. I will provide that case in outline here.

If one picks Russell one usually appeals to his winning record. The Celtics were immediate winners in Russell's rookie season in 1957 and went on to capture 11 of 13 NBA championships with Russell in the pivot. That's the only case for Russell, for it's impossible to build a case that his individual statistics are better than Chamberlain's. It is possible, however, to make a case for Russell versus Jabbar using statistics. You could add his points, rebounds and assists versus Jabbar's. I would not make this case, for I think the difference in scoring between the two is too great in Jabbar's favor. But if you do add those three numbers, Russell's T.O.P. (Total Offensive Production) is 41.9, while the sum of Jabbar's numbers is 39.3.

Those picking Chamberlain first will point to his individual scoring and rebounding. If one ranks players based on statistics alone, then it is a forgone conclusion that Chamberlain is the best in the history of the game or at least even with Jordan. But if you choose on the basis of titles and contribution to team effectiveness, then he is not the best, having played on just 2 title winners in 14 years.

The case for Kareem Abdul-Jabbar is roughly a combination of the cases for Russell and Chamberlain. Jabbar has both individual magnificence and NBA championships. He played on six title winners and averaged 24.6 points for 20 years! So one could argue that Jabbar combines a piece of Chamberlain's solo brilliance with some of Russell's maestro team play.

Since I have outlined the cases that can be made for the three, I realize that these three greats are very close, closer than many experts make them out to be. So while I go with the order of Russell, Chamberlain and Jabbar, I have heard good cases for turning that order upside down. I have even heard some experts say Chamberlain is the best, Jabbar second and Russell third.

# Bill**Russell**

Nobody's done it better than Bill Russell if "it" is winning.

Forget columns and columns of data. The numbers that Russell, Red Auerbach and the New England faithful would have you remember most are 11 of 13.

To be sure, the other 15 candidates in this section have numbers and many impressive distinctions. But in sports, as George C. Scott snarled to Paul Newman in *The Hustler*, "you don't count yardage." There's only one question worth asking when it's over: did you win?

Arrogant yet cooperative, selfless but self-assured — such were the complex endowments of the greatest center of all time. His Celtics won 11 championships.

In sports, where it sometimes seems that everything recent is applauded as best, events and people gone by get buried and are forgotten in a flurry of words about the present. A strong case can be made that Russell, who started his NBA career 40 years ago before people were watching regularly on television, was the greatest that ever played.

Russ was the ultimate winner. Now there's a cliche. From some quarters we hear that Pat Riley's a winner, that Johnson was a winner, that Bird was a winner. True statements all. But try a little exercise. Take the number of times anybody won as a numerator and the number of years they played as a denominator. Then we'll talk. With Russell that's 11 over 13. That means Russell played on World Championship teams in 85% of the years in which he played.

In this fast food, short-attention span, think-fast-when-we-think-at-all society, guys are christened winners after one World Series, one good season, one spectacular week, even after one dazzling play on TV whose duration makes a campaign sound byte seem lengthy. We're often too easily impressed.

Russell's skills were not some flash in the pan. The Celtics measured their success by their number of championships. And if you talk to most any of the great Celtics of his era — Cousy, Heinsohn, Havlicek and others — you will find them saying that Russell was the man.

People tend to analyze Russell's greatness under four guises: his team play, his skills, his tenacity and his intelligence.

## TEAM PLAY

"The highest compliment you can pay a man is that he made other people around him better," says John Havlicek. "Russell did that more than anyone else. *Ever.*" Says Satch Sanders, a defensive specialist who played with Russell from 1960-1968, "We were the players we were because of Russell. We also rose higher because of him. A quick man like Havlicek could make four to six more lay-ups because of Russell. I'm not saying that we were better because of him. Russell made people *more effective*. We all added to our games because of him."

## INTELLIGENCE

When Russell came to the Celtics in 1957 the Boston faithful didn't yet know the nuances of the game. Says teammate Tommy Heinsohn. "They didn't understand his game in Boston. Red had to tell the sportswriters what he was doing; they weren't knowledgeable about defense and shot blocking. He brought chess to the game; everyone else was playing checkers."

Sanders recalls Russell's psychological repertoire. "He was a consummate shot blocker. His defense was intimidation. He might goal tend a couple of shots on purpose to begin a game. He understood the psychology that pros hated to have their shots blocked. At other times all he had to do was take a step toward the ball handler and he'd do something else with the ball. He did a lot of thinking. In blocking shots he could use either hand, depending on whether you were driving from the right or left and he'd have one hand free below to stop the pass. It's because of things like this that his reputation has lasted so long."

And when Russell blocked a shot he did not swat it out of bounds. Look at old films and you see teammates retrieving his blocks off the glass or near the baseline and then starting a fast break the other way. "Russell kept his blocks in-bounds," said Nate Thurmond, another great defensive center. "I always blocked them into the third row. I wanted to let the guy know I didn't just tip it. I was making a statement."

Heinsohn learned of Russell first hand, so to speak, when Russ swatted six or eight of his shots at a Holy Cross-San Francisco game at Madison Square Garden in 1954. "Russell had the technique. He timed it so that he blocked the shot an inch or two after it left a guy's hand. He was a cunning fox. He brought intelligence, he brought a new dimension, he had a book on everyone. I remember that only Jerry West, Cliff Hagan and Dick Barnett gave him trouble on the drive; West and Hagan would use the net and rim to pick him off on lay-ups and Barnett would arc an alley-oop shot over Russell down the middle.

"With Wilt he'd find a way to beat him. When Wilt came to Boston, Russ would invite him out to dinner to take the edge off him. He was into it. He was a brilliant man; a thinker."

Havlicek recalls that Russell the head coach (beginning in the 1966-1967 season) would call three plays in the huddle. "Today guys wouldn't remember three plays. We'd call a 2, 44 and a 5 say. The defense would be set for a 44 and we'd run a three. Having a veteran team helped; we did things by habit.

"We had eye contact on that team, without having to say anything. I'm relying on you, you on me. We have to do this together."

Said Cousy, "He'd never repeat the same mistake. He made adjustments. He had that kind of intellect where it went into the computer and it wasn't repeated."

## TENACITY

When the game started, Russell, the man Heinsohn called a "Raging Thing," was "the fiercest most competitive person I've ever been around. He refused to lose."

And if one wants to know about Russell's commitment, there's the well-worn story that he frequently retched before games. "It was a *disturbing* sound," Sanders recalls, "especially in those small locker rooms." "Dry heaves from Russell made us know we were o.k," says Bob Cousy. Says Heinsohn: "There was a standing joke; if Auerbach didn't hear him vomit he'd yell 'Get back in there and throw up.'

"Speaking of intensity, one instance stays in my mind," Heinsohn says.

"Russ missed a stuff, and got tangled in the basket support out of bounds. Now there's a fast break the other way. Russ untangles himself from the supports. Now remember he's the fastest man on our team; he used to beat the Jones boys in wind sprints. I ran 30 feet and Russell goes by me like I was standing still. He blocks a guy's shot at the other end, all in a matter of seconds.

"Focus is the word people use now. This was the most focused player when you had to get something done."

Still, Russell was often attacked, both during and after his career, for possessing an aloof bearing. When he avoided the Hall of Fame induction in 1974, many people assumed that Russell was making a statement about the sparse representation of black basketball players in the Hall. In fact, Russell — having retired in 1969 before the greatest black players like Chamberlain, Baylor and Robertson did — was the first great black player in the NBA to make the Hall. Russell had no comment on the incident. But Heinsohn defends him on this score. "He didn't show up at the Hall of Fame induction because the thing to him was doing it; he loved to play. That's who he was. That was his statement."

On the subject of Russell's motivation, Heinsohn added another little known story about the big man. "He called Boston a racist city after his career. They broke into his house in Reading once, left excrement all over the place, robbed him, wrote 'NIGGER GO HOME' on the walls. He never told the press." Said Cousy, who spoke at length about Russell's view of Boston, "'Russ' competitive anger was even more fueled by Boston. I never discussed it intimately with him. In the Celtic unit there was never the slightest discord; we needled one another, he entertained in the locker room with that raucous laugh. We used to say 'He was the first to shatter glass, not Ella Fitzgerald.' Within the unit he felt secure; though I've always regretted not being more sensitive. We were the toast of Boston, we were the most successful sports franchise in the history of America. But we didn't go home with him and we didn't get turned away from playing golf...."

And there was also a racial incident at the Phoenix Hotel in Lexington, Kentucky in 1961. Five black players from the Celtics and two more from the St. Louis Hawks were refused meal service at the hotel on October 17th. The players quickly gathered their belongings and left town before they were to play an exhibition game, the proceeds of which were to be used for the Kentucky Alumni Endowment Fund.

According to the New York Times the Celtics who left town were Bill Russell, K.C. Jones, "Satch" Sanders, Sam Jones and Al Butler. The Hawks refused service were Woody Sauldsberry and Cleo Hill.

Coach Red Auerbach drove his players to the airport and sent them home. "I couldn't possibly order them to play," Red explained. "It would have been a different situation if they had gone out in town, but they stayed at the hotel and yet were refused service in the hotel's coffee shop."

So if it is true that racial incidents fueled Russell's tenacity, there was no doubt enough for him to be annoyed about.

## SKILLS

Russell captured a gold with the Olympic team, after having won two NCAA titles and 55 straight games at the University of San Francisco with the Dons. But Boston didn't know if they'd get him.

Landing Russell took some of Auerbach's best tactics. Auerbach did not have a low draft pick in the 1956 draft. He made a call to Ben Kerner, owner of the St. Louis Hawks. Kerner had the second draft pick and his needs were painfully obvious: he wanted warm bodies — preferably drawing cards — to keep the franchise going.

Spinning another ball, Auerbach needed to know what Rochester intended to do with its number one selection. He didn't want to sell the farm for St. Louis' second pick and have Rochester select Russell. Russell was one of the most coveted players in the nation because of his dominance in college. But Celtics' owner Walter Brown was friendly with Rochester boss Lester Harrison and gave him a call. Two factors favored the Celtics: the Royals were strong up front with the 6-7 forward Maurice Stokes and they feared Russell's twenty-five-thousand dollar contract demand. Brown gave them further incentive to avoid Russell.

If Lester passed up Russell, as Dan Shaughnessy explains in *Ever Green*, Brown would arrange for Lester to get the Ice Capades to come to Rochester two weeks a year. Elated, Lester announced that he couldn't wait until December for Russell to finish his Olympic commitment. According to Harold Furash, a Celtic insider for 45 years, "Lester made more money from the Ice Capades than he would have made with Russell..." Short term perhaps, but not over the long haul.

Auerbach verifies the story. "...Lester said 'Look, you gave me the Ice Capades, I'll give you my word we won't take Russell.'"

So Rochester planned to draft Duquesne guard Sihugo Green, who would play with three teams before retiring in 1965. Auerbach called Kerner in St. Louis and offered St. Louis University grad and NBA all-star, "Easy" Ed Macauley. Auerbach used a little psychology, telling Kerner that Russell planned to play in the Melbourne Olympics and wouldn't be immediately available. Kerner wanted more, asking for guard Cliff Hagan as well.

Auerbach agreed.

Russell went to Walter Brown's office and signed for $19,500, taking a cut because of the time he missed due to the Olympics. Kerner got Hagan, a 13-year guard with a 17.7 lifetime scoring average and Macauley, a forward who played nine years averaging 17.5. Lester got two weeks of the Ice Capades. Auerbach got a legend-to-be. Auerbach's victory cigar routine may have been born right then and there.

Even though he played only 48 games in his first year, Russell still led the team's second-place rebounder, Jim Loscutoff, by 213 rebounds. "We were good before he came," Heinsohn recalls. "But now we ran away with it."

Russ's first game was against St. Louis. "We were in first when he joined us," says Cousy. "We beat St. Loo on national television and I remember thinking after the game 'Arnold was right.' Now we went from long shot to probable. The round peg for the round hole had been found. But no one thought we'd win 11 of 13.

"If there was a talent measuring machine, Kareem is a 10. Russ might measure last with Wilt in between the three. I think Russ would agree with me. Still Russ was the most productive center of all-time.

"No one played defense on his level. Chamberlain won't admit it, but he developed his famous fall-away shot because of Russ. With other centers Wilt would put it on the floor and take it to the basket. Thurmond was the second greatest defensive center, but was so far behind Russell in quickness, everything. I've never seen anyone that fast. Russ got after any penetrator. I thought Ewing and Olajuwon might develop that way, but they've been disappointing. They both have the physical skills, the quickness. All the skills are in place, but rebounding and defense are reaction.

"In one old film you see Russ rejecting Wilt three times in a row. Wilt would come back and say 'I averaged this many against Russ.' But that's not an adequate rebuttal. Russell worked only hard enough to accomplish the task, which was victory. Wilt always had his stats. Sure, it took me one game and three overtimes to score what he averaged in 1962: 50 points. But he still doesn't understand to this day why there were four people around him."

Adds New York Knicks' announcer John Anderiese, "Russell took away and nobody did that as much. He blocked shots, he screwed up offenses." His broadcast partner Marv Albert simplifies it. "We'll never see anything like that again; you just don't see that position played that way. He made the blocked shot important; with Russell it was a weapon."

Walt Frazier remembers playing against Russell for the first time in 1967. "I was in awe; I don't think there's any question that if they kept blocked shots statistics that he'd have more in his time than anyone now. And if he wasn't blocking your shots he caused a lot of 'hurries and worries' on the defense."

Says Sanders, "I watched him help players into retirement. That slow hook shot centers practiced then was prime for a man like Russell. He eliminated those kinds of centers."

Said Cousy, "Russell had great body control, blocking with the outside or inside hand. He'd invariably keep it in-bounds, lots of guys block loud — knock it out of bounds to get attention. Not Russell."

To show how much Russell was a part of the offense, Havlicek points out "we had 7 plays on offense and they all involved Russ. He either handled the ball, picked, screened or shot. The 7-play was for his shot. He called the plays on the court after Cousy left."

And Heinsohn makes a different point about Russell as an offensive player. "You hear of defensive pressure — with Russell we developed *offensive* pressure basketball. Indeed in Russell's first year Boston averaged 105, 109 the next, then 116, then 124, not dipping below 115 per game until the 1963-64 season, Russell's seventh year.

## VERDICT

Harvey Pollack keeps vigil on the statistical annals at the Philadelphia Spectrum. If one goes solely by what personal stats show, there is little doubt about who the victor is. Russell and Chamberlain played 142 regular season games against each other, with Russell scoring 2060 points for an average of 14.5, while Wilt scored 4077 for an average of 28.7. Even in rebounds, Chamberlain grabbed 4072 for an average of 28.7, while 3373 for Russell gave him an average of 23.7.

The playoff picture doesn't get rosier for Russell either. In 49 playoff games in which they both played, Chamberlain scored 1260 points for an average of 25.7 and had 1393 rebounds for an average of 28.4. Russell meanwhile had 730 points for an average of 14.9 and 1243 rebounds for an average of 25.4.

These numbers eliminate one tired adage: that Chamberlain was superior for the regular season but wilted in the playoffs. They also show that *any* attempt for Russell defenders to win the argument statistically are dashed. Chamberlain outscored him almost two-to-one and out-rebounded him to boot, regular season and playoffs. In the game's history no one — outside of Jordan — owns Chamberlain's numbers. Even with nine scoring titles in his pocket, Jordan has failed to achieve many of Chamberlain's scoring statistics.

But the debate can be shifted from an emphasis on statistics to that of overall effectiveness. If one isolates Wilt on Russell –forgetting that basket-ball is a team game–then one must conclude that Wilt was the victor. But the game *is* a team game and Russell thought of himself not as a solo act but as one of five. Due to this mind-set, his overall effectiveness was greater. His mastery was many faceted; sweeping the boards and igniting the Celtics' leg-endary fast-break, deducting options on defense, making everyone around him more vital. Pollack points out that Chamberlain did win the assist title one year. Precisely speaking, he had the most total assists during the 1967-68 season, but finished second to Oscar Robertson who averaged 9.7 to Wilt's 8.6. But Wilt was rarely the selfless player that Russell was.

More than in baseball where people frequently perform in isolated moments, in basketball one hardly ever plays alone. Rather, one is leading or following, always part of an ever-changing unit, one thinking as five when things are really working. So while Walt Frazier's opinion — "What matters most is the one-on-one battles and Russell got the better of those" — is an oft repeated misconception and is false on the statistical level, it may be true on another level that measures overall impact.

Pollack thinks Chamberlain and Russell are one and two with Jabbar third.

Matt Guokas, who played on the Sixers' 1967 championship team with Chamberlain, picks Chamberlain over Russell. "But I don't think Russell cared so much that Wilt was scoring 35 or 40 points on a given night. The object, of course, was to win the game. Russell was ahead of his time in that he said 'hey, if Wilt is scoring, the other guys are standing around.'"

Says NBC announcer Marv Albert, who has broadcast games since 1967, "there's no doubt in my mind Russell was greater. With Wilt you never knew what you were getting, all that excess baggage. Which Chamberlain would show up?"

But Sanders defends Chamberlain on this score. "Wilt did other things when he scored less; even the two years he won (1967 and 1972) he scored fewer points." Wilt loves to point out that the former team — when the 76ers finished 68-13 — was the greatest squad ever assembled.

But to keep insisting about this year and keep resisting Russell's 11 titles is like a Dodger fan pointing to the 1955 World Series and forgetting all the other years the Yankees lambasted them.

Cousy saw in Chamberlain an inability to adjust. "He averaged 50 and they gave him grief in the Philadelphia papers, so he vowed to win an assist title. 'Tonight I'll get assists,' he thought. Basketball, though, is free flow and you can't decide before the game to do this or that. You must do what the defense allows."

No one takes away from Wilt his tremendous basketball skill. But others see selfishness, lack of focus and inability to mesh with a team as his debits in the Chamberlain-Russell debate. He usually played a lone Salieri to Russell's many-splendoured Mozart. And Cousy, while placing Chamberlain beyond Russell in talent, wonders about what kind of mix the Big Dipper would have made with the green wave. "We might have won one with Chamberlain but no more than that," comes his astounding conclusion.

*Boston Globe* columnist Bob Ryan thinks that conclusion is off. "With Chamberlain the Celtics would have won five or six titles," he claims. Nate Thurmond thinks the Celtics would have won as many titles with Chamberlain as they had with Russell.

Says Sanders, "if you can read, then you know the truth. Forget coulda, shoulda, might haves — the record is 11 out of 13." "I still hear people talk about that Celtic system" recalls Tommy Heinsohn. "The *Celtic system* was Bill Russell."

Even after Russell's announced retirement at 35 — his last game was a seventh game championship victory over the Lakers in Los Angeles in 1969 — Auerbach still thought the had two years left in him. "He was burnt out." After a summer of rest, he could have played. But travel in those years took so much out of you. Now you have a private jet for each team.

"In those days you looked for something to eat at night after a game. You got up at 6 a.m. to catch a plane at eight. He was unsuccessful at coaxing me when I retired from coaching (after the 1966 season) and now I was unsuccessful at coaxing him to continue."

Russell teamed with all Hall of Famers and that explains his championships if you listen to those people looking to explain away his 11 of 13. 'Give Wilt that same cast and watch out...' some say. 'Russ couldn't play offense,' others say. What we do know is that between 1960 and 1973 Wilt Chamberlain played with Paul Arizin, Tom Gola, Billy Cunningham, Hal Greer, Luke Jackson, Chet Walker, Elgin Baylor, Jerry West, Happy Hairston, Jim McMillan and Gail Goodrich and won just twice. There is no question that the Celtics — with Cousy, Sharman, Ramsey, Sam and K.C Jones, Heinsohn, Havlicek and Sanders, had the deepest talent in the league during Russell's career, but was it deep enough to justify an 11 to 2 difference in titles?

Unlikely. It is more likely that Bill Russell did more to contribute to his team's success than any other player in basketball history.

"His 11 titles may never be equalled again," says Mike Gminski. "I still think Russell was the greatest team player of them all," says Bob Ryan. "He won. He got the job done. Unlike Walton, he wasn't always hurt. The one time he was hurt (1958), they didn't win. And it took a 50-point job by Pettit to get that job done."

Said teammate Don Nelson, "Russell could dominate a game without scoring." That statement may be true of only one other player in history–Magic Johnson.

"Russell was my favorite," said Hall of Fame center and NBC analyst Bill Walton. "Russell was a player that I tried to be like — being the team player and not being just a dominant offensive force. Just doing whatever it took to win the game."

# Wilt**Chamberlain**

If you're evaluating the game using only numbers, then one player holds most of the keys to the kingdom. Wilt Chamberlain stalked and ravaged NBA courts for the first seven years of his career, staging an all-out assault on the record book. What he did to the basketball record book was no less than what Babe Ruth did in baseball and Gretzky in hockey.

Starting with his rookie season, Chamberlain led the league in scoring seven straight times and in rebounding 11 of his 14 seasons. He scored 50 or better in a game a record *118* times. The next on that list in Michael Jordan is 36. Stop please.

Wilt has lifetime averages of 30.1 points, 22.9 rebounds and 4.4 assists. Add those three figures and you get a gargantuan number, a Total Production Average (T.O.P.) of 57.4, which is unlike what anyone ever had. In the midst of his 1965-1966 season, he became the all-time scorer, passing Bob Pettit's total of 20,880 points. It thus took Wilt six and a half years to destroy what Pettit had taken 11 years to build. The man was proving what he once said: "where there's a Wilt, there's a way."

Even the out-of-town press could not resist Wilt as a subject. Look at some of the headlines in the *New York Times*. On February 9th, 1960 — the same day that Red Auerbach coached his 1000th game — a *Times* subhead noted "Scoring Mark for Season Set by Chamberlain." By scoring 41 points against Detroit, Wilt had recorded 2,134 points for the season (in just 56 games), breaking the previous record of 2,105 set the year before by Bob Pettit. The article noted "the 7-foot 2-inch star has eighteen games in which to add to the record." His 16 rebounds ran his season total to 1,613, also breaking Russell's season record. This was his rookie season.

Two weeks later a banner head proclaimed "Chamberlain's 58 Points Set Garden Record." The Garden record irritated the Knicks, who were mathematically eliminated by the loss. Shouts of "look at those elbows" and "he's leaning and backing up" were shouted at the officials from the New York bench. Paul Arizin scored 29 and Tom Gola added 23 in the 129-122 Warrior's victory. Less than a month later, on March 15th 1960, a small box of print with a small head noted "Chamberlain is Named Most Valuable Player." He was the first player to win Rookie of the Year and MVP in the same season.

A year later, on March 10, 1961, Chamberlain became the first player to score 3,000 points in one season. On March 15th, on the last day of the season, the *Times* noted "10 Records Set by Chamberlain." Of the ten records he broke — including field goal percentage, .505; rebound average 27.2; most games 50 or more points, 8 — eight of them had belonged to Wilt. Eight days earlier, in type just as large, a headline read "Bill Russell Will Get Basketball Award." He had won the MVP. And on April 22nd the sports pages said "Boston Keeps NBA Championship." It was their third consecutive title.

At the beginning of Wilt's third season on December 8th we read "78 points Scored by Chamberlain." But the Lakers used 32 points from West and 63 from Baylor to beat Wilt's Warriors in three overtimes, 151-147. Wilt had 53 points at the end of regulation play. A month later Wilt got our attention again. The morning *Times* on January 14th boomed "Chamberlain Sets Scoring Mark with 73 points." He had broken Baylor's regulation record set one year before. 40 of Wilt's 73 came in the second half in front of a sparse

Chicago crowd of just 3,516. The Warriors beat the Packers 135-117.

And on March 2nd, 1962 a two-column head read: "Chamberlain Scores 100 Points." The Warriors beat the Knicks 169-147, establishing a new two-team record of 316 points. A crowd of only 4,124 people in Hershey, Pennsylvania cried "give it to Wilt, give it to Wilt" as Wilt repeatedly dropped in his fallaway shot. Aside from the 100-point record, he sets league records for field goals (36), free throws (28), points in a quarter (31), and points for a half, (59). Two years before Bill Russell had said "the only way to stop Wilt and his dunks is to lock him in the dressing room or use a shotgun. He has the size, strength and stamina to score 100 some night." And now Wilt proved Russell a prophet. The most remarkable thing about the game was Chamberlain's unexpected showing at the foul line. He hit 28 of 32 attempts. But Wilt's Warriors were still ten games behind Boston in the standings.

Two days after the feat, *The New York Times* gave him front page coverage. "Wilt, 100% Player, Reaches 100 Goal" read the bold headline. The article was a broader effort to cover Wilt's exploits from college to the Globetrotters to the pros. In counter-point to Wilt's individual achievements, the Celtics again broke a record, racking up their 60th victory on March 13th. Not to be outdone, Wilt got a bolder head by passing the 4,000-point mark on March 15th, leading the Warriors past the "Packer Five" with just 34 points. Walt Bellamy, in the midst of his fine rookie season, netted 38 points of his own.

When the season ended two days later, Chamberlain had broken ten records. Of course, he had shattered most of his own records. One was his 4,029 points for the season. Another was his 50.4 scoring average. The second leading scorer, Walt Bellamy, averaged 31.6. The gap between the first and second scorer has never been that wide.

Nonetheless, Bill Russell was named the Most Valuable Player for the second year in a row on March 24th. In a truly baffling vote, The United States Basketball Writers' Associates gave Russell 19 first place votes to Chamberlain's 5, with Russell finishing more than 100 points ahead of Chamberlain. According to The United States Basketball Writers, a man can score 100 and average 50.4 and score 50 or more *44 times* in one season and still not win the MVP. Incidentally, anyone thinking that voting writers have progressed since then ought to look at the MVP the Baseball Writers gave to Moe Vaughan in 1995. Cleveland's Albert Belle led the A.L. in homers (50), runs (121), RBIs (126), doubles (52), total bases (377), and slugging (.690) — 115 points higher than Vaughan's .575 slugging average! Vaughan tied for the league lead in RBIs and led the league in one category: strikeouts (150). I will describe the moral of the story in my own headline: "From 1962 to

1995: Chronic Stupidity Afflicts Many Sportswriters."

To add further insult to Wilt, in a thrilling seven-game Final the Celtics, who had finished 11 games ahead of the Warriors, topped the Lakers for their fourth straight title on April 18th.

Wilt's first three years were now complete. A 25 year-old man, he could rest content that no one had ever put up three such seasons in his first three years in the league. And no one has since.

Fans today will hear broadcasters excusing the free throw shooting of Shaquille O'Neal, and you can hear what they're doing. It is as if they are validating O'Neal's comparison to Chamberlain by showing that the two had free throw shooting *in common*. Forget it. That is all they had in common. It must insult the intelligence of anyone with an IQ above room temperature to hear that comparison being made. Wilt Chamberlain gave the world a textbook lesson in how to take a league — any league — by storm.

He put up scoring averages of 37.6, 38.4, 50.4, 44.8, 36.9, 34.7 and 33.5 in his first seven years in the league. No, those are not misprints. No one, — ever, ever, ever — will duplicate that sort of effort. Chamberlain in 1960 through 1966 — like Ruth in the 1920s — utterly rewrote the record book. Chamberlain's dominance was so vast, that when the *Times* on March 26th 1960 announced "Wilt Quits Warriors After One Record-Breaking Season," many players took a moment to breathe a sigh of relief.

"Good, now we can all get back to playing normal basketball," said Bob Cousy. Cousy and others around the league thought that Chamberlain's dunking and shot-blocking had dramatically changed the way the game had been played. They were right. Chamberlain's "quitting" after his first season was because of all the rough tactics being used to defend him. He felt the referees were letting opposing players get away with too much illegal contact. In a statement attributed to him by the *New York Post* Wilt claimed, "If I continue, I feel it may be bad for me and bad for my race. If I come back next year and score less than I have, I may have to punch eight or nine guys in the face. I may lose my poise. I don't want too." Chamberlain's coach Neil Johnston had often encouraged Wilt to fight back. When Wilt had to miss two games in February to have two teeth removed that were damaged by elbows, Johnston said "they're getting away with murder against Wilt. It would help if he would belt a few, but's he's only fought back a couple of times when he got mad." Fortunate for the health of opposing players, Wilt never hauled off and belted anyone. He decided to return for the following season.

If you find delight in numbers even a little bit, you owe it to yourself to ease into your favorite chair, stock up on chips and feast on what this man did. When Ruth slugged .846 in 1920 and .847 in 1921 he was singular, a monster who terrorized opposing pitchers. So, too, with Chamberlain.

"The numbers were astounding," said Mike Gminski. "He is the greatest offensive force ever to play the game," says Hubie Brown. Brown was coaching high school basketball while Chamberlain was realigning the basketball universe. Jerry West saw it all at close range. Wilt's numbers confirm what Jerry West said recently in a *Classics Sports Channel* special on Chamberlain. Said West: "It was funny watching people try to stop him."

How funny? Here's how funny. Taste this small appetizer of his records and don't hold your breath waiting for them to be broken. He led the league in field goal percentage nine times. He finished with 23,924 rebounds, more than anyone. He is thus the only member of the 30,000-20,000 club — the only player to score 30,000 points and grab 20,000 rebounds. Don't look now, but besides Wilt there is no member of the 20,000-20,000 club either. We know he had the highest points-per-game average in a year, when he notched 50.4 per game in 1962.

Perhaps his least known but utterly staggering achievement is his record for the most minutes played, 3,882 in 1962. In his bio *A View From Above* Wilt said he was proudest of this one. Including overtime games, that equals 48.5 minutes a game. He missed only seven minutes in the entire 80-game season!

In his second year in the league, he put up the highest rebound average *ever*, 27.2 per game. He owns 26 of the top 48 rebounding games ever. He holds the record with 55 in one game and in 25 more games he grabbed 38 or more rebounds.

And in case you hadn't noticed, Wilt led the league in rebounds his last three years in the league — at 34, 35 and 36 years of age! That should give you some idea of what a physical specimen he was. But here's more of an idea. In those last three years — 1971, 1972 and 1973 — his average minutes per game were 44.3, 42.3 and 43.2. How the game has changed! Either of those totals would have led the league in 1996, when New York forward Anthony Mason posted the league-high average with 42.2. In 1997 Mason averaged 43.1 minutes a game, which would have barely topped Wilt's 1972 total. Chamberlain's minutes tell you that he could have kept on going had he wanted to.

What about scoring? *The Official NBA Guide Book* lists the top 107 scoring games of all-time. Wilt Chamberlain owns 61 of those games, all of them between 56 and 100 points in a single game.

Wilt ran the floor, shot fadeaways, used spin moves to the baseline that ended in reverse layups or dunks. It was easy to see why he was attractive to the Globe Trotters, with whom he played for a year following his college days at Kansas. Any notion that a man that big couldn't be mobile and athletic was put to rest by Chamberlain's entry into the league.

*The 1960 Basketball Yearbook* collected the opinions of several players after Chamberlain's first year in the pros. Perennial all-star Dolph Schayes said, "I don't know what's going to become of the game with Chamberlain in it — this guy is just fantastic." "Basketball will have to have a new concept," said Neil Johnston, Wilt's coach on the Warriors. "He's everything Russell is and more."

Several of the players who had played against both weighed in with a comparison. "Chamberlain's much better than Russell because of the many things he can do," said Red Kerr of Syracuse. "He's just as good or better on blocking shots and he can get the points for them. When he learns a little more about boxing out under the boards, he'll be rebounding just as well, if not better."

Early on, even Cousy was in Chamberlain's corner on the Wilt-Russell debate. "Potentially, I'd have to say Chamberlain's got to have the nod," says Cousy. "He's never played against the pros and he can do so much already. He shoots so much better than Bill, but this is a challenge for Russell and he's always been able to meet all the challenges." Cousy would later change that view as the Celtics kept right on winning.

"I don't know what we'll have to do to nullify him" said Jack Twyman, the Cincinnati Royals' star. "He'll have to be boxed out, of course, and I imagine somebody'll have to try to belt him around for a while, but he's got so much I don't know if he can be cut down to size."

In February 1962, Hall of Famer Red Kerr held Wilt to 55 points in one game. "I don't feel bad about it," Kerr said to a reporter when asked about his defensive showing after the game. "Look what else he's been doing lately."

Chamberlain's Philadelphia Warriors won 49 that season, the Celtics won 60 and eliminated them in the Eastern Division Finals, 4 games to 3. The Celtics then beat the Lakers in a classic Final.

In January, 1963, a Time magazine staffer wrote:

*At 26 Chamberlain is the best basketball player who ever lived. Alone Chamberlain cannot make his team a consistent winner — last week the Warriors trailed the first-place Lakers by 17 games — but he gives San Francisco fans plenty to crow about. In 1960, his first season as a pro he was named the NBA's rookie of the year and its MVP as well. Nobody ever did that before. Nobody ever averaged 42 points a game through a pro career (as Wilt averaged for the first four years of his career) either or scored 100 in a single night. And no one comes near matching*

*Wilt's all-time record for minutes played (3,882), points scored (4,029), and rebounds (2149); records that Chamberlain himself breaks almost every year. The NBA record book lists 86 players who have scored more than 50 points in one game and 57 of them are named Wilt Chamberlain.*

"Wilt has something that separates the great from the near-great," said Bill Russell at the time. "It's a sort of anticipation. You never know what he's going to do, but you know it's going to be out of the ordinary. The most important thing about him is his originality. Nobody ever played basketball the way Wilt Chamberlain does."

After seven seasons of skewering the competition with statistics, and seven Boston titles, Chamberlain helped the 76ers to a World Championship with a different approach to the game. For the first time in 1967, Wilt *didn't* win the scoring title but still averaged 24 points, 24 rebounds and eight assists per game.

Matt Guokas played on that Philadelphia team, a team that set a league record with 68 wins and 13 losses. "I remember watching that (Russell-Chamberlain) rivalry when Wilt first came into the league," Guokas recalls. "And I was a part of it for a couple of years. And I was with Wilt when he changed his style because of the types of players he was surrounded by. I think that even though all those years when Wilt seemed to get the better of Russell statistically — Wilt was a scorer, Russell was not and both were great rebounders, shot blockers and defenders — Wilt publicly and through the media always took the hit because Russell's teams always eventually won the championship."

Was that unfair? "I think so," Guokas continues. "Russell was surrounded by a great team. The nucleus always seemed to stay together for long periods of time, whereas Wilt jumped around a bit, from the Warriors to the 76ers to the Lakers." Wilt added, "Russell only had to play Wilt Chamberlain; I had to play the whole Celtics team."

The Sixers followed that 68-win season with 62 wins. The Philadelphia fans had raised banners and chanted "Boston's Dead, Boston's Dead." Boston won the opener but the Sixers took the next three in a row. Even though Philly forward Billy Cunningham broke his wrist in game four, people figured the Celtics were done. Down three games to one in the Eastern Division Finals, the Celtics rose again, eking out the seventh game at Philly, 100-96. Chamberlain took only two shots in the second half. Jack Ramsay recalls that when Wilt was asked why he didn't shoot instead of passing the ball to his cold teammates he said, "the coach didn't tell me to shoot." And that was it for Chamberlain and the 76ers.

Jack Ramsay was the coach for the 1968-1969 Sixers and finished 55-27. But it was without Wilt Chamberlain, who had been traded to the Lakers on July 9, 1968. Ramsay wanted a motion offense and it looked liked Wilt was not going to fit into that. The Sixers got Archie Clark, Jerry Chambers and Darryl Imhoff.

Wilt was starting with his third team. The Celtics were usually stronger up and down than Wilt's squads. Were Chamberlain's teams horrible? Definitely not. The truth lies somewhere in between the statements that the Celtics were great and Wilt's teams were untalented. From the outset Wilt had good teammates. With the Warriors in Philadelphia and San Francisco he played with Hall of Famers Tom Gola and Paul Arizin. Guy Rodgers was the assist man. They never won in five years.

With the 76ers starting in 1965 he played with Hal Greer, Luke Jackson, Billy Cunningham, Wali Jones and Chet Walker. With that bunch he won once in four years.

He played with Jerry West for all of his five years with the Lakers. And he had other fine teammates. He played with Gail Goodrich (3 years), Elgin Baylor (3 years), Happy Hairston (4 years) and Jim McMillan (3 years). They won once in those five years, the 1972 season, when they stormed to a record 69-13 season.

So Wilt won two titles in 14 years. He won the Finals MVP in 1972 and deserved it. He averaged 19.4 points and 23.3 rebounds in leading the Lakers past the Knicks in five games.

But one of the lasting legacies of his career was that no matter what he accomplished in the way of individual exploits, some would always attack him. "Nobody roots for Goliath," Chamberlain once said. And thousands of people have repeated it since.

Compounding the problem, of course, was Russell and the Celtics. They won and won often. So the argument went that if the Warriors couldn't win, then there must be something wrong with Wilt. Why couldn't he rally them to victory?

But arch-rival Bill Russell once expressed a measure of sympathy. "Wilt got tricked," Russ said. "Most fans and writers emphasized points, so he went out and got points. Then they said rebounds, so he went out and got the most rebounds. In his mind he had done everything required of a player, because he had led in all the categories that they had told him about. And he still could not win."

So the most eternal argument in all of sports goes on. Who was the greatest center, Russell or Chamberlain? Or Abdul-Jabbar? How a person answers depends on what criteria for greatness he selects. What is the *deci-*

*sion rule?* Russell meshed with his Celtic mates right from the get-go and ended up with all the titles, including a title on the last night of his career. That title was won against Chamberlain, who was sitting on the sideline in the fourth quarter of game seven with a bruised knee.

The Lakers were down 17 points in the fourth quarter but when Chamberlain banged his knee with 5:13 left, the lead was down to 9 points. "I just needed a breather for a second," said Wilt to Terry Pluto in *Tall Tales*. "After a minute I said I was ready to come back in but (coach) Butch (Van Breda Kolff) ignored me."

Said Van Breda Kolff "I put in Mel Counts, he hit a couple of shots and we made a comeback. I said to Wilt, 'We're playing better without you.' It was nothing personal against Wilt." In fact, the game got back to a 1-point deficit with 1:17 left to play. Havlicek had the ball and Keith Erickson batted it away as the 24-second clock ran down. The deflected ball went right into Don Nelson's hands and he hoisted a shot from near the foul line which hit the rim hard, bounced straight up in the air and fell back down through the basket.

The Celtics ended up winning 108-106 as Jerry West's shot rimmed the basket at the buzzer. Mel Counts shot 4-13, while Chamberlain scored 18 points on 7 of 8 shooting and had 27 rebounds.

For the longest time Wilt saw himself as essentially an individual in a team game. Few people read his 1992 book *Wilt: A View from Above*. The media print-byte that Wilt slept with 20,000 women got all the attention. Too bad. For he had many interesting things to say. In the book he talks about track and field, checkers, dominoes, volleyball and the rest — all of which he is proficient at — as if they were individual contests. Predictably, his perspective is that of a person who saw himself as a solo act. Part of that perspective is a defense mechanism, a response to how his performance was usually attacked. And part of that perspective is just Wilt.

But with all the distinctions he collected, Chamberlain is very much entitled to the stream of conscious historical perspective he has on the game. Here's a sampling of what the five-time MVP has to say:

- He complains of guys making "$2 million a year for six points and four rebounds a game. I'd be making $20 million today," he concludes. No argument there.
- He notes that when he started pros were only making about $9,000. "But we were playing for love of the game," he continues, "something today's players don't know a lot about."
- "In my third year," he recalls, "the year I averaged 50 points a game, I scored in the twenties only three times. I never scored below 20 that year. Every other game was 30 points or more."

171

- He recalled missing only seven minutes in the entire season. "I went fifty-one straight games without missing a minute, then came out for three minutes. In one other game I came out for four minutes. Think Patrick Ewing or David Robinson could ever match that?"

No, I don't. And part of Wilt's charm is that he tells us about it. Wilt is forever knowledgeable about his numbers and here's one more for Mr. Jordan: Jordan scored his 15,000th point in 460 games, faster than anyone except himself, Wilt points out. Wilt did it in 358 games.

And then he insists he would have beaten Muhammad Ali if that fight had ever come off.

Chamberlain is never boring. Still isn't. "He dominated a room when he walked into it," says Matt Guokas, "and not just because of his size. But because of his personality and tremendous sense of humor. He would needle people but he would always keep it in certain guidelines. He was a thoroughly entertaining guy."

While many of the things he says have to be looked at with a jaundiced eye, the points he makes about the hype surrounding many of today's stars is right on.

Chamberlain's individual assault on the NBA record book will stand and stand and stand. "When you talk about size, it tends to cloud your vision of everything else," says Mike Gminski. "You see the size, but he was such an unbelievable athlete that it was sometimes overlooked."

And was he the best ever? "It's been intriguing for me to talk to guys who have been around the NBA for a long time and talking about the greatest player ever and they say that one knock they hear about Chamberlain is that he didn't have the competitive fire that Michael Jordan has. That's one constant. It's almost as if he would sometimes get bored with the game."

"At various points in my career I led the league in scoring, assists, and blocked shots," Wilt said in *A View From Above*. "Show me the one player in the history of the game that did all that — and maybe I'll admit that you've found someone better than or as good as I was."

Large. That's the way we like to think of Wilt. There's no way anyone that big could ever or *should* ever play it small. When asked once which nickname he preferred, "Wilt the Stilt" or "The Big Dipper," he said he preferred "The Big Dipper," opting for the name of the heavenly constellation.

In basketball he was that vast. 24 years after his retirement, he is still larger than the game.

# Kareem**Abdul-Jabbar**

The one outstanding constant in Kareem Abdul-Jabbar's career was winning. Whether at Power Memorial High School in New York, U.C.L.A. or the pros, his teams won and won often.

After putting up a .639 field goal percentage and leading the UCLA Bruins to three NCAA titles as Lew Alcindor, he began his pro career averaging more than 30 points per game in three of his first four seasons. Only Wilt Chamberlain and Oscar Robertson began their careers so auspiciously. The only difference? Alcindor's teams won.

Take a look at the record of the Milwaukee Bucks before and after he arrived. The year before Lew Alcindor began, Milwaukee was 27 and 55. In his 1969-70 rookie season, the team catapulted to 56 and 26. Milwaukee won the title in the 1970-1971 season.

The reasons are pretty simple. He had the most unstoppable shot in the history of the game. He said he first took the shot in a junior high school game in 1956. He had developed the shot out of necessity, as a way of playing with tough kids who were beating on him. "It was the only shot I didn't get smashed back in my face," he once explained. He missed the shot often at first, but his coach Jack Donohue insisted he keep at it.

Thirty-three years and 38,387 points later, no one still had a clue about how to stop it. In the book *ShowTime* Pat Riley once said, "Kareem's sky hook was the most deadly and unstoppable weapon in any sport. For years and years the Lakers picked up their paychecks regularly because Kareem dropped that shot in, right hand or left hand, whenever the game was on the line. In our half-court offense we went into Kareem in the low post so much it was an act of arrogance. We didn't even try to disguise it. It was like saying, 'Here's what we're going to do. It's what we always do. We don't think you can stop it.'"

Nate Thurmond, the one defender that Kareem gave credit to for defending him well, said that guarding against his sky hook was a "sickening experience." Added Thurmond, "when he got into his rhythm it was over. You could have fallen out of the ceiling and never blocked that shot."

Despite averaging 31.4 points over his first *four* years and winning an NBA title and two MVPs, Abdul-Jabbar was often criticized for being a slacker on the court! An assistant coach with Milwaukee, Hubie Brown can't figure it out. "I came to Milwaukee in 1973. Kareem was 26. He won another MVP (his third) that first season (in the spring of 1974). Three MVPs at 27 years of age. How many guys have turned around a franchise like that?"

After six years in the league he had four MVPs, two scoring titles and a rebounding title to go with his 1971 world championship. Still, he was attacked and generally not liked by the media and public. His lifestyle was ahead of the times. Had he switched his name to Kareem Abdul-Jabbar in 1997, few people would notice. But he did this in 1971, when his conversion to Islam raised eyebrows among a news media and sports fandom that was more than a little xenophobic. In 1968 he had already refused to play in the Mexico Olympics, as a protest against racism in his own land. "He was extremely private off the court," Hubie Brown recalls. And his on the court play might look disinterested because he played with such grace. He felt no need to display the rah-rah emotions that gets lesser players noticed. "He was a man of few words to the media and people took that as sullenness," says Brown. "He was misunderstood."

This dislike of the person often translated into dislike of the performance. In his rookie year, the Madison Square Garden faithful displayed questionable taste in serenading Alcindor with a chorus of "Good bye Louie, Good bye Louie, Good bye Louie, We hate to see you go." Never mind that he had done everything to help the Bucks win. The Knicks were a better team and won in five games. After the game, several Knicks' players fumbled for reasons when asked why the fans chanted.

## MYTHS ABOUT KAREEM

One of several myths about Kareem was that he couldn't rebound. Looking back, it seems odd that anyone would claim that. Not only did he win four MVPS in his first seven years, but he posted the following rebounding totals:

| YEAR | REBOUNDING AVERAGE |
|------|--------------------|
| 69-70 | 14.5 |
| 70-71 | 16.0 |
| 71-72 | 16.6 |
| 72-73 | 16.1 |
| 73-74 | 14.5 |
| 74-75 | 14.0 |
| 75-76 | 16.9* |

*Denotes a league leading total*

Those same figures would earn him five or six rebounding titles in the nineties.

The second myth concerns the substantial revisionist history about Jabbar and the centers he played against. Starting with the 1970 playoffs with New York, one never stops hearing about the list of great centers who supposedly "outplayed" Kareem in big series. The view seems to go like this: the opposing team won; therefore, they won because the opposing big man outplayed Jabbar.

In 1970, he faced Reed and averaged 34 points and 18 rebounds, outscoring *and* outrebounding Reed in four of the five games. Reed played an excellent series, averaging 28 points and 12 rebounds. Reed had neutralized Jabbar. But he had not outplayed Jabbar, as the press suggested.

Jabbar matched up against another Hall of Fame center the next year, the 1971 Finals. With the Bucks sweeping the Bullets four straight, Jabbar averaged 27 points and 18.5 rebounds to Unseld's 15 points and 19 rebounds.

In the 1972 and 1973 playoffs, yet another Hall of Fame center, Nate

Thurmond, held Jabbar in check. In 1972, Thurmond kept him to 21 points per game on 40 percent shooting. The Bucks won despite Thurmond's great effort. In 1973, Thurmond stymied him again, "holding" Jabbar to 22.8 points and 16 rebounds over the six-game series, which Golden State won. Jabbar shot only 43 percent from the field, compared to his 55 percent efficiency for the regular season.

It was after the 1973 season that several more myths got a foothold. Milwaukee made the finals in 1974, in a thrilling see-saw, seven-game series. Boston had a better team, Bob Ryan recalls, and he says it was only Jabbar's excellent play that got them to a seventh game. This time the Celtics won in seven, with John Havlicek taking the series MVP. Eyes turned to Cowens versus Abdul-Jabbar. One writer, in a special to the *New York Times,* described Cowens "the hustling center" as having "more than equalled" Abdul-Jabbar's performance. Did this vague phrase "more than equalled" mean that he played better than Kareem? Sounds that way to me. You be the judge. Cowens averaged 23 points and 8.5 rebounds for the series. Abdul-Jabbar averaged ten more at 33 and rebounded better at 13 per game. In what universe, pray tell, did Cowens "more than equal" Abdul-Jabbar? Cowens played a good series and a great seventh game but the problem for Milwaukee was more Havlicek and the Milwaukee guards, who had to play without Lucius Allen and John McGlocklin and had to leave the guard duties to an aging and ineffective Oscar Robertson.

A year later, a New York fan wrote that the Knicks, now without a dominant center since Willis Reed had retired, should not even consider trading Walt Frazier to Milwaukee for Jabbar, who was looking for a new home after playing six seasons with the Bucks. The three-time MVP Jabbar was "overrated," the fan said and he said that *Times* columnist Dave Anderson was missing this point by suggesting the trade. Jabbar, the overrated center, settled with Los Angeles and went on to play 14 more years. Frazier had five more. With Reed gone, do you think management at Madison Square Garden might have, you know, found room for Kareem? So "overrated" was Abdul-Jabbar that in both 1976 and 1977, his first two years in L.A., he took league MVP honors.

In the 1977 playoffs another myth got a foothold. The Portland Trailblazers caught fire at the end of the year and turned a 49-33 season into a World Championship. On the way, they swept Los Angeles four straight in the Western Conference Finals. Those listening to talk radio stations in New York — and perhaps other ports — shouldn't be surprised to hear that Bill Walton outplayed Abdul-Jabbar, too. Walton went on to be the deserving MVP in the finals against Philadelphia. But he did not outplay Abdul-Jabbar.

To be sure, he was the best player on the floor for Portland. It is also true that he got major scoring help from Maurice Lucas, 23 points per game; Lionel Hollins, 22; and Johnny Davis, 14. Abdul-Jabbar averaged 30 points and 15 rebounds for the series. Walton averaged 19 points and 15 rebounds. What goes down in history is that Walton outplayed Jabbar. More accurately, the rest of the Blazers outplayed the rest of the Lakers by a country mile. "He was the best I ever played," said Walton, recalling that series. "He set the standard. The opponent's entire game plan had to be what you were going to do about Jabbar."

Three years later Kareem rose to the top again, taking his record sixth league MVP. As good as he was during the regular season in leading the Lakers to 60 wins, he was even better in the Finals. Los Angeles beat Philadelphia in six games and Abdul-Jabbar averaged 33 points and 14 rebounds, both far above his regular season numbers. But he sprained his ankle badly at the end of game five and had to miss game six in Philly. Then Earvin Johnson had a game for the ages, logging 42 points, 15 rebounds and seven assists, while playing most every position on the court. In a controversial choice, the voters gave the series MVP to Johnson. Despite the five titles that Johnson and Jabbar won together in the eighties, more often than not those squads are referred to as "Magic's teams." In actuality, neither won a single title in the eighties without the other. In 1980, he was 33 years-old but Kareem would nonetheless go on to have incredible playoff Finals in 1982 (35 years old), 1984 (37), 1985 (38) and 1987 (40).

In all, Abdul-Jabbar's teams made the post-season in 18 of his 20 seasons. Entering the 1982 Finals, Kareem had 10 playoff years under his belt. He had totaled 97 playoff games and held the highest post-season average in *playoff history* with 30.3 points per game. Jerry West was second with 29.1 per game. Kareem also averaged 15.7 rebounds per game. He was then 35.

The following year he did encounter a center who outplayed him. Moses Malone was all-everything in 1983. He led Philly to 65 wins, won his third MVP and was voted the best defensive center in the league. To his credit, Abdul-Jabbar, 36, posted 20 or more points every game against the irrepressible Malone. He still averaged 23 points and 7.5 rebounds for the series. But 1993 was Moses' year. He put up 28 points and 18 rebounds in a series sweep.

In 1984 the Celtics beat the Lakers in a seven-game Final. Jabbar averaged 26 points to Parish's 15. In 1985, Jabbar, now 38, outscored Robert Parish, this time 26 to 17 per game. He was awarded the Finals MVP. And in 1987, at the age of 40, he outscored Parish in a six-game Lakers victory. Jabbar averaged 22 and Parish averaged 16.

I don't recall Jabbar getting a lot of credit for those performances.

Instead the rivalry of Bird and Johnson was played to the hilt. Jabbar was so graceful at the game that he made it look easy. Grace was more a part of his game than the rough play that other centers displayed in the pivot. Oscar Robertson, Abdul-Jabbar's teammate from 1970 through 1974, once described his shot as "like a ballet-type shot. There's so much rhythm and balance in it...it's almost like a pirouette."

"The sky hook was the single most potent weapon in the history of the game," said Mike Gminski. "Playing him is probably the most helpless feeling I ever had out on the court. Because all you do is try to force him as far away as possible, and then when he went into his stride you had to stand there and look. There was going to be nothing that I was going to do when he was in his shot that was going to alter it.."

And did the refs allow even more shoving against Jabbar? "You did whatever you could," Gminski confesses. "I tried to meet him at the free throw line and make him shoot it at a place where he was uncomfortable. Many people would start playing predominantly on his left shoulder, trying to keep him from swinging to his right hand. Many times he would back you into the lane and if he did ever turn to his right he had an easy finger roll. But he wanted to come back to that hook so much. All he had to do was go that way one time and dunk it and you'd have to honor him. Then he'd get five or six hooks."

Jabbar went on to play 20 years. He attributes much of that success to his training regimen. When it comes to physical conditioning, players now are following the training regimen Kareem employed 25 years ago. "Every training program now involves stretching," Abdul-Jabbar explained. "People used to look at me like I was a male dancer. They would say, 'what is that, ballet?' It certainly contributed to my playing 20 years. I could not have played as long without it. I didn't get the injuries people usually have as their years advance. Now everyone does it."

That stretching allowed Abdul-Jabbar to play 75 or more games in 18 of his 20 years. Consider that *no one* before Abdul-Jabbar had even played 17 years!

Not wishing to be confused with the facts, people held to the misperception that he didn't put out the effort or lacked fire or didn't hustle. In his first seven years in the league he averaged forty-plus minutes per game! If that's loafing, then a lot of players in the nineties should start loafing right now.

Aside from his physical readiness to play, Jabbar was always concerned with the team. "He was totally coachable," Brown continues. "He never demanded the last shot verbally. But he demanded it with his eyes. And then he had the ability to win the game for you and handle disappointment. He was so special. He had a cerebral understanding of the game."

And that included defense. "Kareem was the ultimate team player," recalls Brown. "He was the pivotal force behind the defense of those great teams. Very few centers would leave their man to help on traps and double teams. He anchored those defenses and made them great teams." Four times he would lead the league in blocked shots.

Despite this incredible average, if you listen to the press given to the teams that beat the Milwaukee and Los Angeles teams Kareem played on, most of the centers outplayed him. These we-beat-his-team-so-our-center-outplayed-him *myths* are the most incredible of all.

Kareem had the last laugh. He is the only player in history to win six MVPs. In addition to his 38,387 points he grabbed 17,440 rebounds. Add 5,762 more points in the playoffs. He owns or shares another two dozen records — like most career minutes, field goals made, playoff points — including playing in 18 All-Star games, more than anyone.

There is no one remotely like him now, and no one on the horizon either. Like the other two members of the Big Three, Kareem is far away from the pack.

# Hakeem**Olajuwon**

After giving a post-season performance for the ages in 1995, Hakeem Olajuwon was being talked about with the greatest centers that ever played. Prior to 1994, I had Olajuwon ranked fifth behind the Big Three and Moses Malone. Despite all Moses Malone's distinctions — his three MVP's, his 29,580 points, his rebounds, and his playing on one of the great unsung teams, the 1983 Sixers — Olajuwon has moved past him to earn the fourth slot in the pantheon of great centers.

"He prays five times a day, he's a gentleman and if he played in New York, there would be a statue of him outside the Garden," says Hubie Brown. Brown thinks that only Olajuwon's Houston address had kept him from getting the star treatment and superstar recognition he deserved before 1995.

But Olajuwon's second consecutive Finals MVP in 1995 made him the only player ever to achieve that distinction. Two things can be said. One, the award has only been given since 1969, else Russell would no doubt have captured it in consecutive years. Second, Magic Johnson deserved his second consecutive Finals MVP in 1988, but it was awarded to James Worthy instead.

But a league MVP, the two championships and 12 All-Star appearances in twelve years will catapult a man into an all-time ranking, but fast.

"I only played against Hakeem early in his career," says Walton. "But he is at a different level now. He wins with his mind."

"He is up there with Kareem, Wilt and Russell," said Hall of Fame center Nate Thurmond.

"This is a guy who changed what the center does," says Mike Gminksi. "He's so mobile and quick. He's perennially in the top five in scoring, rebounding, blocked shots and steals."

But the man has to show his age some day. He turned 35 on January 21, 1998. Nothing, not even a heart condition, seems to have slowed him so far. Amazingly, the most productive three seasons of his career on offense came when he was 30, 31 and 32, his ninth, tenth and eleventh years in the league! And his 12th season, while showing a slight decline in production, wasn't exactly free fall:

### OLAJUWON's REGULAR SEASON STATISTICS: 1993-1997

|      | PPG  | RPG  | APG | BLOCKS PER GAME | STEALS PER GAME | T.O.P. |
|------|------|------|-----|-----------------|-----------------|--------|
| 1993 | 26.1 | 13.0 | 3.5 | 4.2             | 1.8             | 42.6   |
| 1994 | 27.3 | 11.9 | 3.6 | 3.7             | 1.6             | 42.8   |
| 1995 | 27.8 | 10.8 | 3.5 | 3.4             | 1.8             | 42.1   |
| 1996 | 26.9 | 10.9 | 3.6 | 2.9             | 1.6             | 41.4   |
| 1997 | 23.2 | 9.2  | 3.0 | 3.6             | 1.5             | 35.4   |

In 1996, Olajuwon's numbers against the Lakers in the first round were good, and then fell off as Seattle steamrolled them in four games in the conference semis:

### OLAJUWON's PLAYOFF STATISTICS: 1993-1997

|      | PPG  | RPG  | APG | BLOCKS PER GAME | STEALS PER GAME | T.O.P. |
|------|------|------|-----|-----------------|-----------------|--------|
| 1993 | 25.7 | 14.0 | 4.8 | 4.9             | 1.8             | 44.5   |
| 1994 | 28.9 | 11.0 | 4.3 | 4.0             | 1.7             | 44.2   |
| 1995 | 33.0 | 10.3 | 4.5 | 2.8             | 1.2             | 47.8   |
| 1996 | 22.4 | 8.1  | 3.9 | 2.1             | 1.9             | 34.4   |
| 1997 | 23.1 | 10.9 | 3.4 | 2.6             | 2.1             | 37.4   |

After producing magnificent post-seasons for three years running, Olajuwon averaged just 18 points and 10 rebounds on .475 shooting against Seattle.

Was this the beginning of the end for the center from Lagos, Nigeria? No. Look at the improvement in his 1997 playoff numbers.

"He has the feet of a dancer and the touch of a surgeon," wrote *New York*

*Times* columnist Harvey Araton before the 1994 Finals against New York. And that was before he outplayed Ewing, Robinson and O'Neal in succession over the next 13 months. If there was any question prior to the 1994 and 1995 seasons that Olajuwon was the best active center, there was no question afterward.

Olajuwon possesses a package of skills not seen before at the center position. He does not have the unstoppable hook that Kareem had, nor the defensive and rebounding prowess of Russell or the scoring of Wilt. But his spin-turn-around on the left baseline is as deadly a move as there is anywhere. "It falls into the category of the unstoppable," says Gminski.

His spin move in the lane — what Gminski calls his "Dream Shake" — is equally dizzying. "Against him I would try to guess," Gminski recalls. "If I guessed wrong, I would end up 15 feet away from him.

"There's a story that Olajuwon went to Pete Newell's Big Man Camp, Gminski continues. "Newell looked at his footwork and asked him, 'who taught you that?' Olajuwon said 'nobody, that's my footwork" Everything is this country is based on hand-eye coordination. The rest of the world is foot-eye, usually from soccer."

While Hakeem doesn't seem driven by statistics, he has every right to be cocky about his by now. He is now one of only 14 members in the 20,000-10,000 club — 20,000 points and 10,000 rebounds — and has an outside shot of being only the second player to get into the 30,000-10,000 club, a club inhabited only by Wilt Chamberlain. I asked Olajuwon if he would reach 30,000 points and he replied, "God willing." Though it may not take divine intervention, it won't be easy either.

Comments by some of his awestruck teammates that he is "the best ever" are kind, but probably inaccurate. Sure, Olajuwon's 1995 post season was an astounding run of games. But to hear some broadcasters, writers and radio folk talk, you'd think that no center ever had such a post season before!

Think again. People have short memories. Look at Kareem Abdul-Jabbar's 1980 playoff line — 31.9 points per game, 12.1rebounds, 3.8 blocks and a .572 field goal percentage. Look at Chamberlain in 1967, when he posted a mind-blowing 21.7 points, 9 assists and *30.2 rebounds* per game, while shooting .579 from the field. And Mr. Russell might have trouble picking his favorite playoffs but the guy averaged 29.9 rebounds, 19 points and 5 assists in 1961 when — surprise, surprise — the Celtics won another title. So if your awareness of sports history begins around the time of U-2's first album or the arrival of Bon Jovi, it's time to expand your frame of reference. Don't expect *anyone, ever* to be as dominant as those three guys. Their achievements are like Baccarat crystal — on the shelf to be viewed but probably not touched.

But Hakeem is no doubt the best of his time. Despite Shaquille's premature proclamation that he is "The Man," the real man plays in Houston. While Olajuwon etches his name into the record book, O'Neal is trying to find out where his heart of hearts is. O'Neal has said Olajuwon is his idol. Well, Olajuwon has played his entire career with one team, has come up big in big spots and has the respect of all his peers and those who know the game as being the best.

People who care about the game hope that Olajuwon returns to the form that he displayed between 1993 and 1995. But even if he never returns to that level of play, he has carved out a place in basketball history. He is the greatest center of the nineties and has a firm hold on the fourth spot among the greatest pivot men that ever lived.

# Moses**Malone**

Whether people liked his style of play or didn't, Moses Malone did a lot of things in the league and they shouldn't be forgotten. Basketball isn't figure skating and so players don't get one rating for achievement and then have points added or subtracted for artistry. Malone's entire game was about results.

If style were the major consideration, then some guys who were long on style but short on lifetime achievements would have made this list. Besides, if you like style, you noticed that Moses Malone had his. It's not at all surprising to me that Malone is sometimes forgotten and even left off the list of great players. He and Isiah Thomas were both left off the Barcelona Dream Team in 1992, despite being two of the best players of the 1980s. When each played his last game there was little of the fanfare that attends the retirement of great players.

Be that as it may, if you want to move Moses out of the fifth spot, you had better come with your elbows out, head down or lead with your shoulders. Because brother, no one is in miles of Moses Malone for that slot.

"Sit down and list the accomplishments," says Hubie Brown. "List the three MVPs and five rebounding championships. List the four All-NBA First Team selections and four All-Second Team selections. List six times leading the league in free throw attempts and the fact that he never went to college. Then add the title in 1983. Put all that on a piece of paper without his name next to it and ask someone to pick out the guy who did it!" Many people wouldn't know who did it all or believe it once they found out.

Moses lit the scoreboard for 29,580 points — the fourth highest total of *all-time*. And Moses parted clusters of bodies under the boards, too. The rebounds ended at 17,834, for *third best all-time*. "He is the greatest offensive rebounder of all-time," says Hubie Brown. Bob Ryan and Mike Gminski agree.

Cynical observers — happy to own any thought as long as it is sufficiently bizarre to be regarded as interesting — will maintain that Malone padded these offensive rebound totals off deliberately missed shots. Rather than make an awkward or obstructed shot attempt, Malone would at times purposefully bounce the ball off the glass and go retrieve it. The result was either an easier second field goal attempt or a foul and some free throws. That tactic confirmed how cocksure he was about rebounding. People who say that he did this to pad his rebounding stats are the same people who tell you that they are *sure* that certain losses are fixed, resulting from league conspiracies.

Malone just never got the credit. "Some of the guys didn't have the outgoing personality that allowed them to become more famous," says Bill Walton, speaking of Malone and Robert Parish. "Their on-the-court demeanor and their relation with the public was a very quiet one by their choice." In fact, Malone was thought to be a sullen guy from early on in his career. The voice of the Seton Hall Pirates, Warner Fusselle recalls that when Malone was with the St. Louis Spirits in the ABA, a reporter with the *St. Louis Post Dispatch* interviewed Malone and included all the stutters and pauses and "uhs" in his responses. That hurt him and he avoided the press. He became the kind of player as likely to walk away without warning in the middle of an interview as he was to analyze his career.

If a man is taciturn we may conclude he is dim. If he's quiet, then he must be surly. Malone's most impressive expression occurred *on* the court. He always had a tough time expressing himself. But then he is not given credit for his savvy or his sense of humor. He attributes a part of his success to his name."My mother gave me that name and said I had to do the right thing with it," he smiles to himself.

But his chief aptitude was in playing the game, not in talking about it. "People talk about *academic* IQ," said TNT analyst Hubie Brown. "That's bull. It's IQ for the game that counts." When it came to playing the game, Malone displayed a high IQ in several unexpected ways.

Then New York coach Hubie Brown recalled how the Knicks tried to stop Malone in the famous "fo-fo-fo" (it actually became "fo-fi-fo") year of 1983. Prior to procuring his third MVP award that season, Moses had already stockpiled a few tricks in his arsenal. "When a shot went up, he would go behind the backboard and then step back inbounds, into your man's chest," Brown recalls. "He picked that up from George McGinnis. So when he went behind the backboard, we'd go get him. But if he goes behind the backboard, comes back, turns and faces the boards, he would back himself in and get inside position. Dumb like a fox."

For those observing Moses at the dawn of the Magic-Bird era, the 1982-83 76er team leaps to mind first. That squad, comprised of Erving, Toney, Cheeks and Bobby Jones, was the only team other than the Celtics or Lakers to win in the nine-year span from 1980-88. And they went through the post-season with unprecedented ease. The team represented the end of an era of frustrations for the Sixers and their eternally skeptical fandom. It was, after all, an era when heartbreaking losses in Finals and conference finals were the norm in Philly, an era when Julius Erving often had to go one-on-two or three without success in the closing seconds of tight games, an era when behemoth Darryl Dawkins got chewed up and spit out in the 1980 Finals by a hitherto unseen pivot man by the name of Earvin Johnson.

Malone's arrival in Philly put an end to that. Had he come to the team in 1980, they may have won two or three titles. No team had ever gone through three playoff series in 13 games (the 1970-71 Milwaukee squad made it in 14). Philadelphia won 12 and lost one, the lone loss coming to Milwaukee at the buzzer. The gifts of Julius Erving and the steady, heady control of Mo Cheeks needed Malone's unquenchable fire to complete them. All Malone did was average 24.5 points and 15 rebounds a game for the season. In the playoff Finals against Abdul-Jabbar he upped the ante, averaging 26 points and 18 rebounds. "He owned Jabbar for four games," Gminski recalls. He took the playoff MVP and — of course — the league MVP. To assess the greatness of Malone and that Sixer team, consider just one fact:

they swept a Laker squad that included Abdul-Jabbar, Magic Johnson, Jamaal Wilkes, Michael Cooper and Curt Rambis.

"I have to give the devil his due," said Bob Ryan. "My God he was a great rebounder. That Philadelphia team with him was very, very good."

Malone put a feast of distinctions on the table, enough to get him elected to the Hall of Fame twice. He played in 13 all-star games. Moreover, Malone always played his game. What center ever forced Malone out of his style of play or got the better of him? Would Moses Malone ever run from contact, abandon the pivot and fire jumpers from the perimeter?

Ask some of the centers he routinely carved up in the early eighties. Malone seemed more physical, more effective and just plain better than the rest. The strongest centers of his time were Jabbar and Gilmore, Lanier and Unseld, Issel and Walton, McAdoo and Cowens, Ruland and Sikma, Cartwright and Webster, Laimbeer and Parish. Not a bad list. Seven of them are in the Hall of Fame and two others are on their way. New York fans witnessed two other Hall of Fame centers just before Malone's time: Bellamy and Reed.

How many of these guys were better than Malone? Only Abdul-Jabbar. Malone never got whipped by any of them over a period of time. Who played more of an irrepressible power game than he did? Who was more consistent? "He was right there with the best that ever played," said Jeff Ruland, who played against Malone as a member of the Washington Bullets. Ruland mirrored Malone's physical style on many occasions. "He brought out the best in me."

As for the fine unfinished centers of the eighties and nineties — Olajuwon, Robinson, Ewing, O'Neal and Mourning? Well, we'll just have to wait. Olajuwon is ahead of him. But the others have a lot of catching up to do. While Moses pushed 30,000 points, how probable is it that Ewing, Robinson and O'Neal will ever get than many? It's not likely. Will they match Malone's rebounding totals? Forget it. If one acknowledges something called the 'burden of proof' in argumentation, then the burden of proof falls on those who maintain that people who didn't accomplish what Malone did belong ahead of him. He was a ravenous rebounder and his accomplishments are immense.

Yet Moses still gets less credit than he deserves. For one, Malone's teams have won only one championship. Wilt Chamberlain played on only two champions in 14 years, but people make allowances for that due to his enormous individual talent. Abdul-Jabbar and Russell — besides possessing abundant talent — played on six and 11 championship teams respectively.

Malone's gritty, unadorned style of play is also taken for granted. At his best, Malone was a stick-a-shoulder-in-your-chest center. He rarely played with splash and panache. There was little basket shattering or flying that translated into sneaker deals, though I believe sports marketers missed the boat by not having Moses endorse Timberland boots and camouflage clothing.

Then there's the media market problem. Malone never played in the largest three markets — New York, Los Angeles and Chicago. "You can parallel his career with Olajuwon," notes Brown. "If Olajuwon played in New York he'd be ranked with the greatest ever. The same with Malone. He labored in Houston all those years instead of with one of the mainstream teams."

His lone public peccadillo was a statement made before the 1981 Finals. "Me and four guys from Petersburg High (in Virginia, Moses' hometown) could beat the Celtics," he crowed before the series. The Celtics won the series four games to two. "I don't regret the statement," Moses smiles. "We were just 40 and 42 that year and look what we did." For the most part, Malone's basketball days were full of production and empty of scandal.

But he kept to himself for many years, marching to his own drummer. Anyone capable of objective measurement of his achievements would have to admit that he could flat out play. The word "relentless" is often heard when Malone's career is discussed. You also hear desire. You should also hear "consistency." Until the 1992-1993 season — when he missed 71 games due to back surgery — he hadn't missed 10 games in a season since 1978. Desire has always been the constant in the Malone weaponry. Beginning in 1978 and ending in 1988 he scored 20 points a game and 10 rebounds each year, for 11 consecutive years. Jabbar scored as many points, but never could rebound with Malone. He was a physical presence.

"Moses was so quick he would just wear you down," says Walton. "And he was so quick mentally. People think quickness is just a physical skill but it's a mental skill, too. It's anticipation. That's what set Bird apart and what set Malone apart. He was just so quick and didn't have to develop a great shooting touch because he could always get by guys." How did Walton play him?

"I just tried to keep him away from the basket. He would position himself so magnificently for rebounds. Like Rodman and Barkley and all the great rebounders, he knew where the ball was going. And he would go get it and stick it back in."

Bad games for Moses just weren't on the menu. If offense comes and goes but defense shows up every night, the same could be said for rebounding. And Malone always rebounded. And even when he shot badly, Malone got to the free throw line. His uncanny manner of throwing his bulky frame into the lane always drew fouls, even on off balance not-a-prayer shots in the lane on the baseline, anywhere. Malone got more whistles than Cindy Crawford. He was adept at it.

The late referee Earl Strom, who worked NBA games from 1957 through 1990, thought that Moses had an even temperament that kept him out of trouble. "He never got in a position to lose a call because he was a pain in the ass," recalled Strom. "The game is made up of calls on the margin and Moses was well-liked." Moses shrugs at the suggestion. "You get to know how to use your body, draw the contact, get fouled." And he did that to the hilt, shooting 11,864 free throws, more than *anyone* in NBA history.

"People like to mention things in threes," Isiah Thomas explains, noting Moses' exclusion from the hallowed company of the great NBA centers. "You know, Larry, Michael and Magic." "In order to go to the line that many times, then put the offensive rebounding in its place, then sustain it without missing games — that alone should command reverence," says Hubie Brown. "It's sad that the reverence is not universal."

But those who know the game know his place. Though he acknowledges Artis Gilmore as the toughest of his opponents, he says that no one but himself could stop him at his best. And man, does the record ever prove it.

# George**Mikan**

With thick-rimmed glasses, looking not unlike Clark Kent, George Mikan peers out from photos taken during the dawn of the NBA in the nineteen-forties and fifties. He has the look of one who would eventually run for congress, which he did. A glance at George Mikan's stat line turns up nothing that would give anyone pause. Yes, he did average 22.6 points per game for his nine years. But he scored just 11,764 points and that total wouldn't make the top fifty.

Then you must take that second look. In six consecutive years from 1947-1952 he led either the National Basketball League (NBL), Basketball Association of America (BAA) or NBA in scoring. There's more. From '47 through '54 he played on seven championship teams, including the NBA champion Minneapolis Lakers from 1950, 1952, 1953 and 1954. This 6'10" center made his bones during times when blocked shots and steals were not even recorded. Minutes played, rebounds, field goal percentage and assists were only available in certain years. Record keeping was spotty.

It was a time when the sports world was attuned to the Brooklyn Dodgers and the New York Yankees, DiMaggio and Ted Williams, Army and Navy football. Basketball was an afterthought. The Harlem Globetrotters and college doubleheaders were far more popular than the pro game.

But George Mikan, whose brother Ed had played ball with the NBA and Basketball Association of America, was thought highly of. How highly? Consider that Mikan would be named Associated Press top player of the half century in 1950. "Mikan called Best Netter" read the head on an Associated Press story. It was one of those awards for the ages. "Today," the copy read, "George Mikan was named the greatest basketball player of the last 50 years by sportswriters and broadcasters participating in the AP mid-century poll. He received 139 of the 380 votes cast, winning out over Hank Luisetti, Stanford's whiz of 13 years ago. Luisetti got 123 votes." Quite an honor, heh?

How did he get to that point? With great difficulty. At the time that Mikan began his career, there was certainly an opening for a man of his size — 6-10, 245 — and brawn. But his road to hardwood success would be bumpy. All he had won early in life was the marble-shooting championship of Will County in Illinois.

Then he tried out for the basketball team at Catholic High School in Joliet, Illinois. When the coach, Father Gilbert Burns, noticed Mikan squinting, he demanded an explanation. Mikan explained that he squinted because he wasn't wearing his glasses. The good Father Burns would not accept that explanation. Basketball success and eyeglasses did not go together, he thought, and he cut Mikan from the squad.

At his next stop it got worse. Notre Dame coach George Keogan claimed that Mikan was "too awkward, lacked talent and wore glasses." His condescending advice to young Mikan? "You should become a scholar."Bob Pettit confirms the story, recalling that Mikan was so ungainly that Notre Dame turned down his application for a scholarship.

But Mikan did not take the scholarly path. Rather, he took the road less travelled, the road he was advised not to take. Under the watchful eye of De Paul coach Ray Meyer, Mikan gradually built his skills. "Ray was a slave driver," Mikan said later. "But he was just what I needed. He taught me everything I know." Coach Meyer's first lesson was to teach Mikan, still lean and still growing at 6-8, how to use his height in getting up in the air and over his rivals.

Mikan constantly worked on his game and made All-American in 1944, 1945 and 1946. He was the nation's leading scorer these last two years, with averages of 23.9 and 23.1. His 120 points in three games enabled De Paul to win the 1945 National Invitation Tournament in 1945.

While Mikan was still at De Paul in 1945, James Enright of the *Chicago Herald American* wrote a story for *Converse Yearbook*. "With the war over and pro basketball expected to boom along with all other sports," Enright pointed out, "there is a lot of money awaiting Mikan when he gets ready to take up the cash register game. Already one performer has offered the pride of Joliet $1,000 per month on a game-per-week basis."

$1,000 a month. Think of it. By 1949 Mikan was playing for the Minneapolis Lakers in the Basketball Association of America and drawing the league's top salary: $17,500 per year.

Mikan's game had broadened. He employed a sweeping hook in the lane, a shot he could make left-handed or right-handed. It was a shot that no one could stop. He swept the offensive boards and he scored in the lane or on the baseline. Printed on his shirt was "MPLS," with the number 99 across the front.

As Roland Lazenby wrote in *The Lakers*, Mikan made use of his broad shoulders and "and a bruising pair of elbows." He would get low position, back in and pivot and lead with the elbow. Teammate Jim Pollard said "he didn't get called for the offensive foul because he had both hands on the ball. He'd take it up in the air with both hands. If he took a hand off the ball and threw the elbow, he was going to get called for the foul. But George seldom did that. He was smart."

In 1949, the year that the New York Yankees won their first of five consecutive World Championships, Minneapolis quietly beat the Washington Capitols in six games. It wasn't the NBA, but it began a trend for Mikan. Winning would become his hallmark. His 28.2 points per game gave him his third scoring title in a row. He had led the NBL in scoring while playing with Chicago and then Minneapolis in the previous two years.

With Mikan scoring 40 in the final sixth game, the Lakers beat Syracuse 110-95 for the NBA championship in 1950. Minnesota got a bonus of $19,500, enough for each player to enjoy a "nest egg of $2,027.27," the *New York Times* reported.

Mikan won the scoring title that year, too, with an average of 27.4 per game. He went on to win three titles in a row, the first of six NBA players to accomplish that feat. The remaining five were Neil Johnston, Wilt Chamberlain, Bob McAdoo, George Gervin and Michael Jordan.

In the playoffs he put up phenomenal numbers, too, averaging 30.3, 24, 23.6 and 19.8 in the Lakers' title years.

Mike Gminski chose Mikan as the fourth best center in history, behind only Jabbar, Chamberlain and Russell. "Mikan *was* the league early on," Gminski points out. "He was the drawing card."

"He set the table for everybody," says Bill Walton. "He came in and showed it wasn't about just being big but about being skilled and being smart. It's not the biggest strongest guy who wins all the time. Shaq and Wilt have only two titles between them in 19 years of play. They're phenomenal players, but look where the titles are: with Russell, Mikan, Jabbar. The titles are with Magic, Bird, Jordan, Hakeem, Isiah."

With the combination of winning and the scoring titles, it is no wonder that he was elected to the NBA 25th Anniversary All-Time Team in 1970 and the 35th Anniversary Team in 1980. His greatness and historical importance are beyond dispute.

Despite this, I have heard the argument from keen observers of the league that Mikan would not have played well in today's game. "The game has expanded much further than Mikan's physical ability would have taken him," says Bob Ryan. But wouldn't he have been a brute down low, as he was in the forties and fifties? "Guys would block his hook shot today," Ryan thinks. "They would just block it. I know he's a great *competitor*; no one can achieve what he's achieved at any time in history without being a competitor. But I don't think it would have added up to enough. He just wasn't the athlete the guys are today. I could name ten back-up centers who are better athletes and I just don't think he could deal with them."

Mikan was large for his time and would be comparatively small in the pivot today. But centers no larger than Mikan — Reed, Unseld, Cowens, to name just a few — enjoyed brilliant NBA careers. So it's not clear that "The Mighty Mikan" would have flopped. Could he have gotten along down low? "I think great players adapt," says Gminski. "Alright, maybe that hook shot wouldn't fly. But he was great and would have found a way to score by doing something else. He did win five titles in six years!"

Mikan was known for mixing it up underneath and getting many of his points off of tip ins. "Grandmother gets credit for that," came Mikan's innocent explanation. "She made me practice the piano two hours every day for eight years and I finally earned a conservatory diploma. The keyboard practice made my fingers strong and sensitive and gave me the quick instinctive touch you need in those under-the-basket scrambles."

Bill Walton is also convinced that Mikan would still flourish in today's game. "Coach Wooden had a very famous saying: it's not how big you are, it's how big you play," says Walton. "It's not how high you jump, it's where you are when you jump. It's not a game of size and strength; it's a game of skill, timing and position. That fits George Mikan to a tee. People say he wouldn't be able to do it today, but he was about 6-10 and 250. I don't see why he wouldn't be a talented player. All the great players from the past would be great ones today. The reason they got to be great was how hard they worked, how smart they were, and their competitive greatness and that's something you can't measure."

Mikan stayed around for the 1955-1956 season, long enough to see the game change significantly with the advent of the 24-second shot. "This new rule," a reporter wrote for *Time* in December, 1954, "adopted for the 1954-1955 season, has made the game a better, faster, more exciting sport. In other years "freezing" the ball in the late stages was the name of the game. A team that found itself a few points ahead near the end would simply pass the ball around from player to player without trying for a basket. The trailing team would then deliberately foul to get possession, risking a one-point foul shot for a possible two-point basket. The leading team would then foul back and the game would dissolve in a *dreary welter*."

Mikan retired for a year after Minneapolis' last title in 1954 and then returned for the 1955-1956 season. But he played only 37 games. After he retired for good in 1956 he turned to coaching. "It was the shortest coaching career on record," Mikan said. With Mikan guiding the team from the bench, the Lakers won 9 games and lost 30 for the 1957-1958 season. The next year Elgin Baylor was a rookie for the Lakers.

In 1959 he was elected to the Hall of Fame. He became the first commissioner of the newly formed ABA in 1967.

The Clark Kent look alike was the first Superman in the early years of the NBA. What type of player would Big George be today? Like Reed? Cowens? Unseld? "He would be a George Mikan-type player," says Walton. "And the game would be better for it."

# Willis**Reed**

Bill Bradley, then Senator Bill Bradley, wrote a letter to the Honors Committee of the Basketball Hall of Fame in November 1980. The purpose of the letter was to endorse Willis Reed's nomination to the Hall of Fame. These sorts of letters are typically chock full of hyperbole and enough rhetoric to make presidential candidates blush. But look at what "Dollar Bill" wrote and see if any of it is untrue.

*For ten years, I had the opportunity to play with Willis Reed*
*in the NBA. There is no player more deserving of the honor of*

*being elected to the Basketball Hall of Fame than Mr. Reed. He was the captain and leader of the New York Knicks during two championships in 1970 and 1973, in addition to being selected as the league's Most Valuable Player in 1970. His past exploits while injured are well known to the public, but they are merely a small indication of the tremendous "heart" that he exhibited throughout his basketball career.*

*I wholeheartedly endorse Willis Reed's nomination to the Basketball Hall of Fame.*

Dollar Bill nailed it. Because of the way he played, Reed was a coach's dream. If you could pick a 12-man squad of players who got everything out of their talent, Reed would have to be on that team. And maybe captain. He was a self-starter who led by example.

Listed at 6-10, 240, the consensus is that he was shorter — and probably heavier. Some said he was only 6-8. Reed gave the Knicks a rebounder, 20-point scorer and a physical presence who would give you a maximum effort night in and night out against the top centers of his time — Russell, Chamberlain, Abdul-Jabbar, Wes Unseld, Dave Cowens, Nate Thurmond and Bob Rule. In the most center-rich period in the history of the NBA, the Knicks rarely got embarrassed by the opponent's pivot man. And if the Knicks could win the center match-up or get a standoff, then they were going to win with the rest of their starting five and their bench.

A force right from the start, Reed won Rookie of the Year in the 1964-65 season. He entered a league dominated by the legendary Russell-Chamberlain wars and scored 19.5 points and grabbed 14.7 rebounds per game in his first season. As a result of a trade in November 1965, he and Walt Bellamy were together the following season. The pivot now belonged to Bellamy, and Reed's numbers declined significantly. A crowded pivot was not producing wins, either. Despite decent scoring from Dick Barnett and Bellamy, the Knicks were not getting it done. They won 30 and lost 52. Mediocrity was the norm for the Knicks — nothing new to a team that had been one of the league doormats for nearly 15 years.

But the trade of Bellamy was the emancipation of Reed. The pivot now belonged to the second round pick from Grambling. He responded with his best seasons in 69-70 and 70-71. The 1969-1970 season will forever be unparalleled in the history of the Knicks. They had lost four games to two to the Celtics and Bill Russell the year before. The Knicks had won 54 and the Celts 48 that year, but Boston had Havlicek and Sam Jones, Russell and Bailey Howell, Don Nelson and Larry Siegfried and that is all you need to know. Even Celtics teams that rated about a six in talent had a way of becoming a nine once the playoffs began.

Boston won four of the seven regular season games the next season, but without Russell the Celtics didn't make the playoffs. The Knicks won 60 and lost 22 and Reed won every honor under the sun. With 21 points and 11 rebounds he won the All-Star Game MVP. With 21.7 points and 13.7 rebounds for the season he won the league MVP. After dispatching the Baltimore Bullets in seven games and Milwaukee in five, the Knicks had to play the Los Angeles Lakers, who had Chamberlain back. Wilt had missed 70 games with an injury, but he averaged 22 points and 22 rebounds in the post-season. They also got big seasons from Jerry West, Elgin Baylor and Happy Hairston.

With the Knicks behind 25-15 in game five of a series tied two-two, Reed drove left but his weak right knee buckled and he fell, pulling a ligament in his right hip. He had to leave the game. In his absence the Lakers panicked. Instead of continuing the balanced attack they had used to build the lead, having hit 15 of their first 15 jumpers, they now started forcing the ball in to Chamberlain, who was being doubled with various combinations of Dave DeBusschere, Dave Stallworth and Nate Bowman. The Knicks made up the deficit with some extraordinary defense and won 107-100. But a funny thing happened on the way to the Forum.

Reed would sit out game six. Chamberlain unleashed his fury on the Knicks in game 6, scoring 45 points (on 20 for 27 shooting!) and getting 27 rebounds. Jerry West added 33 points, 6 rebounds and 13 assists as the Lakers rolled, 135-113. In game seven the ending was a forgone conclusion if the Knicks played another game without Reed. Even the home cooking of Madison Square Garden would not be enough to keep Chamberlain out of the lane.

No one knew if Reed would play. Not coach Red Holzman, not Reed, certainly not the Lakers. "If there's any way he can play, he'll play," said West right after game six. "He might hurt them if he's not at his best but he might help them, too. I think they have to take the chance. You don't like to see a team lose when it's not at its best. It's like stealing something. Seeing him on the bench took something out of it." Wilt sounded a similar tune. "This may sound corny," he said, "but I know this means a lot to Willis and us. We don't want to come in the back door."

With a stiff dose of cortisone, Reed decided he would give it a go and drag his right leg up and down the floor. The talk in the Garden that year was about the "decibel levels" of the noise. Reed's entrance onto the floor that May 8th evening was greeted with a deafening roar, a roar so great that Reed's face seemed to tighten against the emotion that was building in him as he tried to concentrate on his warm-up tosses. Everyone on the Knicks tried to look busy with his warm-ups, but to no avail. They were shooting and dribbling but looking at Reed. If you were breathing at all, the storm of noise made you shudder.

"This is a helluva predicament to be in," Reed later said, recalling what was going through his mind. "Everybody in Madison Square Garden is saying everything's all right, the captain's here. And I have to go out and play the best big man who ever's been around. Not with two legs but one leg."

Unchecked on the perimeter by Chamberlain, Reed hit two 18-footers with that six-inch jump and left-handed stroke. In no time the Lakers were down 9 to 2. At the end of the first quarter they were down 38-24 and at half-time 69-42. Frazier had one of the most clutch games ever played, putting up 36 points, 7 rebounds and 19 assists. While Chamberlain had 21 points and 24 rebounds, Baylor had 19 and West 28, the impact of the immortal three-some was strangely lacking.

Frazier had 31 by the middle of the third quarter, and the Lakers were still down by 27 points. Reed hit just two of five shots but he had contributed in two major ways.

For one, he had given his mates an indescribable boost by just appearing on the court. And then he kept Chamberlain out of the middle. Chamberlain still rebounded but his finger roll attempts were not coming from three feet away but eight or ten feet from the hoop. Reed kept Chamberlain from making the power moves in the paint that invariably led to easy baskets.

In the Finals Reed averaged 23 points and 10.5 rebounds (but 32 and 15 in the first four games before the injury) and deservedly won the MVP of the series. Chamberlain averaged 23 points and 24 rebounds for the series.

In 1973, Reed's next to last year in basketball, he struggled through a season in which he missed 13 games due to injury, averaging only 11 points and 8.6 rebounds. In the Finals he upped that total to 16.4 points and 9.2 rebounds in 30 minutes per night. But Frazier was the Knicks' work horse that series, giving the Knicks 16.6 points, 5.2 assists and 7 rebounds. Still, Reed was awarded the finals MVP. One rationale for Reed winning the award was that he shot 28 for 53 from the field over the last three games. He outscored Chamberlain 61-41 in those games, all won by the Knicks.

But the Knicks — perhaps as much as any great team in the history of any sport — embraced a team philosophy that made the question "who was the high scorer?" an utter impertinence. Coach Red Holzman had imposed a team philosophy on New York and the players absorbed it. They stressed "hitting the open man" and their number of passes in one sequence would have pleased the high school in "Hoosiers." Several elements made them a great team. They had perimeter shooting at all five starting positions. Their team defense kept opponents from rolling over them. Between DeBusschere, Frazier and Reed, they had the best team defense in the league *four times* between 1969 and 1973 and 3rd best the other time.

A sign of that team philosophy was evident even after the second championship. When Reed appeared at Mama Leone's to accept the MVP award he said, "If I had a vote I would have selected Walt Frazier, maybe because I'm a big Walt Frazier fan." Then he said, "four or five guys on our team deserved to win." No matter, Frazier and the rest of the Knicks recognized who the captain was. Frazier once said that Reed was "the backbone" of the team.

"Reed was a phenomenal competitor," recalls Bill Walton, who missed playing against Reed by one year. "He used to be able to go *right at* all centers. He got hurt; when he did play he was special. Willis Reed was a combination of everybody. He had the heart, the body, the power, the skills. He had great teammates and really fit into that team. He was a fierce, fierce competitor."

"He *really* knew how to play," says Bob Ryan, "every aspect of the game. There wasn't a bigger heart or a tougher guy. He was a great offensive player and excellent rebounder. Just knew how to play and a tremendous body, but unfortunately the knees went on him. If you're talking about guys who have big games, he is right there."

And Mr. Ryan wasn't just thinking about game seven against Los Angeles in 1970. In a very tough first round series against Baltimore that year, Reed had 36 points *and* 36 rebounds in game five, to give the Knicks a three-games to two lead.

As odd as it is to highlight an individual on a collective that was always known as a *team*, it was on Reed's broad shoulders that the Knicks' hopes often rested.

# Dave**Cowens**

Dave Cowens was the Celtics' next great center after Bill Russell. Can you imagine what is was like trying to fill that job? Henry Finkel had been the Celtics' center the year after Russell and fans had made it a living hell for him. The fans booed him so much at home that he contemplated retirement. One reward of that season with Finkel was that Boston finished 34 and 48 and would get the fourth draft pick in the 1970 sweepstakes.

People all over the league had waited for the Celtics to lose. Now that Russell was gone, GM Red Auerbach keep hearing the same refrain dinning in his ears: 'just let's see you win without Russell.'

Now, for the first time in 24 years, the Celtics would draft from the top four picks. Detroit selected first and took St. Bonaventure's Bob Lanier, the San Diego Rockets took Rudy Tomjanovich and Atlanta got Pete Maravich. A litter of talent still remained — Sam Lacey, Geoff Petrie, Calvin Murphy, Nate Archibald. Coached by Bob Cousy, Cincinnati picked next. Some confusion exists about whether Auerbach wanted Sam Lacey and was talked out of it by Ernie Barrett, the Athletic Director at Kansas State, who insisted that Lacey would not pan out as an NBA performer. Others said that Red knew exactly who he wanted.

In no uncertain terms, Tom Heinsohn, then head coach, said that Red had his eye on Cowens months before the draft, having seen him play in a college game. To give the appearance of being disinterested in Cowens, Auerbach left the game at half-time.

So Auerbach selected fourth and got Cowens and Cinci got Lacey. Cowens' first year was a wild ride. His irrepressible enthusiasm got him a league-leading 350 fouls and he fouled out of 15 games. But the team won 10 more games than the year before with Cowens giving them 38 minutes a night. People who didn't like the way Cowens played were usually enemy coaches, fans and players.

Despite the fouls, Cowens was tireless. While he couldn't match a 7-2 Jabbar or a 7-1 Chamberlain in the pivot, he could run those guys on the perimeter, taking take them away from the paint where they wanted to be. And at 6-8 and a half, Cowens rebounded like a devil, averaging 15 a game on desire and jumping ability. That plus 17 points gave him and Geoff Petrie a share of the "Rookie of the Year" voting. "Cowens could go inside, too," Walton reminds us. "He was wildly enthusiastic. He risked *life and limb*. He could absorb all the punishment and pounding inside."

So Red had himself another red head. In Cowens' second year Boston won 56 games. Cowens still led the league in personal fouls but he fouled out of only 10 games this time. But the 1973 season was the ultimate for Cowens. Boston won 68 games and Cowens won MVP. He was all everything, averaging 20.5 points and 16.2 rebounds. Perhaps only Havlicek's separated shoulder kept the Celtics from winning the title. The Knicks beat them in seven games.

But the next year belonged to Boston. They took on Milwaukee in the Finals and Cowens, while he didn't outplay Kareem the entire series, played a terrific seventh game in Milwaukee and helped Boston to win that nip-and-tuck, fabulously undersold series. "He had a terrible game 6, shooting 5 for 18," recalls Bob Ryan. "And he wanted to redeem himself. No one thought more in terms of redemption than Dave Cowens; he made it a biblical thing. And then he went out and had 8 for 13 in the first half of game seven." He ended up with 28 points and 14 rebounds. Havlicek won the series MVP as Boston walked off with its 12th NBA title.

"He always played much bigger than his size," recalls Ryan. "He was living proof that you are as big as you play and that you are a center if you believe you are a center and act like a center. That was true of Unseld, too, who played center at 6-6. Compare this with David Robinson who is 7-2 and acts like a small forward."

Hubie Brown has a similar recollection of Cowens. "If Willis Reed was undersized, Cowens was *definitely* undersized. Yet, I don't think there was a night when Cowens didn't participate at 100 percent of his athletic talent. He always played to his potential. Any loose ball on the floor was his."

Like the New York teams of the early and mid-seventies, Boston — with Havlicek, Cowens and Paul Silas on the front line and Don Chaney and Jo Jo White in the backcourt — was a force to be reckoned with. When they weren't winning 60 plus games a year, they were winning in the mid-fifties. And they were at it again in 1976. Now instead of Chaney they had Charley Scott, who brought extra offense to the mix. With Scott, Jo Jo, Big Red and Hondo they had four players averaging between 17 and 19 points per game. Aside from his 19 points, Cowens had his second best rebounding season, putting up 16 per game.

They emerged from a six-game series with Buffalo and scoring machine Bob McAdoo. Then they topped Cleveland in six and went to the Finals against Phoenix.

Since Phoenix had finished just 42 and 40, Boston was heavily favored. After Boston went up 2-0, Phoenix evened it 2-2 on their home wood. Boston took big advantage of their rebounding edge with Cowens and Silas, and word circulated how these two were beating up on poor Phoenix off the glass. Silas admitted as much and seemed amused by all the controversy. Cowens didn't deny it either. Silas was a rebounding specialist his entire career, a rare player who rebounded more than he scored in his best years. Despite having 12 years of wear on his body, Silas grabbed 14 per game for the Phoenix series. Cowens was his usual maniacal self off the boards, adding 16.4 more. Try to think of better one-two punches off the boards in playoff history and you won't come up with many better than that duo.

But the Celtics still had to win two of the last three games to get past an over-achieving Phoenix squad. Those watching the fifth game will tell you that it was as fine a game as was ever played. The Celtics had led by 22 points, but the Suns rallied behind ex-Celtic Paul Westphal to put the game in overtime. At the end of the second overtime it seemed that Havlicek had won the game by hitting a jumper with two seconds left. With Cowens, Scott and Silas fouled out of the marathon 63-minute game, Gar Heard then hit a bomb with a second left and sent the game into the third overtime. But the Celtics had enough left in the tank — and enough players on the court — to win 128-126.

In game six the Celtics shot a cock-eyed 39 percent from the field but brought their best defense and rode the hot shooting and all-around play of Charlie Scott. Scott scored 25 points, and added 11 rebounds, 3 assists and five steals to lead Boston to a 87-80 victory. Cowens was the only Celtic to hit half of his shots, making 10 of 16 from the field for 21 points and 17 rebounds. Jo Jo White took Finals MVP honors. The Celtics had their 13th title and their last of the Havlicek-Cowens-White era. The Celtics didn't get deep into the playoffs again before Havlicek retired in 1978 and Cowens retired for two years in 1980.

Looking back at Cowens' career, Bob Ryan recalls Big Red with great admiration. "Cowens was a sensational rebounder, great at running the floor, good outside shot. Guys he could take inside he took inside, guys he wanted to take outside he took outside."

"He was a rugged, rugged, post-up player who through sheer hustle and determination averaged 14 rebounds a game," says Hubie Brown. "He had to overcome the superstars of his time — Wilt, Kareem and Thurmond."

Cowens backed down to no one. I can see him yet, the trailer on a fast break, nailing that left-handed 18-footer. If you rooted for any other team but the Celtics, you just hated that he wasn't on your team, because he was just never beaten. The seven-time All-Star was elected to the Hall of Fame in 1990.

A different kind of center, he was still the Celtics' second great center in their storied history. Those who said that the Celtics would not win without Russell were not making any noise at the end of Big Red's 11-year career.

With Cowens they won twice.

# Wes**Unseld**

Continuing the theme of undersized centers with oversized hearts, I give you Wes Unseld. If you think that increased height always correlates with better results, then you ought to get familiar with the facts about Unseld's career. At his best he was a rebounding machine. His was a game of picks and passes and muscle and he did all the intangible things that help teams to win.

Wes Unseld was indescribably proficient as a scorer and rebounder at

Louisville, and was picked second overall in the 1968 draft. Only Elvin Hayes, his future teammate, was picked ahead of him. Unseld then began as a force in the NBA and stayed that way, a great rebounder even in his last year.

When he was inducted into the Hall of Fame in 1987, Unseld said "I didn't do anything very pretty. My contributions were more in the intangibles. But they were the type of things that help to lead a team." Amen.

Those who think that style points are required for excellence, save yourself time and don't bother reading any further. Skip to the next best center. Unseld had many productive points but, by his own admission, few style points. He was good enough to lead *four* Bullets' teams to the Finals. He was 6-7 and 245 at the start, though Bob Ryan will tell you that was "only 6-6 plus big haircut." By the end he was near 300 pounds, thinks Ryan, but no one called him fatso. His frame was big enough to distribute the excess, even if those horizontal stripes on his Bullets' shirt made his chest and shoulders approach the dimensions of the pickle barrel in the butcher's store or of those Olympic weightlifters in Atlanta.

A story goes that as Bullets' head coach he got the team's attention one day by saying to his charges, "if any of you guys thinks he can take me, go ahead." There were no takers. But there was nothing different between that and his playing days.

At the outset he made the NBA his home. He played 36 minutes per game in his rookie season and went steadily up from there. His first year was Russell's last, and besides Bill the league was littered with big men like Chamberlain, Walt Bellamy, Reed, Nate Thurmond, Elvin Hayes and Wayne Embry. That's some litter. You'd have to argue your tail off to maintain that the competition in the pivot, with just 14 teams in the league, was ever better than that. So a rookie in the league had every right to a have bad year and write it off as intimidation.

Not Unseld. He averaged 18.2 rebounds and 13.8 points, winning Rookie of the Year *and* MVP in 1969. He lead Baltimore to a 57-win season it had never seen the likes of it before. The year prior to his arrival, Baltimore won 36 games.

The late sixties and early seventies featured several fevered rivalries, and none would get any better than Baltimore-New York. In that first year Unseld and the Bullets got swept out in four games by New York. It wasn't Unseld's fault: he upped his points (18.8), rebounds (18.5) and field goal percentage (.526) in the playoffs, but the Knicks were a better rounded team.

The following year the Knicks deflected the Bullets in seven. Here Unseld grabbed an astounding 23.6 rebounds a game but scored only 10.6 on .414 shooting. He had just 2 points in game seven. Willis Reed put up 21.3

points and 17.7 rebounds. While Willis' higher scoring would be a regular feature of this competition, Unseld was no slacker. With his team down two games to none, Unseld scored 23 points and grabbed 34 rebounds to lead them to victory in game three!

The next year he took the Bullets a step further, leading them to the Finals. The Bullets had accomplished the improbable, beating the Knicks in game seven at Madison Square Garden.

In the Finals against Milwaukee, Unseld gave the Bullets 15 points and 19 rebounds, but it wasn't enough to avert a Milwaukee sweep. He gave away eight inches to his 7-2 counterpart, Abdul-Jabbar, who logged 27 points and 18.5 rebounds.

Four years later the Bullets were back in the final round again, this time with the high-scoring duo of Elvin Hayes and Phil Chenier, both of whom averaged well over 20 points. They got additional scoring help from Mike Riordan and Kevin Porter was their assist man. They squared off against the Golden State Warriors. Unseld averaged 12 points and 17 rebounds but the Warriors executed down the stretch, putting the ball in Barry's hands when it counted, and ended up winning two one-point games. Phil Chenier gave the Bullets another 23 points, 5 rebounds and 5 assists and Hayes put up 21 points and 11 rebounds. Regardless of those efforts, Rick Barry owned the series and the Bullets, now in Washington, lost four close ones. That made two sweeps in a row. So the Bullets were still an also-ran. They were a consistently good playoff team, but at various times they lacked the one superstar and overall team excellence to overcome the better teams.

In 1978 the bridesmaid tag disappeared. The Seattle SuperSonics lead three games to two in the Finals, but the Bullets stormed back. They beat the Sonics by 35 points in game six and then got key contributions from Charles Johnson and Mitch Kupchak to win game seven in Seattle, 105-99. Unseld was selected the MVP for the series. "Unseld was our inspirational leader," Chenier recalls. "His outlet passing and rebounding — he was always dependable. He would go 40 or 46 minutes, setting picks, and doing all the little things you need done. He was the established leader of that team. He reinforced that leadership with his style of play and mannerisms on the court — and by age, too."

The Lakers current GM Mitch Kupchak played on that Washington team, too. "Unseld was the consummate team basketball player; his only objective was to win. Statistics were never ever important to him. You can't begin to imagine what he did to make his teammates better — set picks, made outlet passes, guarded the bigger center. He was the MVP of that series."

The Sonics took the Bullets in five in the 1979 Finals, winning because of the dominance of their guards, Dennis Johnson and Gus Williams. Johnson won the series MVP as the Sonics took four straight after the Bullets' opening game victory.

Age would soon catch up with the former MVP. During his 13th year in the league, Unseld could no longer play on one good leg and he called it quits. On March 16, 1981 he announced he'd be retiring at season's end. "All right-handed people do things off their left foot," he explained. "But when I hurt my left leg (in his second season, which was followed by a knee operation) I couldn't anymore, so I had to all of a sudden switch and do things off my right leg. It's awkward, but I had to do it if I wanted to keep playing. I knew it was only a matter of time before my right leg wore out. I'm surprised it lasted this long."

The appraisals followed his retirement announcement. "Wes was," said Red Auerbach, "the greatest outlet passer of them all, the only one I'd rate better than Russell." On that subject, Hubie Brown recalls how Unseld, with sportcoat still on, used to throw a 94-foot seed with that two-handed, over-the-head pass and hit the other backboard. "He was the greatest outlet passer in the history of the game," says Brown. "No man in history ever began more fast breaks with 50-foot outlet passes than Wes Unseld did," says Bob Ryan. Ryan also remembers the picks. "I will always think of Unseld's crunching picks," says Ryan. "Someone once said, 'he sets a pick and it takes you 24 seconds to run around it.'"

"He was a great passing center," said Bill Walton. "McAdoo, Unseld and Cowens were three guys who had totally different games than most centers. Unseld was a phenomenal passer. He could shoot the spot-up shot. He was not a power inside player. That was never his game. His game was team-work; rebounding, passing, very much like Russell's. Though he was not as mobile as Russell."

"With Walton and Russell he was *the* consummate outlet passer," Ryan sums up. "He was better on offense in his early years. Later in his career he stopped shooting altogether. If you ever saw him in college, you knew how good he was. I saw him when he was 6-7 and 235; he was solid and reasonably mobile then."

At the end he averaged 14 rebounds and 10.8 points per game. That puts him in a category with Thurmond and Russell, two other dominant centers who rebounded more than they scored. No, the Unseld style wasn't pretty. But it sure did bring results.

# Patrick**Ewing**

While David Robinson is a better shot blocker, rebounder and scorer than Ewing, Ewing just keeps on going, putting up numbers. He has played 12 years to Robinson's seven and will become only the 15th player to join the 20,000-10,000 club next season.

If Robinson can be criticized for not getting mentally tough when the game is on the line and for not taking a mediocre cast of characters to a championship, then consistency demands that those same critics give Ewing the same rap. At times it appears that Ewing relies exclusively on 17-footers and in 1996 his field goal percentage of .466 — the lowest of his career — proved that this perimeter game was drawing more iron than nylon. An 11-time All-Star, Ewing had a comeback year in 1997, hitting 49 percent of his shots and averaging 22 points and close to 11 rebounds.

People refer to the 35-year old as "the ultimate warrior." There is no question that Ewing is all of that. He owns just about every New York Knicks' record that you can name. He has been the franchise player on a team that would often have been hard-pressed to play .500 without him. But unless he gets a title over the next three years, while the window of opportunity is still open, what else will there be to talk about?

Far less talk surrounded his New York predecessor Willis Reed — mostly because basketball was a less popular game in the sixties and seventies — but Willis Reed was more productive. Reed played at a time when there were more great centers than there have been during Ewing's career. But Reed still flourished and seemed to grow larger as the games got bigger.

This is not the case with Ewing. As is the case with Admiral David, Ewing's field goal percentage drops off significantly in the post-season — from 51 percent to 48 percent. His crunch time free throw shooting frequently goes south, too. In the 1994 Finals Ewing shot an anemic .363 from the field against Olajuwon, and yet all one hears in New York was how Starks hit only 2 of 18 field goals attempts in game 7. In 7 out of his 9 post-seasons, Ewing's points per game dipped *below* that year's regular season total. All the cries are familiar by now. "He needs to get his head under the basket," "he misses important free throws" "he needs to come up big in the fourth quarter." And the litany continues.

But Knicks' management and people around the league tend to look at Ewing's career as half-full, rather than half-empty. There is evidence enough to justify that perspective. "I know it's a cliche, but Ewing is a warrior," says Matt Guokas. Ewing doesn't jump teams. He never said anything screwy like 'me and Starks are the Wilt and Hal Greer of the nineties.' He basically shuts up and plays big minutes. And the organization is treating the Garden as a place where smaller tress should be planted around their redwood. The acquisition of Larry Johnson, Chris Childs and Allan Houston in 1996 was very flattering to Ewing. In essence, the moves say 'you're our franchise player and we think enough of you to help you with all this high-priced talent.' Will it work? Only time will tell.

"Ewing works his ass off," says Bob Ryan, who put Ewing behind Bob Lanier in 13th place. "Ewing never gave up an easy basket or was guilty of a non-hustling moment on a basketball court. This goes back to high school, which I saw him play. He absolutely goes out there to play. It doesn't always come out the way people want, God knows. He's got a great turn-around jump shot in traffic. We want him to be a better rebounder, we want him to be better at a lot of things.

"His offensive game has broadened and I don't think he was done any favors by going to Georgetown in terms of his *offense*. It gave him some grounding as a person. Thompson retards all these guys; he just doesn't have any offensive sense. When Ewing got the 29 points in the championship game in 1982 when he was a freshman, you'd think a bell would have gone off in Thompson's head saying 'I've got to go to this guy; he's got to score 25 points a game for me the rest of his career, that's just gotta be.' Instead he averaged 15 and 14 a game there. Ewing's a great offensive player but they're just not going to win a title."

Said Bill Walton, "Ewing's great, a terrific player. He's worked really hard but never had the good teammates. This year will be a huge test for Ewing." And then the Knicks blew a three games-to-one lead against Miami in the conference semi-finals. Ewing and several other key players left the bench during a skirmish between Charlie Ward and P.J. Brown with seconds remaining in game five, which Miami already had salted away. Suspensions resulted to Ewing, Houston, Starks, Johnson and Ward and the Knicks lost the next two games.

The window of opportunity is open wide for the Knicks. But with a aging Ewing, don't expect the window to stay open forever.

# David**Robinson**

Mr. Robinson, or "St. David," as he was facetiously referred to in a *Sports Illustrated* cover story, has done some amazing things. But those amazing things have been overridden of late by harsh criticisms.

First the accomplishments. He is 32, despite having played only seven years. He hadn't completed his military obligation to the Navy and so he was 24 years old in his first season. He won the Rookie of the Year award right out of the gate and hasn't stopped earning big distinctions since. Scoring

2,000 points in an NBA season requires night-in, night-out scoring plus durability. And Robinson averaged that many for *seven* years, before playing only six games in the 1996-1997 season due to an injury. He also rebounds, blocks shots and has made four appearances each on the All-Defensive team and the All-NBA team. He's also won an MVP (1995), led the league in scoring (1994) and is routinely among the top of the centers in assists. "You step back and say, 'What's wrong with this guy?'" says Hubie Brown. "He averages 26 points and 12 rebounds for his career. He's loved by his teammates and is probably the quickest and most athletic center ever to play. But because of his team's lack of ability to win a championship..."

"David is ahead of Hakeem Olajuwon at similar stages in their careers," says Bill Walton. "Hakeem's team went to the Finals in just his second year in the league (1986 against Boston) and then there was a long dry spell there." The dry spell lasted eight years, until they went to the Finals in 1994 and won the championship. "Robinson already has an MVP. He's been an All-Star every single year, everything."

If you asked the first ten fans you saw who had the better career numbers, Olajuwon or Robinson, nine of ten would answer that is was Olajuwon. They'd be right as far as totals are concerned but wrong as far as *averages* are concerned. Robinson's career points per game (25.5) and field goal percentage (.53) are higher than Olajuwon's. Yet the prevailing wisdom says that Olajuwon is the best center in the league.

Why? Several reasons. One, Olajuwon appears the more dominant center. "They're both tough but Hakeem's tougher," says Patrick Ewing. "Olajuwon's more a post-up player like myself," said Hall of Fame center Wes Unseld. "Of the centers now I would pick Olajuwon," says Brown.

Two, Olajuwon has that other thing you never stop hearing of: a ring — two to be exact. But it took him ten years to get his first and also ten years for an MVP. Robinson, whose eighth year was a wash out, probably won't get two titles over the next two seasons.

Third, there's a question about Robinson's toughness, especially in playoff competition. He fades in playoff games. He doesn't raise his game as he needs to. They never level such a criticism against Olajuwon. And it's obvious why. Robinson has played in 53 career playoff games and Olajuwon has played in 115. Here are their playoff records:

|  | F.G. PCT. | P.P.G. | R.P.G. |
|---|---|---|---|
| Robinson | .49 | 24.0 | 11.8 |
| Olajuwon | .54 | 27.3 | 11.6 |

Both Robinson's field goal percentage and his points per game are less than his career regular season averages. His regular season percentage of .526 is significantly better than his playoff average of .488. And 25.6 points per game during the regular season is also significantly different than his 24 points per game during the playoffs. And in the losing effort to Utah in the second round of the 1996 playoffs, Robinson and the Spurs looked feeble, averaging just 83.9 points per game. Robinson shot .475 from the field, .580 from the foul line and averaged just 19.3 points and 9.2 rebounds. And Utah has no dominant center to defend him!

Olajuwon, on the other hand, ups his career average of 24.2 to 27.3 during the playoffs and raises his field goal percentage of .52 to .54. His playoff demolition of Robinson in 1995 is the stuff of legends.

In Robinson's defense one might ask: who has he played with? His supporting cast since 1989 isn't about to make opposing coaches run and hide. But does he need to change his style of play in fourth quarters or for the playoffs. "I think it's his teammates; he's never had the great teammates," says Walton.

Bob Ryan won't let Robinson off that easy. "David Robinson is a seven-foot-two, wonderful, graceful athlete who doesn't have the heart of a center. If he had what Cowens had and Russell had, then he'd be up there in the top six. (Ryan's top six all-time are Bill Walton, Russell, Chamberlain, Abdul-Jabbar, Thurmond and Olajuwon). He would just step right ahead of everyone. He just settles for something less; I don't know what it is."

Anyone who watched the Spurs' offense against Utah in 1996 must acknowledge that there's truth in Ryan's remarks. Ryan says what a lot of people are thinking. Throw in the poor playoff performances and we might conclude that this officer is too much of a gentleman. His mental toughness is questionable at crucial times. In mentioning his fifteenth best center of all-time, Ryan picks Bill Laimbeer, saying "he got more out of less than any of these centers here, including Dave Cowens, who was only 6-8 but could jump." But then he praises Laimbeer's fire: "It really mattered to him who won the game; a lot more than it did to Robinson.

"I think Dennis Rodman has Robinson pegged," Ryan continues. "He should quit now and go into the clergy. In his book, Rodman is tough on Robinson. He's a wonderful *man* but the act is wearing thin on the basketball court." Until he wins, Robinson, a born-again Christian, is likely to hear the usual murmurs about born-again athletes and their supposed less than all-out desire to win. If that is true, then Robinson will have to make some changes. Perhaps the addition of Tim Duncan will get San Antonio the help they need.

"David Robinson is going to have to play well in the playoffs," says

Gminski. "He's established himself and won an MVP. But especially recently, he has not played well in the playoffs. I've seen him do incredible things and then in the playoffs he disappears."

Robinson should have at least five years left if he desires to play that long. Who was it that said "slow and steady wins the race?" An NBA title would surely add to his already impressive list of distinctions.

# Nate**Thurmond**

Nate Thurmond played with as even a balance between offense and defense as anyone who ever played. When he is remembered at all, Thurmond's calling card is the way that he played defense on Kareem Abdul-Jabbar. This is a worthy accomplishment in itself, and the reputation is firmly established by Kareem's own testimony. But to hear some people talk, you'd think that Thurmond never did anything else but make things difficult for Jabbar in the first five years of his career.

He did a lot of other things. His points almost match his rebounds. Check this out: in 14 seasons he scored 14,437 points and logged 14,464 rebounds. That's a virtual dead heat. His career points per game were 15.0 and his rebounds per game were 15.0. Despite this impressively democratic attention to offense and defense, Thurmond is one of the NBA's forgotten men.

Too bad. It is now 20 years since Nate retired and that's part of the reason for his reputation fading into the past. The other reason is that as tall as Thurmond played, there were always taller trees on the landscape. When he began with the San Francisco Warriors, they already had a guy named Chamberlain in the pivot. Wilt averaged 46 minutes that season and it's a wonder that Nate logged any playing time at all. But he played some forward and averaged 26 minutes a game and contributed 10.4 rebounds a game, making the NBA Rookie Team.

But Thurmond was surrounded by excellence. "I played against Thurmond a little bit," says Bill Walton. "He was a great all-around basketball player. Like Bellamy, he was often lost in the attention that was given to Russell and Chamberlain and Jabbar. He had all the skills. He could shoot, rebound, block shots, everything."

Since those who watched the game were immersed in the epic battles between Chamberlain and Russell, Thurmond was never chosen All-NBA First Team or MVP. Then, mid-way through his career, Abdul-Jabbar came into the league.

But Nate had quite a career before Jabbar came along and quite a career afterward. At the All-Star break during the 1964-1965 season the Warriors decided they could no longer handle the $200,000 salary of Chamberlain and traded him to Philadelphia.

Thurmond then began a *nine-year* run of years which deserve a second look:

### NATE THURMOND: 1965-1973

|      | PPG  | RPG  | APG | TOTAL OFFENSIVE PRODUCTION |
|------|------|------|-----|----------------------------|
| 1965 | 16.5 | 18.1 | 2.0 | 36.6 |
| 1966 | 16.3 | 18.0 | 1.5 | 35.8 |
| 1967 | 18.7 | 21.3 | 2.6 | 42.6 |
| 1968 | 20.5 | 22.0 | 4.2 | 46.7 |
| 1969 | 21.5 | 19.7 | 3.6 | 44.8 |
| 1970 | 21.9 | 17.7 | 3.5 | 43.1 |
| 1971 | 20.0 | 13.8 | 3.1 | 36.9 |
| 1972 | 21.4 | 16.1 | 2.9 | 40.4 |
| 1973 | 17.1 | 17.1 | 3.5 | 37.7 |

While all the league MVPs between 1965 and 1973 (in fact, right through 1980!) were won by centers, Thurmond was putting up these totals. Russell (1965), Chamberlain (1966-1968), Unseld (1969), Reed (1970), Abdul-Jabbar (1971-1972) and Cowens (1973) won the MVP during these nine years. But look at what Thurmond was doing. Averaging 20 points and 20 rebounds in 1968, Thurmond accomplished something done by just three other players — Wilt Chamberlain, Bob Pettit and Jerry Lucas. Thurmond had an accurate turn-around jumper. And that's just the offense.

Thurmond was no shrinking violet while defending. Said Willis Reed about Thurmond, "I scored my fewest points against him. When the ball went away from most guys, you were open. When the ball went away against Nate, he went with you." So while Reed could drill the 18-footer against centers who didn't follow him away from the paint, he couldn't against Thurmond.

And then there were "Nate the Great's" contests against Abdul-Jabbar. Thurmond had Kareem's number from the outset. "The first time Kareem came to the West Coast, he was playing Wilt down in Los Angeles the night before he was coming to San Francisco," Thurmond told Chuck Connors on a "Where are They Now?" feature produced by NBA Entertainment. "I was about 23, 24 years old (actually, he was 28 in Kareem's rookie year). I really didn't need sleep, but I needed an advantage. So I got on a flight and flew down and watched that game. I could see, that night, the moves that he tried to do, or didn't do, against Wilt and what he liked to do best.

"The next night, the first time I played against Kareem, he only got 13 or 14 points. And that one game helped me for the next 10 years."

In two crucial spots Thurmond put the clamps on Kareem and brought his sky hook back down to earth. In the Western Conference Semifinals in 1972, Milwaukee won 4 games to 1 over Golden State (who had changed their name from San Francisco in 1971). "Thurmond," wrote *San Francisco Chronicle* beat writer Gary Tobin, "went into the series expecting to hold Jabbar to 25 to 30 points per game. He held him to 21 on a poor percentage of 40, but still the Warriors lost...When Kareem went to his right for a hook, Thurmond was there; when Kareem fell back for a jump shot, Thurmond was there. And, finally, went to his left for a hook, Thurmond was not only there but slapped the shot back in his face." Said Thurmond afterward, "I could do it because I think I'm the best defensive center in the league. I don't think I could psyche him, but I know he knew I was there, you dig?"

I dig. Seventies-speak and all, that was accurate. And he did it against Jabbar again the next year. This time Golden State knocked Milwaukee out in six in the semis. And again Thurmond held Jabbar to 22.8 points on 43 percent shooting, far less than his 55 percent shooting for the year. Nate's teammates were a little over-zealous in the aftermath. "Right now," said Warrior guard Jeff Mullin, "Nate Thurmond has to be regarded as the top center in pro basketball." "This was almost like winning the World Series of baseball," said Thurmond afterward. "Of course, I know it isn't as big as that because I'm well aware we have a long way to go."

Indeed they did. The elation of the Warriors — who had Rick Barry and Cazzie Russell besides Mullin and Thurmond — was short lived. In the

Western Finals against L.A. they lost in five games.

Thurmond was traded to the Bulls for Clifford Ray and a first round draft pick after the 1974 season. Too bad for him. The following year, Barry led the Warriors to an NBA championship. With Chicago — and later Cleveland — Thurmond's teams would never challenge for a title.

But he had done enough. He retired after the 1977 season and his legacy lives on in the words of Kareem Abdul-Jabbar. "He was agile and quick and played aggressive defense really well. He positioned himself well. At the beginning of my career Nate Thurmond played great defense on me. A lot of people beat up on me and said they played great defense. Nate really did. Nate was the first and Walton second."

That from the player with the sky hook, the single greatest scoring weapon in league history. Thurmond seemed to get into Jabbar's chest and straighten him up on that shot. Wilt Chamberlain also said that Thurmond was the greatest defender he played against. Nate should be remembered for that, and for everything else he did.

# Walt**Bellamy**

It has been said that "timing is everything." If that is the case, then everything would have been different for Walt Bellamy if he had different timing. As a talented center, his career could not have begun at a worse time. "He had longevity, he played a lot of years," said Matt Guokas. "He just came along at a time when Chamberlain and Russell were dominating and Thurmond, too."

Though Rookie of the Year with the Chicago Packers in the 1961-1962 season, Bellamy was a third wheel in the NBA. The basketball world was more attuned to the exploits of Russell and Chamberlain than they were to the 31.6 points, 19 rebounds and .519 field goal percentage that Bellamy accomplished that year. The field goal percentage was then an a*ll-time record*, and seemed like the only significant record that Chamberlain did not hold.

Despite that impressive achievement, Bellamy is only talked about in connection with the knees he stuck out on picks, the elbows he threw and the horrendous teams he played on. Once reputations like that are entrenched, aided by those who write the game's unofficial "official" history, then a player, even a gifted player, hardly has a chance.

"I should eliminate him," said Phil Chenier, "since he stuck his knees out when he set picks." Jack Ramsay and Hubie Brown also grumble about his temperament.

And while no one knows about the field goal percentage, everyone knows about "the trade." In 14 years Bellamy is most famous for getting traded from New York to Detroit with Howard Komives for Dave DeBusschere in December of 1968. Next to that he is known for never having played on a winner. True. He played for six teams in 14 years and not one of them was memorable. And he holds an unusual record, playing 89 games in the 1968-1969 season as a result of the trade. I'm about to revive some of the respectable things about Bellamy's career. I can hear the groans, already.

First off, I want compare his first four years in the league to the first four years of another center of note, Shaquille O'Neal.

### WALT BELLAMY's FIRST FOUR YEARS

|  | GAMES | MINUTES | FG PCT. | PPG | RPG | APG | TOTAL OFF. PROD. |
|---|---|---|---|---|---|---|---|
| 1962 | 79 | 43.5 | .519* | 31.6 | 19.0 | 2.7 | 53.3 |
| 1963 | 80 | 41.3 | .527 | 27.9 | 16.4 | 2.9 | 47.2 |
| 1964 | 80 | 42.4 | .513 | 27.0 | 17.0 | 1.6 | 45.6 |
| 1965 | 80 | 41.3 | .509 | 24.8 | 14.6 | 2.4 | 41.8 |
| AVG. YR. | 80 | 41.8 | .517 | 27.8 | 16. | 72.4 | 46.9 |

And now O'Neal:

### SHAQUILLE ONEAL's FIRST FOUR YEARS

|  | GAMES | MINUTES | FG PCT. | PPG | RPG | APG | TOTAL OFF. PROD. |
|---|---|---|---|---|---|---|---|
| 1993 | 81 | 37.9 | .562 | 23.4 | 13.9 | 1.9 | 39.2 |
| 1994 | 81 | 39.8 | .599* | 29.3 | 13.2 | 2.4 | 44.9 |
| 1995 | 79 | 37.0 | .583 | 29.3* | 11.4 | 2.7 | 43.4 |
| 1996 | 54 | 36.0 | .573 | 26.6 | 11.0 | 2.9 | 40.5 |
| AVG YR. | 74 | 37.8 | .582 | 27.2 | 12.5 | 2.4 | 42.1 |

Shaquille O'Neal leads Bellamy in only one category, field goal percentage. He shows up for less games, plays less minutes in those games, averages *slightly* less points, far fewer rebounds and has a 42.1 T.O.P. compared to Bellamy's 46.9. O'Neal's blocks and rebounds have dropped off each year. No wonder that Bob Ryan points out, "Shaq is a disgracefully sub-par rebounder for a man of his size."

So if you're going to line-up around the block to praise Shaquille O'Neal, as members of the frequently cheerleading media do, then you must be consistent and not denounce players who did even more than he did. O'Neal was voted to the list of the best 50 players of all-time, after having played just four NBA seasons. Many of us would like to know the rationale for that selection. I suspect it was based more on marketing than on merit. Meanwhile, Bellamy was left out.

Not everyone in Bellamy's time denounced him. In *Tall Tales* former Laker's coach Fred Schaus recalls the Lakers squads in the 1960s and what the team lacked.

*I tried to trade for a center a couple of times, but I wouldn't give up Elgin or Jerry. Those guys were great players, the guys who got us to the championship. Once, I thought we had a trade worked out for Walter Bellamy, but that fell through. Walter was no superstar, but put him in the middle and we would have been a different team. Even without a big-time center, we nearly beat them (the Celtics) in 1966.*

If you give Bellamy's points and rebounds and presence in the middle to the Lakers, they would probably have won one of those titles against the Celtics.

And Chamberlain talked about how difficult it was to score points in the early sixties when there were only eight teams in the league and he had to go against Johnny Kerr, Bill Russell, Wayne Embry, Nate Thurmond and Walt Bellamy eleven times a year each.

Bellamy is also a member of one of the most exclusive clubs in basketball history, "The 20,000-10,000 Club." Here are the members of that exclusive club.

### "THE 20,000-10,000 CLUB"
#### Players with 20,000 Points + 10,000 Rebounds

| | POINTS | REBOUNDS | TOTAL PTS. + REBS. |
|---|---|---|---|
| Abdul-Jabbar | 38,387 | 17,440 | 55,827 |
| Chamberlain* | 31,419 | 23,924 | 55,343 |
| M. Malone | 29,580 | 17,834 | 47,414 |
| Hayes | 27,313 | 16,279 | 43,592 |
| Gilmore | 24,941 | 16,330 | 41,271 |
| Erving | 30,026 | 10,525 | 40,551 |
| Issel | 27,482 | 11,133 | 38,615 |
| Parish | 23,334 | 14,715 | 38,049 |
| K. Malone | 25,592 | 10,542 | 36,134 |
| Olajuwon | 23,650 | 11,739 | 35,389 |
| Bellamy | 20,941 | 14,241 | 35,182 |
| Baylor | 23,149 | 11,463 | 34,612 |
| Pettit | 20,880 | 12,849 | 33,729 |
| Barkley | 21,756 | 11,027 | 32,783 |

*\* Wilt Chamberlain is the only member of the 20,000-20,000 club and the 30,000-30,000 club.*

There are only 14 members of the 20,000-10,000 group and Bellamy is in eleventh place among all those who ever played if you add their points and rebounds. If you didn't know the name but learned that it took Olajuwon and Karl Malone until 1997 to surpass him in this category, wouldn't you place him among the top fifty of all-time? The answer is obvious.

Bob Ryan quotes George Kiseda, who covered the NBA for the *Philadelphia Bulletin.* "Kiseda once said, 'Walt Bellamy is the skeleton in the closet of the 20,000-point club.'" Still, everyone on the 20,000 point list is either in the Hall of Fame or on their way. Though Bellamy retired in 1975, he was not elected to the Hall of Fame until 1993. That delay was too long in coming. Bob Lanier was elected in 1991, long before Walt Bellamy and his statistics were *not even close* to Bellamy's. Neither player won a title, so what is the rationale for putting the one player in but not the other?

The answer, I think, is that a groundswell of opinion begins for one player, or *against* another and a bandwagon effect occurs. Perhaps we feel for one player because he never played on a winner. Public opinion seems to embrace some players and reject others, often for insubstantial reasons.

Walt Bellamy owns some of the best numbers of any center than ever played. He also has another little known distinction, since the Chicago packers of 1961-1962 were the very first team to play five black players on the court at once. In *Tall Tales* former official Pete D'Ambrosio recalls officiating the 1961 game and the five players were Woody Sauldsberry, Horace Walker, Walt Bellamy, Andy Johnson and Sihugo Green.

The omission of Bellamy is yet another case in which the experts missed the boat. He belongs on the list of the greatest centers and I hope that this information will change some minds about him. "Walt Bellamy was a terrific player," said Bill Walton. "But he played in the shadow of Russell and Chamberlain. The focus was on them. Those were two guys who defined the game, really."

In 1983, ten years before Bellamy was elected to the Hall of Fame, another Hall of Famer wrote a letter on his behalf. The letter said:

> *In 1965-1966, his first year in New York, Walt led the Knickerbockers and placed fifth in the league in both scoring (23.2) and rebounding (16.0). During the four years that Walt played in New York, he averaged 18.9 points and 13.4 rebounds. In each of those years, Bellamy finished in the top ten in rebounding. His four-year scoring average is fourth best in Knickerbockers' history behind Bob McAdoo, Richie Guerin and Walt Frazier.*
>
> *Walt was a major contributor here in New York with the Knickerbockers as I am sure his statistics indicate. I hope this information on Walt will be useful in your overall evaluation of his fine NBA career.*

The letter, written on New York Knicks stationery, was signed: "Sincerely, Dave DeBusschere, Executive Vice President." The man whose trade helped make the Knicks a champion recognized the value of the player he was traded for. "Bells was an all-around player," said Nate Thurmond, who played many games against Bellamy. "He could drive around you, shoot the jumper, block shots, rebound." Bellamy is the second of three players with 20,000 points and 10,000 rebounds ranked here to be left off the NBA's top fifty list. They left off a combined six players who either 25,000 points or scored 20,000 points and grabbed 10,000 rebounds.

Should we demand another vote?

# Bob**McAdoo**

Bob McAdoo was an offensive force in the 1970s, one of just four centers in the history of the game to win three or more consecutive scoring titles. This he did for the Buffalo Braves in 1974, 1975 and 1976, leading a good team into the playoffs in those years. With McAdoo, Jim McMillan, Randy Smith, Gar Heard, Ernie DiGregorio and Jack Marin, the Braves were a fun team.

Matt Guokas played on Buffalo for 27 games that season. "I played with McAdoo in Buffalo for about six weeks. He was not really a true center. But he could play like a forward and was a great jump shooter. I think that the thing that always impressed me about Bob was that he played as hard in practice as he did in the game. Every time he stepped on the basketball court he had the same temperament. It really rubbed off on his teammates. You just don't see that, because everyone has that feeling in practice that you go to a certain level and stop there. Consequently, practices under Jack Ramsay were very short, an hour at most, because these guys were all tired."

"Bob McAdoo's ability to get a shot off with minimal daylight was better than any player's I've ever seen," said Bob Ryan. "He was too quick for most of these guys to guard him at the center spot. He had great battles with Cowens. Cowens would take him down and pound him low, and he would take Cowens out."

"McAdoo was an incredibly tough scorer," says Guokas. "He really shot a jump shot and got up in the air and it really took a toll. Bob was a good rebounder, too," says Guokas, "he had the long arms." While people tend to remember McAdoo as a great scorer and indifferent at the game's other skills, that isn't really true. In the years he did his best scoring, he was rebounding awfully well. Not convinced? Take a look at these seven seasons from 1974 through 1980.

### McADOO: 1974-1980

|      | MINUTES | PPG   | RPG  | APG | TOTAL OFFENSIVE PRODUCTION |
|------|---------|-------|------|-----|----------------------------|
| 1974 | 43.0    | 30.6* | 15.1 | 2.3 | 48.0                       |
| 1975 | 43.2*   | 34.5* | 14.1 | 2.2 | 50.8                       |
| 1976 | 42.7    | 31.1* | 12.4 | 4.0 | 47.5                       |
| 1977 | 38.9    | 25.8  | 12.9 | 2.8 | 41.5                       |
| 1978 | 40.3    | 26.5  | 12.8 | 3.8 | 3.1                        |
| 1979 | 37.2    | 24.8  | 8.7  | 2.8 | 36.3                       |
| 1980 | 36.2    | 21.1  | 8.1  | 3.4 | 32.6                       |

"True center" or not, those numbers tell the truth. From 1974 through 1978 he was always ranked between third and eighth in the league in rebounds. "His real run was very short," Bob Ryan points out. But that great seven-year run was only ended by injuries.

"When people look at him they think of him as a big forward, but for many years he was always a center," says Hubie Brown. "He was the heart and soul of that Buffalo team." Especially in the playoffs. In 1974 they took the Celtics to six games. "He had great series and put up some of the best scoring games I've ever seen," Ryan recalls. "Buffalo got what they should have. Boston was better and Buffalo pushed them to two very excellent six-game series." In the 1974 series, won by the Celtics in six, McAdoo averaged 31.7 points and 13.7 rebounds. The Celtics went on to win the title.

The following year Buffalo took Unseld and the Bullets to seven games in the eastern semi-finals. McAdoo was completely out of control. He scored 50 in game four to bring the series even. He averaged 37.4 for the series, to go with 13.4 rebounds. But Washington, on their way to the Finals, won in seven games.

In 1976 the Celtics took them in six again. McAdoo "slumped" to 28 points per game and the Celtics went on to win the title. "He and Cowens would really go at it," Guokas says. From an individual standpoint, McAdoo's last six years in the NBA were uneventful. He never averaged more than 15 points a game. But he was traded to the Lakers in December, 1981, just in time for their 1982 championship. He was also with them in 1985 when they won the title. "At the end he was able to get the two titles," says Brown. "He played the back of that 1-3-1 Lakers trap, which was the best I've seen to this day. McAdoo had the jumping ability and foot quickness. In high school he jumped 6'9". Unfortunately he ended his career in Europe (in Italy, playing from 1987 through 1993). He refused to play as a backup in the United States for what he considered limited money."

"McAdoo's game was just offensive brilliance," says Walton. "He was just a phenomenal, flat-out scorer. He could score at will. Not in a power game, but in a finesse game; facing the basket and in a transition game. Bob McAdoo was a very special player. In my opinion he is a cinch NBA Hall of Famer.

"He didn't have the bulk for the inside game. He would give up 50 and 60 pounds to everybody inside."

So he went outside and made people chase him. No center ever shot jumpers off the dribble like McAdoo. And few players at any position matched his output as a scorer. He played with seven teams in his career and that blemished his record a bit. The Knicks traded him to the Celtics for draft picks, one of whom turned out to be Bill Cartwright. And the Celtics were happy to be rid of him. They disliked his selfish concern with points and minutes and lack of concern with what Red Auerbach called "the Celtic ways," which Dave Cowens was trying to teach McAdoo for the last 20 games of the year in 1979. The Celtics then traded him to Detroit. From there he went to New Jersey, Los Angeles and finished with Philadelphia.

But his travelling ways didn't erase his legacy of scoring, one of the most awesome in NBA history. McAdoo was another great left off the NBA's list of the top fifty players. He complained that he was the only league MVP winner — an award he won in 1975 — not to make the NBA's list. He might also have added that he had three consecutive scoring titles, a feat accomplished by only five other players in NBA history.

# Robert**Parrish**

After playing 21 seasons in the NBA, Robert Parish announced his retirement on August 25th, 1997. Playing his last season with the Chicago Bulls, Parish had been around since the end of the Gerald Ford administration. He finished with a record 1,611 games played. The *NBA Register* also claims that he holds the record for "most defensive rebounds" (now 10,117), but Chamberlain, Russell, Abdul-Jabbar, Hayes and Moses Malone certainly had more than that, though the league didn't start keeping offensive and defensive rebound stats until the 1973-1974 season.

Aside from records based on longevity, Robert Parish doesn't hold any records. He is the Don Sutton of basketball. Sutton pitched 23 years and won 324 games. What is remarkable about that is that Sutton won 20 games only once and at no time was the best pitcher in the game. So, too, Robert Parish was never the best center in the game.

But like Sutton, Parish played well for a long, long time and by virtue of playing so long and well had a Hall of Fame career. Mike Gminski picks him sixth best all-time among centers. He was broadcasting Hornets' games during Parish's two-year stay in Charlotte. "I've played against him and seen him play here for the last two years," says Gminski. "They should put his body in the Smithsonian when he passes away. There has been an appreciable drop-off in his skills, still I don't think anyone can comprehend what it means to be 43 and running up and down the court."

"He's had incredible longevity," says Bob Ryan, who picks Parish as the ninth greatest center of all-time. "He had the great turn-around jump shot and incredible ability to run the floor." Parish's first four years in Golden State were uneventful. Then he was traded in June, 1980 and began a 14-year stay with Boston. Said Ryan, "the big difference in Boston was that Bill Fitch exploited his great ability, which for some reason Al Attles (in Golden State) didn't want to do. Fitch encouraged him to run and made him part of the deal. And he got caught up in the whole Boston thing and became a better player. That was a great run in Boston."

With a jumper that went so high it came down moist, Parish shot a very high percentage of his shots and was the anchor of the greatest front line ever assembled. He played with Bird and McHale and outlasted both of them. "Playing with Bird and McHale overshadowed a lot of what he did," says Gminski. "It was unfortunate, for whenever there was a lull up in Boston, he was the target. And I don't think that was deserved."

Not for a guy who gave Boston double-digits in points and rebounds eight different years. "He was just getting started in Golden State," said Walton. "But we loved the Chief. He was a great player and a very determined person." And the Celtics of the eighties didn't win a title without him.

Boston's getting Parish is a swindle that matches the Lufthansa heist and the Brinks job multiplied. In 1980 Boston got Parish and Mchale for Joe Barry Carroll and Ricky Brown. The Celtics had won 13 titles to that point. By 1986 they would own three more.

In *Drive*, Larry Bird's autobiography, he told Bob Ryan:

> *There's no question that Parish and McHale made us a better team. Once Dave (Cowens) retired and Robert got in shape, he showed us he was going to be a great player. He was filling the*

*lanes on our fast break, he was dunking, he was blocking shots and he had a good outlet pass.*

*Then when you brought Kevin off the bench, it was double doses of everything. Kevin was the total package. He also rebounded and blocked shots and ran the break — and he was a killer inside. We didn't really have a shot blocker the year before. The only team with fewer rejections than us was San Diego. When Robert and Kevin showed up, we went right to second place in blocks, trailing only San Antonio. Their presence certainly made me a much better defensive player. I could now guard anybody I wanted to because I knew I could run my man to either one of those big men.*

And then there was his offense. "His baseline jump shot falls into the category of the unstoppable" said Mike Gminski. "The guy held the ball straight up. I couldn't block it with a broom." With that shot and solid defense and rebounding, Parish could help you in many ways. "What a nice, solid package, an all-around player," said Bob Ryan. To prove Ryan's point, in nine of his first eleven seasons in Boston, Parish made the All-Star team.

He finished his career with another team that has a dynastic run. After his 21st season ended with a title, he retired.

# Artis**Gilmore**

For most experts, the first adjective that comes to mind in describing Artis Gilmore is "strong." "He was definitely one of the strongest guys I ever played," said Mike Gminski. "One time I was driving down the lane. Gilmore took the charge and caught me in mid-air and just kind of put me down. I was 250 pounds at the time. He had amazing strength and not real refined offensive moves. But he was a bull around the basket."

He was a bull in both leagues. He began his career in 1971 and played for 17 years. The first five were in the ABA with the Kentucky Colonels and then he played 12 more years with Chicago and San Antonio and Boston.

During that time he put up 24,041 points and 16,330 rebounds, good enough for fifth place in history if you add the two numbers. Still, he was a third member of the 20,000-10,000 club that the NBA left off their list of the 50 best all-time.

"He was number 11 for me," said Gminski. "He had this one move, facing the basket on the right side and would wing into the lane with his hand and take the ball and hit you in the chest and make you fall back and then continue on up with the shot. He'd push you out and he was so strong that you couldn't knock the ball out of his hand. A lot of people tried to tomahawk the ball. And he didn't get the offensive foul call. That was his thing; he'd get away with it."

Matt Guokas recalls Gilmore playing in Chicago. "Moses Malone, who was very strong, had all kinds of problems playing against Artis inside. Moses was able to out duel him because of his quickness and relentlessness. He was just more natural than Artis. But he certainly had his problems with the size and strength of Artis Gilmore.

"He was a tough scorer in that right box. He would turn in on you and get you with that hook shot." Gilmore did not make Bill Walton's list of the top centers. But Walton admits, "nothing conventional ever worked against Artis. He was beyond the boundaries because he was so big and so strong."

But enough praise for the 7-2, 265-pound center. Bob Ryan watched Gilmore for years and even caught the last 47 games of Gilmore's career in Boston. "A simple fact of life is that Artis Gilmore played basketball for one reason: he was 7-foot-2. I guarantee that if he was 6-2, he wouldn't have gone near the court. They wouldn't have dragged him near it. He did not like to play. He was not interested. He would rather scuba dive! A nice man but he did have the killer instinct. He had mechanical, easy to stop moves. He was amazingly strong, that body was well-proportioned and boy, he was strong. But he was mechanical, boring and just ultimately beatable by people who cared more." Peter May, then of the Hartford Courant, dubbed Gilmore "Rigor Artis."

"He would never take the next step as far as making his teammates better," says Matt Guokas. "And he wasn't as good a passer as he could have been." What about his leading the league in rebounding four times in the ABA and his 1975 title with Kentucky? "There weren't that many good centers in the ABA," Guokas replies.

No doubt about it. But Gilmore still had a long and notable career. He played in six NBA All-Star games and five others in the ABA. He blocked shots in both leagues and still holds the ABA record for blocks in a year, 422 in 1972. That same year he won the league MVP. He also led the NBA with

366 blocks in 1978. Only Parish, Abdul-Jabbar and Moses Malone played more than Gilmore, who performed for 1,329 games. But his averages in points (22.3 to 17.1) and rebounds (17.1 to 10.1) did drop off significantly in the NBA. His .582 field goal percentage is first all-time among all players who have attempted 5,000 or more shots. Only Mark West is ahead of Gilmore in lifetime field goal percentage, but West attempts less than 5 shots per game for his career.

At no time was Gilmore the best center in the NBA. That's alright. He played long enough and well enough to deserve the last slot among the centers.

# Ten**More**

## 1. Earl Monroe

The hardest player to omit. To my mind Monroe was the most exciting player that ever lived, including Jordan. This is because Monroe's excitement had a build-up, lasting about fifteen to twenty seconds. While Jordan scores in a flash, Monroe worked hard for every edge, like a fullback grounding out yardage. His offense had a beginning (spin dribbling side to side) a middle, (pump faking and twirling in the lane) and an end (a shot — usually below the foul line — which he barely got off) which created great anticipation and drama. Not blessed with great foot speed or leaping ability, he nonetheless was a devastating one-on-one player who shot better with guys draped all over him and hands in his face than he did wide open.

He got his championship in 1973 with New York, proving wrong the rap that he could only play solo and not with a team.

## 2. Neil Johnston

If you haven't heard of him, then look him up. Johnston's three straight scoring titles in the early fifties (one of only six players in NBA history to do so) and a world championship with the Philadelphia Warriors in 1956 put him over the top for me. Says Matt Guokas: "Neil had a fabulous hook shot. He had a sweeping hook not on the right baseline but going toward it, at a 45-degree angle, and he would kiss it off the glass. He had a beautiful touch. He was a battler, about 6-8.

"As a kid growing up, one of the saddest things I ever saw as a spectator — or ever was a part of — was when Neil's career was winding down and Russell's was just starting. In Convention Hall in 1958 Neil took a hook shot — and he used to be able to get that shot off on anybody, but Russell had the long arms and I remember Neil coming across the lane and Russell blocking the shot and Neil crumbled. He had injured his knee. He looked so surprised to see that and his career was effectively over after that." He retired at 30 years old.

Neil Johnston died in 1978.

## 3. Sam Jones

Sam Jones' numbers provide only a glimmer of how good he was. Jones was an integral part of the championship Celtics of the 1960s and when he started getting big minutes, his stats also improved. Said Bob Ryan: "Sam

Jones is the single most underrated guard in the history of the Hall of Fame. What a modern player he was; the most explosive first step ever, a clutch shooter and never asked to take the big shot. They'd say 'take the big shot' and he'd say "oh, all right."

## 4. Lenny Wilkens

Play word association and people no doubt will think of Lenny Wilkens the coach, who began the 1996-1997 season having won 1,014 games since 1969. But Wilkens the player was a sight to behold.

He played on three undistinguished teams — St. Louis, Seattle and Cleveland. "He ran those teams superbly," said Ryan. "People have no idea today about how he played. He was great on the drive and was incredibly acrobatic and one of the great pickpockets of his time." He drove left, defenders knew he was going to drive left and he got by them anyway.

## 5. Hal Greer

Second in scoring and minutes on the famous Philadelphia championship team of 1967, Greer had a stellar career, scoring 21,586 points in his 15-year career. How good was he? In 10 of those years he was an All-Star and won the MVP of the game in 1968. He is the all-time leading scorer for the Philadelphia 76ers.

"Look how many times (seven) he was All NBA Second-Team," said Bob Ryan. "Why was he second team? Because he was up against Oscar and Jerry. That was his heyday. He was a very reliable guy. With Hal Greer there were few 40-point games and few 10-point games. If they played 82, I bet that Hal Greer was good for 18 to 28 points 65 times a year! Every night you're getting that from Hal Greer. And who can forget the great little signature pull-up jump shot." Close in the alphabet, Goodrich and Greer are also close in scoring, Greer managed 21,586 points in his career and was rewarded by being elected to the Hall of Fame in 1981.

## 6. Gail Goodrich

Left-handed money for the Lakers from 1970 through 1976.

Check the morning papers — late edition only on the east coast — and you routinely found that West got 38 and Goodrich 33 more the night before. The lefty stroke from the key area was Goodrich's deadliest weapon, but he had others. Says Bob Ryan: I just loved Gail Goodrich. First of all, I'm a total sucker for small guys who can post up. Gail Goodrich is the greatest post-up guard I've ever seen. Tiny could do it, too, by the way.

"He and West averaged 51 points between them in the 1971-1972 season." Inducted into the Hall of Fame in 1996, Goodrich scored 19,181 points.

## 7. Dennis Johnson

Dennis Johnson was one of the greatest defenders ever to play the guard position and the player Bird called "the most intelligent he ever played with." In a game where offense gets headlines, Johnson won NBA All-Defensive First Team from 1979 through 1983 and then again in 1987. The total of six is more than any guard in NBA history except Jordan and Frazier.

Also a great clutch shooter, the five-time All-Star had better get in the Hall of Fame or someone was asleep at the wheel for the ten-year period from 1979 through 1988. Says Ryan: "D.J. stands apart. The young Dennis Johnson — here's the phrase I always use — was a destructive defensive guard. In the 1979 Finals Dennis Johnson blocked 14 shots and averaged 20 points a game." And he won the Finals MVP award in a five-game revenge thrashing of the Bullets.

"I always know D.J. is up for the big game when he takes it to the basket,'" was Bird's dictum on Dennis Johnson," says Ryan. And he was also a great clutch shooter. "He could go 0-for-17 and you'd have every confidence he'd make the 18th shot. I have to question anyone, anyone who suggests that Dennis Johnson isn't a Hall of Famer. He did not make it this time and the Hall is diminished until he's in."

## 8. Tom Chambers

One of the great offensive players of the 1980s, and a guy who Bob Ryan says "is on the all-white leaper team — one of the most athletic power forwards who ever played the game. He had a whole package."

He had a reputation for being a very selfish player but also put up 20,024 points. His official coming out was the 1987 All-Star game in Seattle, when Chambers took MVP honors with 34 points.

## 9. Walter Davis

"The Greyhound" ran as well as any guard of his time and shot 51 percent from the field for his career, mostly on jumpers. "When Phoenix had Alvin Adams at center, the offense was geared around Davis running off screens," recalls Matt Guokas. "David could go from slow to fast very quickly and had a beautiful looking shot and a great release. He had one of those shots where everything looked good leaving his hands."

Peruse the stat line for "Sweet D" and several things jump right out at you. Not only did he shoot above 50 percent — astounding for any guard — but shot 85 percent from the free throw line and ended up with 19,521 points, good enough for seventh place among all the guards who ever played.

## 10. Bob Lanier

"Titleless in Detroit" (and Milwaukee) became the motif for the end stages of his career. Just missed 20,000 points and just missed 10,000 rebounds, though he missed getting a title by a wider margin. Never the best center in the game, Lanier nonetheless possessed a feather touch and was a fine offensive player for a ten-year period from 1971 through 1980.

# UpandComing

### 1. Grant Hill

If I were writing this book ten years from now, Grant Hill would be in the top fifty. He has emerged as the most complete player in the under-30 crowd. His .496 field goal percentage, 21.4 points, and 9 rebounds and 7 assists per game in '97 makes him a better Pippen than Pippen, at least on offense.

He needs to shoot free throws better than 71 percent and he has not yet learned to take over games, as game five in the first round against Atlanta in 1997 showed. Just 25, Hill has all the needed skill and will to improve.

### 2. Anfernee Hardaway

Forgetting the early comparisons to Magic and the premature view that he would preempt Jordan as the game's greatest player after an early season game in 1995, Hardaway should have an outstanding career.

After sleep walking through the first two games of the Orlando-Miami series in 1997, he said "we have to show some pride." What about pride in the first two games, after the team went down 2-0?

### 3. Gary Payton

Leave it to *Sports Illustrated* to proclaim Tyrell Brandon as the game's best point guard. Did they forget Stockton and Payton? Across the board, Payton's numbers are better than Brandon's. His defense is known. But in 1997 he added 21.8 points, 7.1 assists and 4.7 rebounds, while shooting it at a .476 clip. Not only were those figures better than Brandon's, they were also better than Hardaway's.

### 4. Shaquille O'Neal

The numbers are there. The points, rebounds, field goal percentage — they can't be denied. The next Chamberlain? Want to reconsider, all you guys who made that comparison? O'Neal has missed more games in five years than Chamberlain did in his first ten. Now that his latest movie bombed, maybe Movie Man will decide to become a basketball player for the ages.

His first title will probably come in three to five years. By the time he retires he will have great numbers and even more one liners, some even better than "Me and Penny are the Kareem and Magic of the nineties."

# Lifetime Regular Season and Playoff Statistics
## For the Best 50 Players of All-Time

## THE GUARDS

| YRS. | GAMES | FG PCT. | FT PCT. | PTS. | REBS. | ASTS. | RPG | APG | PPG | T.O.P. |
|---|---|---|---|---|---|---|---|---|---|---|
| **Michael Jordan** | | | | | | | | | | |
| **Regular Season** | | | | | | | | | | |
| 12 | 848 | .51 | .84 | 26,920 | 5,361 | 4,729 | 6.3 | 5.6 | 31.7 | 43.6 |
| **Playoffs** | | | | | | | | | | |
| 12 | 158 | .49 | .83 | 5,307 | 1045 | 948 | 6.8 | 6.0 | 33.6 | 46.2 |
| | | | | | Regular Season-Playoff Differential | | | | | +2.6 |
| **Magic Johnson** | | | | | | | | | | |
| **Regular Season** | | | | | | | | | | |
| 13 | 906 | .52 | .85 | 17,707 | 6,559 | 10,041 | 7.2 | 11.2 | 19.5 | 37.9 |
| **Playoffs** | | | | | | | | | | |
| 13 | 190 | .51 | .84 | 3,701 | 1,465 | 2,346 | 7.7 | 12.3 | 19.5 | 39.5 |
| | | | | | | | | | | +1.6 |
| **Oscar Robertson** | | | | | | | | | | |
| **Regular Season** | | | | | | | | | | |
| 14 | 1,040 | .49 | .84 | 26,710 | 7,804 | 9,887 | 7.5 | 9.5 | 25.7 | 42.7 |
| **Playoffs** | | | | | | | | | | |
| 10 | 86 | .46 | .86 | 1,910 | 578 | 769 | 6.7 | 8.9 | 22.2 | 37.8 |
| | | | | | | | | | | -4.9 |
| **Jerry West** | | | | | | | | | | |
| **Regular Season** | | | | | | | | | | |
| 14 | 932 | .47 | .81 | 25,192 | 5,376 | 6,238 | 5.8 | 6.7 | 27.0 | 39.5 |
| **Playoffs** | | | | | | | | | | |
| 13 | 153 | .43 | .81 | 4,457 | 855 | 970 | 5.6 | 6.3 | 29.1 | 41.0 |
| | | | | | | | | | | +1.5 |
| **George Gervin** | | | | | | | | | | |
| **Regular Season** | | | | | | | | | | |
| 14 | 1,060 | .50 | .84 | 26,595 | 5,602 | 2,798 | 5.3 | 2.6 | 25.1 | 33 |
| **Playoffs** | | | | | | | | | | |
| 13 | 84 | .50 | .82 | 2,231 | 579 | 240 | 6.9 | 2.9 | 26.5 | 36.3 |
| | | | | | | | | | | +3.3 |
| **Walt Frazier** | | | | | | | | | | |
| **Regular Season** | | | | | | | | | | |
| 13 | 825 | .49 | .79 | 15,581 | 4,830 | 5,040 | 5.9 | 6.1 | 18.9 | 30.9 |
| **Playoffs** | | | | | | | | | | |
| 8 | 93 | .51 | .75 | 1,927 | 666 | 599 | 7.2 | 6.4 | 20.7 | 34.3 |
| | | | | | | | | | | +3.4 |

| YRS. | GAMES | FG PCT. | FT PCT. | PTS. | REBS. | ASTS. | RPG | APG | PPG | T.O.P. |
|---|---|---|---|---|---|---|---|---|---|---|
| **Isiah Thomas** | | | | | | | | | | |
| **Regular Season** | | | | | | | | | | |
| 13 | 979 | .45 | .76 | 18,822 | 3,478 | 9,061 | 3.6 | 9.3 | 19.2 | 32.1 |
| **Playoffs** | | | | | | | | | | |
| 9 | 111 | .44 | .77 | 2,261 | 524 | 987 | 4.7 | 8.9 | 20.4 | 34.0 |
| | | | | | | | | | | +1.9 |
| **Bob Cousy** | | | | | | | | | | |
| **Regular Season** | | | | | | | | | | |
| 14 | 924 | .38 | .80 | 16,290 | 4,786 | 6,955 | 5.2 | 7.5 | 18.4 | 31.1 |
| **Playoffs** | | | | | | | | | | |
| 13 | 109 | .34 | .80 | 2,018 | 546 | 937 | 5.0 | 8.6 | 18.5 | 32.1 |
| | | | | | | | | | | +1.0 |
| **John Stockton** | | | | | | | | | | |
| **Regular Season** | | | | | | | | | | |
| 13 | 1,062 | .52 | .82 | 14,468 | 2,833 | 12,170 | 2.7 | 11.5 | 13.6 | 27.8 |
| **Playoffs** | | | | | | | | | | |
| 13 | 127 | .48 | .82 | 1,825 | 422 | 1,366 | 3.3 | 10.8 | 14.4 | 28.5 |
| | | | | | | | | | | +.7 |
| **Clyde Drexler** | | | | | | | | | | |
| **Regular Season** | | | | | | | | | | |
| 14 | 1,016 | .47 | .79 | 20,908 | 6,331 | 5,743 | 6.2 | 5.7 | 20.6 | 32.5 |
| **Playoffs** | | | | | | | | | | |
| 14 | 140 | .45 | .79 | 2,888 | 975 | 868 | 7.0 | 6.2 | 20.6 | 33.8 |
| | | | | | | | | | | +1.3 |
| **Dave Bing** | | | | | | | | | | |
| **Regular Season** | | | | | | | | | | |
| 12 | 901 | .44 | .78 | 18,327 | 3,420 | 5,397 | 3.8 | 6.0 | 20.3 | 30.1 |
| **Playoffs** | | | | | | | | | | |
| 5 | 31 | .42 | .75 | 477 | 85 | 135 | 2.7 | 4.3 | 15.4 | 22.4 |
| | | | | | | | | | | -7.7 |
| **Pete Maravich** | | | | | | | | | | |
| **Regular Season** | | | | | | | | | | |
| 10 | 658 | .44 | .82 | 15,948 | 2,748 | 3,563 | 4.2 | 5.4 | 24.2 | 33.8 |
| **Playoffs** | | | | | | | | | | |
| 4 | 26 | .42 | .78 | 487 | 95 | 98 | 3.7 | 3.8 | 18.7 | 26.2 |
| | | | | | | | | | | -7.6 |
| **Nate Archibald** | | | | | | | | | | |
| **Regular Season** | | | | | | | | | | |
| 13 | 876 | .47 | .81 | 16,481 | 2,046 | 6,476 | 2.3 | 7.4 | 18.8 | 28.5 |
| **Playoffs** | | | | | | | | | | |
| 5 | 47 | .42 | .83 | 667 | 77 | 306 | 1.6 | 6.5 | 14.2 | 22.3 |
| | | | | | | | | | | -6.2 |

# THE FORWARDS

| YRS. | GAMES | FG PCT. | FT PCT. | PTS. | REBS. | ASTS. | RPG | APG | PPG | T.O.P. |
|---|---|---|---|---|---|---|---|---|---|---|
| *Larry Bird* | | | | | | | | | | |
| **Regular Season** | | | | | | | | | | |
| 13 | 901 | .44 | .78 | 21,791 | 8,974 | 5,695 | 10.0 | 6.3 | 24.3 | 40.6 |
| **Playoffs** | | | | | | | | | | |
| 12 | 164 | .47 | .89 | 3,897 | 1,683 | 1,062 | 10.3 | 6.5 | 23.8 | 40.6 Even |
| *Elgin Baylor* | | | | | | | | | | |
| **Regular Season** | | | | | | | | | | |
| 14 | 846 | .43 | .78 | 23,149 | 11,463 | 3,650 | 13.5 | 4.3 | 27.4 | 45.2 |
| **Playoffs** | | | | | | | | | | |
| 12 | 134 | .44 | .77 | 3,623 | 1,724 | 541 | 12.9 | 4.0 | 27.0 | 43.9 -1.3 |
| *Bob Pettit* | | | | | | | | | | |
| **Regular Season** | | | | | | | | | | |
| 11 | 792 | .44 | .76 | 20,880 | 12,849 | 2,369 | 16.2 | 3.0 | 26.4 | 45.6 |
| **Playoffs** | | | | | | | | | | |
| 9 | 88· | .42 | .77 | 2,240 | 1,304 | 241 | 14.8 | 2.7 | 2.7 | 43.0 -2.6 |
| *Julius Erving* | | | | | | | | | | |
| **Regular Season** | | | | | | | | | | |
| 16 | 1,243 | .51 | .78 | 30,026 | 10,525 | 5,176 | 8.5 | 4.2 | 24.2 | 36.9 |
| **Playoffs** | | | | | | | | | | |
| 16 | 189 | .50 | .78 | 4,580 | 1,611 | 841 | 8.5 | 4.4 | 24.2 | 37.1 +.2 |
| *Rick Barry* | | | | | | | | | | |
| **Regular Season** | | | | | | | | | | |
| 14 | 1,020 | .46 | .89 | 25,279 | 6,863 | 4,952 | 6.7 | 4.9 | 24.8 | 36.4 |
| **Playoffs** | | | | | | | | | | |
| 10 | 105 | .44 | .87 | 2,870 | 675 | 456 | 6.4 | 4.3 | 27.3 | 38.0 +1.6 |
| *John Havlicek* | | | | | | | | | | |
| **Regular Season** | | | | | | | | | | |
| 15 | 1,270 | .44 | .82 | 26,395 | 8,007 | 6,114 | 6.3 | 4.8 | 20.8 | 31.9 |
| **Playoffs** | | | | | | | | | | |
| 13 | 172 | .44 | .84 | 3,776 | 1,186 | 825 | 6.9 | 4.8 | 22.0 | 33.7 +1.8 |
| *Karl Malone* | | | | | | | | | | |
| **Regular Season** | | | | | | | | | | |
| 12 | 980 | .53 | .72 | 25,592 | 10,542 | 3,183 | 10.8 | 3.2 | 26.1 | 40.1 |
| **Playoffs** | | | | | | | | | | |
| 12 | 117 | .46 | .72 | 3,165 | 1,339 | 332 | 11. | 4 2.8 | 27.1 | 41.3 +1.2 |

| | YRS. | GAMES | FG PCT. | FT PCT. | PTS. | REBS. | ASTS. | RPG | APG | PPG | T.O.P. |
|---|---|---|---|---|---|---|---|---|---|---|---|
| **Charles Barkley** | | | | | | | | | | | |
| **Regular Season** | | | | | | | | | | | |
| | 13 | 943 | .55 | .74 | 21,756 | 11,027 | 3,741 | 11.7 | 4.0 | 23.2 | 38.8 |
| **Playoffs** | | | | | | | | | | | |
| | 11 | 115 | .51 | .72 | 2,703 | 1,506 | 463 | 13.1 | 4.0 | 23.5 | 40.6 |
| | | | | | | | | | | | +1.8 |
| **Elvin Hayes** | | | | | | | | | | | |
| **Regular Season** | | | | | | | | | | | |
| | 16 | 1,303 | .45 | .67 | 27,313 | 16,279 | 2,398 | 12.5 | 1.8 | 21.0 | 35.3 |
| **Playoffs** | | | | | | | | | | | |
| | 10 | 96 | .46 | .65 | 2,194 | 1,244 | 185 | 13.0 | 1.9 | 22.9 | 37.8 |
| | | | | | | | | | | | +2.3 |
| **Kevin McHale** | | | | | | | | | | | |
| **Regular Season** | | | | | | | | | | | |
| | 13 | 971 | .55 | .80 | 17,335 | 7,122 | 1,670 | 7.3 | 1.7 | 17.9 | 26.9 |
| **Playoffs** | | | | | | | | | | | |
| | 13 | 169 | .56 | .79 | 3,182 | 1,253 | 274 | 7.4 | 1.6 | 18.8 | 27.8 |
| | | | | | | | | | | | +.9 |
| **Scottie Pippen** | | | | | | | | | | | |
| **Regular Season** | | | | | | | | | | | |
| | 10 | 789 | .48 | .69 | 14,146 | 5,431 | 4,190 | 6.9 | 5.3 | 17.9 | 30.1 |
| **Playoffs** | | | | | | | | | | | |
| | 10 | 157 | .45 | .72 | 2,864 | 1,216 | 810 | 7.7 | 5.2 | 18.2 | 31.1 |
| | | | | | | | | | | | +1.0 |
| **Dolph Scahyes** | | | | | | | | | | | |
| **Regular Season** | | | | | | | | | | | |
| | 16 | 996 | .38 | .85 | 19,247 | 11,256 | 3,072 | 12.1 | 3.1 | 18.5 | 33.7 |
| **Playoffs** | | | | | | | | | | | |
| | 15 | 97 | .39 | .83 | 1,887 | 1,051 | 257 | 12.2 | 2.6 | 19.5 | 34.3 |
| | | | | | | | | | | | +.6 |
| **Jerry Lucas** | | | | | | | | | | | |
| **Regular Season** | | | | | | | | | | | |
| | 11 | 829 | .50 | .78 | 14,053 | 12,942 | 2,730 | 15.6 | 3.3 | 17.0 | 35.9 |
| **Playoffs** | | | | | | | | | | | |
| | 8 | 72 | .49 | .76 | 896 | 717 | 214 | 10.0 | 3.0 | 12.4 | 25.4 |
| | | | | | | | | | | | -10.5 |
| **Billy Cunningham** | | | | | | | | | | | |
| **Regular Season** | | | | | | | | | | | |
| | 11 | 770 | .45 | .73 | 16,310 | 7,981 | 3,305 | 10.4 | 4.3 | 21.2 | 35.9 |
| **Playoffs** | | | | | | | | | | | |
| | 8 | 54 | .44 | .69 | 1,061 | 514 | 192 | 9.5 | 3.6 | 19.6 | 32.7 |
| | | | | | | | | | | | -3.2 |

| YRS. | GAMES | FG PCT. | FT PCT. | PTS. | REBS. | ASTS. | RPG | APG | PPG | T.O.P. |
|------|-------|---------|---------|------|-------|-------|-----|-----|-----|--------|

*Paul Arizin*
**Regular Season**

| 11 | 713 | .42 | .81 | 16,266 | 6,219 | 1,665 | 8.6 | 2.3 | 22.8 | 33.7 |

**Playoffs**

| 8 | 49 | .41 | .83 | 1,186 | 404 | 128 | 8.2 | 2.6 | 24.2 | 35.0 |
|   |    |     |     |       |     |     |     |     |      | +1.3 |

*Dave DeBusschere*
**Regular Season**

| 12 | 875 | .43 | .70 | 14,053 | 9,618 | 2,497 | 11.0 | 2.9 | 16.1 | 30.0 |

**Playoffs**

| 8 | 96 | .42 | .70 | 1,536 | 1,155 | 253 | 12.0 | 2.6 | 16.0 | 30.6 |
|   |    |     |     |       |       |     |      |     |      | +.6 |

*Dominique Wilkins*
**Regular Season**

| 15 | 1,047 | .46 | .81 | 26,534 | 7,098 | 2,661 | 6.8 | 2.5 | 25.3 | 34.9 |

**Playoffs**

| 9 | 55 | .43 | .82 | 1,421 | 365 | 143 | 6.8 | 2.6 | 25.8 | 35.2 |
|   |    |     |     |       |     |     |     |     |      | +.3 |

*Adrian Dantley*
**Regular Season**

| 15 | 955 | .54 | .82 | 23,177 | 5,455 | 2,830 | 5.7 | 3.0 | 24.3 | 33.0 |

**Playoffs**

| 7 | 73 | .53 | .80 | 1,558 | 395 | 169 | 5.4 | 2.3 | 21.3 | 29.0 |
|   |    |     |     |       |     |     |     |     |      | -4.0 |

*Bernard King*
**Regular Season**

| 14 | 874 | .52 | .73 | 19,655 | 5,060 | 2,863 | 5.8 | 3.3 | 22.5 | 31.6 |

**Playoffs**

| 5 | 28 | .56 | .73 | 687 | 121 | 65 | 4.3 | 2.3 | 24.5 | 31.1 |
|   |    |     |     |     |     |    |     |     |      | -.5 |

*Dan Issel*
**Regular Season**

| 15 | 1,218 | .50 | .79 | 27,482 | 11,133 | 2,907 | 9.1 | 2.4 | 22.6 | 34.1 |

**Playoffs**

| 13 | 133 | .49 | .82 | 2,936 | 1,255 | 281 | 9.3 | 2.3 | 24.5 | 36.1 |
|    |     |     |     |       |       |     |     |     |      | +2.0 |

*Alex English*
**Regular Season**

| 15 | 1,193 | .51 | .83 | 25,613 | 6,538 | 4,351 | 5.5 | 3.6 | 21.5 | 30.6 |

**Playoffs**

| 10 | 68 | .50 | .86 | 1,661 | 371 | 293 | 5.5 | 4.3 | 24.4 | 34.2 |
|    |    |     |     |       |     |     |     |     |      | +3.6 |

# THE CENTERS

| YRS. | GAMES | FG PCT. | FT PCT. | PTS. | REBS. | ASTS. | RPG | APG | PPG | T.O.P. |
|---|---|---|---|---|---|---|---|---|---|---|
| *Bill Russell* | | | | | | | | | | |
| **Regular Season** | | | | | | | | | | |
| 13 | 963 | .44 | .56 | 14,522 | 21,620 | 4,100 | 22.5 | 4.3 | 15.1 | 41.9 |
| **Playoffs** | | | | | | | | | | |
| 13 | 165 | .43 | .60 | 2,673 | 4,104 | 770 | 24.9 | 4.7 | 16.2 | 45.8 +3.9 |
| *Wilt Chamberlain* | | | | | | | | | | |
| **Regular Season** | | | | | | | | | | |
| 14 | 1,045 | .54 | .51 | 31,419 | 23,924 | 4,643 | 22.9 | 4.4 | 30.1 | 57.4 |
| **Playoffs** | | | | | | | | | | |
| 13 | 160 | .52 | .47 | 3,607 | 3,913 | 673 | 24.5 | 4.2 | 22.5 | 51.2 -6.2 |
| *Kareem Abdul-Jabbar* | | | | | | | | | | |
| **Regular Season** | | | | | | | | | | |
| 20 | 1,560 | .56 | .72 | 38,387 | 17,440 | 5,660 | 11.2 | 3.6 | 24.6 | 39.4 |
| **Playoffs** | | | | | | | | | | |
| 14 | 237 | .53 | .74 | 5,762 | 2,481 | 767 | 10.5 | 3.2 | 24.3 | 38.0 -1.4 |
| *Hakeem Olajuwon* | | | | | | | | | | |
| **Regular Season** | | | | | | | | | | |
| 13 | 978 | .52 | .72 | 23,650 | 11,739 | 2,628 | 12.0 | 2.7 | 24.2 | 38.9 |
| **Playoffs** | | | | | | | | | | |
| 12 | 131 | .54 | .72 | 3,572 | 1,519 | 2,446 | 11.6 | 3.4 | 27.3 | 42.3 +3.4 |
| *Moses Malone* | | | | | | | | | | |
| **Regular Season** | | | | | | | | | | |
| 21 | 1,455 | .50 | .76 | 29,580 | 17,834 | 1,936 | 12.3 | 1.3 | 20.3 | 33.9 |
| **Playoffs** | | | | | | | | | | |
| 13 | 100 | .49 | .76 | 2,213 | 1,400 | 145 | 14.0 | 1.5 | 22.1 | 37.6 +3.7 |
| *George Mikan (not all NBL statistics available)* | | | | | | | | | | |
| **Regular Season** | | | | | | | | | | |
| 9 | 520 | .40 | .78 | 11,764 | 4,167 | 1,245 | 13.4 | 2.8 | 22.6 | 38.8 |
| **Playoffs** | | | | | | | | | | |
| 9 | 91 | .40 | .77 | 2,141 | 665 | 155 | 13.9 | 2.2 | 23.5 | 39.6 +.8 |
| *Willis Reed* | | | | | | | | | | |
| **Regular Season** | | | | | | | | | | |
| 10 | 650 | .48 | .75 | 12,183 | 8,414 | 1,186 | 12.9 | 1.8 | 18.7 | 33.4 |
| **Playoffs** | | | | | | | | | | |
| 7 | 86 | .47 | .77 | 1,358 | 801 | 149 | 10.3 | 1.9 | 17.4 | 29.6 -3.8 |
| *Dave Cowens* | | | | | | | | | | |
| **Regular Season** | | | | | | | | | | |
| 11 | 766 | .46 | .78 | 13,516 | 10,444 | 2,910 | 13.6 | 3.8 | 17.6 | 35.0 |
| **Playoffs** | | | | | | | | | | |
| 7 | 89 | .45 | .74 | 1,684 | 1,285 | 333 | 14.4 | 3.7 | 18.9 | 37.0 +2.0 |

| YRS. | GAMES | FG PCT. | FT PCT. | PTS. | REBS. | ASTS. | RPG | APG | PPG | T.O.P. |
|------|-------|---------|---------|------|-------|-------|-----|-----|-----|--------|

*Wes Unseld*
**Regular Season**

| YRS. | GAMES | FG PCT. | FT PCT. | PTS. | REBS. | ASTS. | RPG | APG | PPG | T.O.P. |
|------|-------|---------|---------|------|-------|-------|-----|-----|-----|--------|
| 13 | 984 | .51 | .63 | 10,624 | 13,769 | 3,822 | 14.0 | 3.9 | 10.9 | 28.7 |

**Playoffs**

| 12 | 119 | .49 | .61 | 1,260 | 1,777 | 453 | 14.9 | 3.8 | 10.6 | 29.3 +.6 |
|----|-----|-----|-----|-------|-------|-----|------|-----|------|----------|

*Patrick Ewing*
**Regular Season**

| 12 | 913 | .51 | .75 | 21,539 | 9,513 | 1,959 | 10.4 | 2.1 | 23.6 | 36.1 |
|----|-----|-----|-----|--------|-------|-------|------|-----|------|------|

**Playoffs**

| 10 | 106 | .48 | .73 | 2,383 | 1,152 | 254 | 10.9 | 2.4 | 22.5 | 33.8 -2.3 |
|----|-----|-----|-----|-------|-------|-----|------|-----|------|-----------|

*David Robinson*
**Regular Season**

| 8 | 563 | .53 | .75 | 14,366 | 6,614 | 1,726 | 11.7 | 3.1 | 25.6 | 40.4 |
|---|-----|-----|-----|--------|-------|-------|------|-----|------|------|

**Playoffs**

| 6 | 53 | .49 | .73 | 1,273 | 623 | 156 | 11.8 | 2.8 | 24.0 | 38.7 -1.7 |
|---|----|-----|-----|-------|-----|-----|------|-----|------|-----------|

*Nate Thurmond*
**Regular Season**

| 14 | 964 | .42 | .67 | 14,437 | 14,464 | 2,575 | 15.0 | 2.7 | 15.0 | 32.7 |
|----|-----|-----|-----|--------|--------|-------|------|-----|------|------|

**Playoffs**

| 9 | 81 | .42 | .62 | 966 | 1,101 | 227 | 13.6 | 2.8 | 11.9 | 28.3 -4.4 |
|---|----|-----|-----|-----|-------|-----|------|-----|------|-----------|

*Walt Bellamy*
**Regular Season**

| 14 | 1,043 | .52 | .63 | 20,941 | 14,241 | 2,544 | 13.7 | 2.4 | 20.1 | 36.2 |
|----|-------|-----|-----|--------|--------|-------|------|-----|------|------|

**Playoffs**

| 7 | 46 | .47 | .64 | 850 | 680 | 136 | 14.8 | 3.0 | 18.5 | 36.3 +.1 |
|---|----|-----|-----|-----|-----|-----|------|-----|------|----------|

*Bob McAdoo*
**Regular Season**

| 14 | 852 | .50 | .75 | 18,787 | 8,048 | 1,951 | 9.4 | 2.3 | 22.1 | 33.8 |
|----|-----|-----|-----|--------|-------|-------|-----|-----|------|------|

**Playoffs**

| 9 | 94 | .49 | .72 | 1,718 | 711 | 127 | 7.6 | 1.4 | 18.3 | 27.3 -6.5 |
|---|----|-----|-----|-------|-----|-----|-----|-----|------|-----------|

*Robert Parish*
**Regular Season**

| 21 | 1,611 | .54 | .72 | 23,334 | 14,715 | 2,180 | 9.1 | 1.4 | 14.5 | 25.6 |
|----|-------|-----|-----|--------|--------|-------|-----|-----|------|------|

**Playoffs**

| 16 | 184 | .51 | .72 | 2,820 | 1,765 | 234 | 9.6 | 1.3 | 15.3 | 24.0 -1.6 |
|----|-----|-----|-----|-------|-------|-----|-----|-----|------|-----------|

*Artis Gilmore*
**Regular Season**

| 17 | 1,329 | .58 | .70 | 24,041 | 16,330 | 3,050 | 12.3 | 2.3 | 18.1 | 32.7 |
|----|-------|-----|-----|--------|--------|-------|------|-----|------|------|

**Playoffs**

| 11 | 100 | .56 | .69 | 1,768 | 1,267 | 232 | 12.7 | 2.3 | 17.7 | 32.7 Even |
|----|-----|-----|-----|-------|-------|-----|------|-----|------|-----------|

# Bibliography

*Official NBA Register*
(The Sporting News)

*The Sporting News NBA Guide*

*The Official NBA Basketball Encyclopedia*
(Villard Books)

*The New York Times*, articles from 1946-Present

*Drive: The Story of My Life*
by Larry Bird with Bob Ryan
(Bantam Books)

*Tall Tales* by Terry Pluto
(Simon and Schuster)

*Loose Balls* by Terry Pluto
(Simon and Schuster)

*A View from Above*
(by Wilt Chamberlain)

*Seeing Red: The Red Auerbach Story*
by Dan Shaughnessy
(Adams Publishing)

*Ever Green: The Boston Celtics*
by Dan Shaughnessy
(St. Martin's Press)

*The Lakers*
by Roland Lazenby
(St. Martin's Press)

**Ken Shouler,** author and City University of New York philosophy professor, writes regularly for *Cigar Aficionado, Inside Sports* and *Biography Magazine.* He lives in White Plains, New York with his wife Rose Marie.